SH NG

GLOBALIZATION AND COMMUNITY

Dennis R. Judd, Series Editor

SHANGHAI
RISING

STATE POWER AND LOCAL TRANSFORMATIONS IN A GLOBAL MEGACITY

XIANGMING CHEN EDITOR
WITH ZHENHUA ZHOU

Globalization and Community / Volume 15
University of Minnesota Press
Minneapolis • London

M IN NE SO TA

Portions of chapter 2 were previously published in Karen Chapple, Ann R. Markusen, Gregory Schrock, Dai Yamamoto, and Pingkang Yu, "Gauging Metropolitan 'High Tech' and 'I-Tech' Activity," *Economic Development Quarterly* 18, no. 1 (2004): 10–29; reprinted with permission of Sage Publications.

Published by the University of Minnesota Press
111 Third Avenue South, Suite 290
Minneapolis, MN 55401-2520
http://www.upress.umn.edu

Library of Congress Cataloging-in-Publication Data

Shanghai rising : state power and local transformations in a global megacity / Xiangming Chen, editor.
    p. cm. — (Globalization and community ; 15)
   Includes bibliographical references and index.
   ISBN 978-0-8166-5487-1 (hc : alk. paper) — ISBN 978-0-8166-5488-8 (pb : alk. paper)
   1. City and town life—China—Shanghai. 2. City planning—China—Shanghai. 3. Social change—China—Shanghai. 4. Economic development—China—Shanghai. 5. Shanghai (China)—Politics and government. 6. Shanghai (China)—Social conditions. 7. Shanghai (China)—Economic conditions. 8. Globalization—Political aspects—China—Shanghai. 9. Globalization—Social aspects—China—Shanghai. 10. Cities and towns—Growth—Case studies. I. Chen, Xiangming.
   HT384.C62S437 2009
   307.760951'132—dc22   2008051138

Printed in the United States of America on acid-free paper

The University of Minnesota is an equal-opportunity educator and employer.

16 15 14 13 12 11 10 09   10 9 8 7 6 5 4 3 2 1

CONTENTS

PREFACE

Shanghai is "hot" not because of the scorching heat in its oven- or saunalike summers but because of its sizzling double-digit annual growth over fifteen years (1992–2007); Shanghai is "hot" also because it arguably has been the most attention-grabbing and heavily studied global(izing) city on the planet during the past decade. As we look back at three full decades of remarkable economic reform and social change in China beginning in the late 1970s, we are struck by how fast Shanghai—China's most cosmopolitan city of the past—has since the early 1990s zoomed far ahead of the rest of the country toward the future. Shanghai "cooled down" in 2008 (with GDP growth falling under ten percent for the first time in over seventeen years), when the global economic crisis decelerated the exports and real estate sectors that drove the city's boom. This sharp turn, however, did not turn around the "Shanghai express" but served only to highlight the tremendous speed at which China's premier city surged toward global city status. In fact, it renders the question of what makes the "Shanghai miracle" even more valid. This book looks for key answers.

Although the book is primarily about Shanghai, it does not begin with it. Instead, it opens with theoretical perspectives and empirical analyses by U.S. urban scholars in order to place Shanghai in a broader comparative context and to offer broader lessons for Shanghai. The lessons range from a better and clearer understanding of the key elements of the global city perspective and its applicability (Sassen) to the more practical lessons of evaluating the opportunities and constraints on developing high-tech industries (Markusen and Yu) and, further, to building efficient international air logistics by integrating Shanghai's old and new airports (Kasarda). The chapters on Singapore and Hong Kong provide analyses and insights from an authentically local perspective on the actions and strategies used by these two cities to compete for global city status and functions. They offer honest and often critical assessments of the varied roles of major actors (national government agencies, local firms) in shaping the competitive advantages of the cities and in coping with the difficult political and social consequences of participating in global economic competition. These two chapters also offer lessons to Shanghai in light of its similarities to and differences from Singapore and Hong Kong and its rapid rise as a formidable new competing city on the regional and global scene, especially with Hong Kong.

Part II of the book features the central case of Shanghai with five chapters written by scholars of Chinese background who are intimately familiar with the city. All these authors (except the book's editor, whose recent research has focused primarily on Shanghai) are native to Shanghai and have lived there for some time. More important, they have all conducted extensive research and published on Shanghai over a long period of time. All of them have been differentially exposed to the research and literature on international and comparative urban issues through training, working, and visiting at American and European universities. This combination puts these authors in an advantaged position to study the multiple aspects of Shanghai as a globalizing city with unique local insights and a broader awareness of the Western urban literature and the characteristics of other competing Asian cities covered in Part I.

The five chapters in Part II deal with local transformations in Shanghai at different scales of analysis ranging from an institutional focus on the local state and governance in chapter 6 to the behavioral choices of individual consumers in chapter 10, with sector-, district-, and community-centered analyses in between. Although these chapters vary in analytical perspectives and levels of data used, they collectively produce a synthetic and nuanced account of how the different facets and elements of local politics, economy, society, and space have been transformed by macro- and microlevel forces emanating locally, globally, and in between. In different fashions, these chapters "rediscover" the varied contents and new meanings of the local in Shanghai as it adapts to the global.

A timely study of Shanghai is a never-ending process, because the torrential pace of growth and change in this dynamic city would make any updated information appear out of date soon. Although it seemed that the book was aiming at a fast-moving target while it was being completed and revised, the authors and I are reasonably content that we have hit several crucial dimensions of local transformations that unfolded during Shanghai's rise as a globalizing city—analyses and findings that should weather the temporary brunt of the global economic maelstrom that erupted in 2008 and continued into 2009 and beyond.

Xiangming Chen

ACKNOWLEDGMENTS

This book has been several years in the making, which threads my recent career through three cities (Shanghai, Chicago, and Hartford), with the book's genesis dating back to the international conference "Shanghai's Development and Global Cities" held in Shanghai, China, on May 18–19, 2002. The conference was organized by the Institute of Economics at Shanghai Academy of Social Sciences (SASS) with financial support provided by the Shanghai Municipal Government through SASS. I was instrumental in bringing a number of international participants to Shanghai. I thank the Institute of Economics of SASS, especially its former deputy director, Professor Zhenhua Zhou, for allowing me to work with him in organizing the conference in 2002 and for his support of the editing process. Other officials, researchers, and staff of SASS hosted a number of my visits and invited me to several other conferences. I would like to single out Professor Xuejin Zuo, executive vice president of SASS, and Renhe Chen of the Institute of Economics for their kindness and hospitality.

Other institutions and individuals provided inspiration and different forms of support (direct or indirect) to the completion of this book. Since becoming part of the Urban Age project (www.urban-age.net) based at the London School of Economics in 2005, I have been invited to conferences in London, Mexico City, Johannesburg, Berlin, and Sao Paulo, and thus become more aware of the broader value of looking at the world's great cities beyond Shanghai. After being invited to join the Board of Trustees of the Alfred Herrhausen Society of Deutsche Bank in 2006, I became more convinced of the continued significance in understanding the problems confronting the world's megacities through both better research and governance. I am grateful to Wolfgang Novak of the Alfred Herrhausen Society for supporting an international conference at Fudan University in Shanghai in May 2008 that would extend some of the work reported in this book.

I thank all the authors of this volume for their tremendous support, patience, and cooperation. I not only benefited from reading Saskia Sassen, Ann Markusen, and John Kasarda as a graduate student years ago but also have learned even more from having their valuable contributions to this book. I apologize to the authors of the chapters on Tokyo, Seoul, and Taipei, which had to be left out of this book due to the issues of fit and space constraint; they made important contributions as participants at the Shanghai conference in 2002 and by providing comparative references from their perspectives and cities. All of the authors of the chapters on Shanghai except me are native to the city and have taught me about this city that I have come to love to study, visit, and live in, even though I grew up in its sometimes-rival Beijing.

I thank the School of Social Development and Public Policy of Fudan University in Shanghai, especially Dean Xizhe Peng and my long-time collaborator Professor Yuan Ren, for hosting me on numerous occasions. In finalizing this book, I benefited from the support of a Faculty Scholar Award from the Great Cities Institute of the University of Illinois at Chicago during fall 2005. David Perry, director of the Great Cities Institute, had a hand in this book, even though it may not appear obvious. Dennis Judd, editor of the Globalization and Community book series at the University of Minnesota Press through March 2007, showed unwavering support and insightful guidance for this project from the outset. I am grateful to former University of Minnesota Press editor Carrie Mullen and current editor Pieter Martin for their confidence in me and this long drawn-out project, and to several anonymous reviewers for their useful comments and suggestions on the manuscript at its various stages of development. The editorial staff (Andrea Patch, Mike Stoffel, and Mary Zemaitis of PubServ) did a superb job in bringing the manuscript to print in a timely manner so that it could become a timely book on Shanghai—the world's most dynamic and rapidly globalizing megacity. Jason C. Percy, my administrative assistant at the Center for Urban and Global Studies at Trinity College, applied his fine proofreading skills to the manuscript at the last stage of its preparation. Finally, I owe gratitude to Hongjun Shi and Xin Cai of Horizon Media Co. for their belief in the value of publishing a simultaneous Chinese edition of the book in

Shanghai, to Hui Zhu of Fudan University for his timely and excellent translation of the book, and to Chang Liu' 12 of Trinity College for his final proofreading of the translated manuscript.

In August 2007, I became the founding dean and director of the new Center for Urban and Global Studies at Trinity College in Hartford, Connecticut. I hope a few of the lessons for and from Shanghai's rise as a globalizing city may carry forward to Hartford. Despite its much smaller size, Hartford ranks as one of the top insurance centers in the United States and the world but is experiencing economic and social inequalities as a result of deep deindustrialization, the legacy of racism, city–suburban divide, international migration, and a host of other factors. In these regards, Hartford is a miniature version of Chicago and in sharp contrast to Shanghai. It is from the new vantage point of an old smaller city— Hartford—that I will continue to carry out comparative studies of Shanghai and other global or globalizing cities. Mutual learning between cities, large or small and from the global or local angles, goes on indefinitely.

Xiangming Chen
Chicago, Shanghai, Hartford

A GLOBALIZING CITY ON THE RISE

SHANGHAI'S TRANSFORMATION IN COMPARATIVE PERSPECTIVE

Xiangming Chen

THE RISE OF SHANGHAI IN THE GLOBAL AGE

Shanghai is recognized as the most rapidly globalizing city in the world. As the first city from the modern developing world, it appears well on its way to host the World Expo in 2010. Shanghai's rise has caught the world-wide attention of urban scholars and casual observers. Shanghai has experienced the fastest economic growth of any megacity from the early 1990s, averaging 12 percent annually. Shanghai attracted over US$120 billion in total foreign direct investment (FDI) after 1992, including US$14.6 billion in 2006, or 23 percent of China's total FDI (Balfour 2007). More FDI flows into Shanghai alone than into any other developing country every year, twice the amount invested in the whole of India. Shanghai is undergoing "the greatest transformation of a piece of earth in history. It's mind-boggling," according to a Baltimore-based architect who does planning work in the city (Balfour 2007, 53).

In the early 1980s, the row of European-style buildings along the Bund by the Huangpu River—the visible architectural legacy of past Western influence (see Figure I.1)—looked distinctively tall against the sea of traditional houses nested along and into narrow alleys. Today they are overshadowed by over four thousand modern high-rises that have sprung up during the past decade, doubling the total number of buildings in New York City. Rumor has it that at some point in the mid-1990s half of the world's cranes were working in the Pudong New Area (east of the

Huangpu River) of Shanghai, turning it into the "world's largest construction project." An agricultural district of rice paddies, farm houses, and scattered state-owned factories largely cut off from the rest of Shanghai through the early 1980s, present-day Pudong boasts the world's fastest train and is dotted with modern factories including semiconductor plants in the booming Zhangjiang High-Tech Park and commercial skyscrapers, such as the world's tallest hotel (a Grand Hyatt reaching to the 93rd floor). Japanese real estate tycoon Minoru Mori spent over US$1 billion constructing China's tallest building and Asia's second tallest (slightly lower than Taipei 101); the Shanghai World Financial Center in Pudong's Lujiazui financial district was completed in 2008 (see Map I.1 and Figure I.2). The Shanghai government recently approved the nearby construction of the Shanghai Center (dubbed the Shanghai Dragon), which may compete with Dubai's Burj to be the world's tallest building.

Some may see Shanghai's rise in the late twentieth and early twenty-first centuries as a "renaissance" from its cosmopolitan and glorious days

FIGURE I.1
The Bund and new Pudong with the Oriental Pearl Tower, Shanghai.
Source: Photograph copyright 2008 Anthony M. Orum.

MAP I.1
The Shanghai municipality and neighboring secondary cities in the Yangtze River Delta Region. This map was drawn by Philip Schwartzberg.

in the 1920s–1930s, when it became known as "the Paris of the East" in a largely impoverished China. Just as Shanghai was poised to rise again after the Chinese Revolution of 1949, its growth stagnated through the late 1970s due to the central government policy of redistributing its economic and technical resources to finance the development of poor interior cities. Shanghai contributed 350 billion yuan (US$40 billion) in revenue to the central government from 1949 to 1985 but got back only 3.5 billion yuan (US$44 million) for building municipal infrastructure (Shi, Qi, and Yuan 2004). Shanghai languished again behind the booming cities in South China such as Shenzhen and Guangzhou, which were favored by the central government during the 1980s (Chen 2005). The onset of the 1990s, when former Shanghai mayors Jiang Zemin and Zhu

FIGURE I.2
Tearing down the old and building the new, Shanghai.
Source: Photograph copyright 2008 Anthony M. Orum.

Rongji rose to power, marked the dawn of a "golden decade" for Shanghai, which has since been groomed and guided by both the national and municipal government along an upward trajectory to becoming China's preeminent global city. "The Paris of the East" of the past appears to be jumping forward to becoming "the New York of China" in the future.

The rise and renaissance of Shanghai has had a measurable impact on major Asian cities that generally see or position themselves as competitors. According to recent reports by the *South China Morning Post*,[1] Taiwanese corporate CEOs lamented that Taipei may be losing to Shanghai in multi-national company competition for human talent, especially IT professionals such as software engineers. Some Hong Kong accounting professionals, especially those at the managerial level, either moved or traveled to work in Shanghai due to a high local demand and competitive salaries, despite increasing competition in competency from their mainland counterparts. In both reality and perception, Shanghai emerged as an attractive new business hub for Asia at some expense to both Hong Kong and Singapore. Fifty-five multinational companies set up regional headquarters in Shanghai after 2003, leading to increased membership for its American

Chamber of Commerce (Amcham), whereas Amcham memberships in Hong Kong and Singapore declined (Lawrence 2002; Overholt 2004). More specifically, three business groups under General Electric (GE) moved their Asia–Pacific regional headquarters from Hong Kong and other Asian cities to Shanghai. Chipmaker Advanced Micro Devices (AMD) moved its South Asia–Pacific headquarters (which is responsible for sales and marketing in Australia, Greater China, India, and Southeast Asia) from Hong Kong to Shanghai in 2002. IBM also moved its Asia–Pacific headquarters from Tokyo to Shanghai, and so did auto parts maker Visteon Corp in 2003. In addition, GM's R&D center in Shanghai has grown from about 100 employees in 1996 to over 1,000 by 2007. In spite of its rapid rise only during the last decade or so, that Shanghai drew a growing number of regional headquarters of multinational corporations from the established Asian headquarters cities of Singapore and Hong Kong (Ho 2000) is highly significant. (Chapters 4 and 5 of this book will address Singapore and Hong Kong in comparison to Shanghai.)

Ranked outside the world's top ten ports just five years earlier and 25th in 1994 (Lambert 1996), Shanghai passed the Korean port city of Pusan (and the 4th-ranked Taiwanese port of Kaohsiung) in both volume and number of twenty-foot equivalent units (TEU) containers to become the world's third-busiest port behind only Hong Kong and Singapore in 2003 (Dunn 2005). With the opening of the new Yangshan deepwater port on an island thirty kilometers offshore in December 2005, Shanghai passed Hong Kong in the number of containers in 2007 and is poised to take over the title of the world's largest port by 2010. Shanghai also is on its way to owning the largest urban rail mass transit system in the world. Already, Shanghai has opened five subway lines and ninety-five stations serving 2 million people per day. With as many as six more lines scheduled to open by around 2010, Shanghai's subway system probably will surpass the world's largest and busiest systems, those in New York, London, Moscow, and Tokyo in the near future.

As Shanghai's economic functions and physical infrastructure improved vis-à-vis major world cities, especially those in Asia, it developed a cultural draw and influence on the latter. Hong Kong and Taiwan's film industries began to shift their operations there; TV series about the history, culture, and romance of the old Shanghai became popular in Taipei; and Shanghai-themed restaurants and nightclubs in Taipei such as "Shanghai Shanghai" and the "Shanghai Parliament Club" are doing a brisk business, connecting with people's combined nostalgia and admiration for traditional Shanghainese food, deco, and atmosphere. The staying power of Shanghai in the consciousness of Taiwanese is not so much the city's colorful history as it is its return to glory as the international gateway for China (Huang 2002).

The growing presence and impact of Shanghai in the Asia–Pacific region and globally, coupled with its dramatic local transformations, have turned Shanghai into possibly the most heavily studied megacity in recent years. Although this is a book about Shanghai, it is more than that. It looks at Shanghai through theoretical and comparative lenses and at multiple analytical scales to make Shanghai a timely urban laboratory for understanding how local transformations occur in global or globalizing cities as a combined function of global impact and state power.

REFOCUSING ON "THE LOCAL" IN GLOBAL CITIES: IS SHANGHAI A SPECIAL CASE?

If Shanghai is rapidly becoming a global city, as the preceding account suggests, the process tends to focus our analytical attention on the external functions and rising ranks of Shanghai in the global/world city hierarchy. Besides the clear evidence of the speed at which Shanghai soared in the hierarchies of the world's top ports and the Asia–Pacific region's top headquarters centers, Ren (2005) showed that on four measures of power and centrality, Shanghai (and Beijing)—the only two Chinese cities—came out of nowhere to rank among the top ten most important cities in 2003 as locations for global architectural firms and their major and even iconic projects in the world-city network. Although still trailing far behind Hong Kong and Singapore, Shanghai (and Beijing), among major East Asian cities, gained momentum in the number and frequency of international flights and international airfreight movements in recent years (Yusuf and Wu 2002). The preceding analyses of relational or network measures provide a striking picture of Shanghai's rapid climb in the world-city hierarchy. This relational approach to treating or comparing Shanghai (with other similar cities) as a holistic unit of observation is consistent with the body of studies on the structure of the world-city network and the mobility of cities within it (see Smith and Timberlake 1995; Shin and Timberlake 2000; Taylor 2004).

As we learn more about the rise or fall of major cities in the world-city hierarchy, we are more intrigued by what brings about the upward or downward shifts of these individual cities. Here the network approach takes us only so far by focusing on such explanatory variables as the concentration of corporate headquarters or branch offices and the connectivity of international flights. Whereas this approach may be sufficient for providing a systemic account of blocks of cities in a world hierarchy, it falls short in accounting for what drove Shanghai to rise so rapidly and simultaneously along several ladders of the world-city hierarchy and the local socioeconomic consequences. In other words, we face a dual analytical challenge. On the one hand, we need to push the causal chain further back and deeper down to uncover the internal and local factors in Shanghai's global rise. On the other hand, we need to better understand the multifaceted, local socioeconomic transformations of Shanghai as it is striving to be a global city. This calls for differentiating the ways in which these local transformations are induced by penetrating global forces as opposed to macrosocietal and local institutional changes that may or may not be linked to globalization (Marcuse and van Kempen 2000a). These institutional changes crystallize around the shifting but still strong role of the state.

The state remains a powerful actor in mediating global forces and local responses in any given global or globalizing city, even as globalization denationalizes or relocates certain parts of the national economy, politics, and society into the global system (see Sassen 2006). Whereas globalizing and localizing tendencies or processes are coexisting, interdependent, and mutually penetrating rather than contradictory and divergent (Rosenau 1997), localizing tendencies tend to reinforce certain indigenous historical and traditional conditions, which significantly modify the impact of global forces (Judd 2003). An even stronger counter to the global city perspective is the embedded or nested argument that national and subnational political-economic contexts such as state-centric bureaucratic and rational-planning practices, rather than global capitalism, are decisive in shaping the spatial and socioeconomic configurations of a global city such as Tokyo (see Jacobs 2006). The logic behind this rethinking about global cities calls for an analytical "(re)turn to the local." What does this mean and how to carry it out in the context of Shanghai, which is globalizing at such a torrential pace behind the purposeful and powerful push by the Party-state? If this makes Shanghai a special or Chinese version of a globalizing city, it behooves this book to focus on how the state operates as a driver and also mediator vs. globalization in bringing about local socioeconomic transformations. This distinctive focus aims at revealing the global and local features of Shanghai as a globalizing city that are both similar to and different from other global or globalizing cities. In the next two sections, I discuss a few comparative thematic threads that run from the first through the second part of the book.

FROM THE WEST TO SHANGHAI: GLOBAL CITIES, HIGH-TECH, AND LOGISTICS

In the wake of John Friedmann's world city hypothesis and research agenda in the early to mid 1980s, Saskia Sassen, with the release of *The Global City* (first edition) in 1991, opened up a new stream of scholarship on what she sees as a new kind of city—the global city. Unlike the world city of the past and present, the global city of the late twentieth and the early twenty-first centuries possesses a host of new and salient functional and relational attributes that reflect the local reconfiguration of the global economy in a few strategic cities with dominant command and control functions. In Chapter 1, Sassen reintroduces the global city perspective by fleshing out seven hypotheses and discerning a number of major trends bearing on all global or globalizing cities. Sassen's chapter sets up the theoretical backdrop against which the other chapters on the Asian cities and Shanghai dialogue in one way or another. A key argument of her chapter is that global economic activities are deeply embedded in place and take on concrete localized forms of a political, social, or cultural nature. It resonates with many discussions and analyses in the other chapters of the book. As an added bonus, Sassen offers several empirical observations on Shanghai through her theoretical lens.

The literature on global cities launched by Sassen's seminal work is concerned with two important questions that have generated unsettled debates. The basic question of "What is a global city?" is addressed by network analysis and in-depth case studies (see chapters in Marcuse and van Kempen 2002b), but the more involved question of "How and why do different global cities differ?" has created more uncertainty regarding whether and how such East Asian cities as Tokyo, Seoul, and Taipei are fundamentally different global cities than New York due to the developmental state of Japan, Korea, and Taiwan in the East Asian context (see Hill and Kim 2000; Sassen 2001b; Wang 2003). Instead of engaging that debate here, I want to consider whether there are certain local transformations that occur during the process by which cities become global cities. This question in the context of Shanghai as a globalizing city calls for understanding the full range of local transformations that can stem from global impact and state power.

To find some comparative reference for understanding local transformations in Shanghai, Markusen and Yu (chapter 2) turn to the restructured and transformed U.S. metropolitan economy under global-ization by providing a broader conceptualization and measure of high-tech industry across U.S. metropolitan economies based on science and technology occupations. As Markusen and Yu argue, this human capital-based measure reflects a growing interest in skilled labor, rather than resources or physical capital, as a driver of economic development. Shanghai's rapid growth, however, has been driven by massive fixed assets investment in physical infrastructure and more high-tech factories in Pudong. In the meantime, the city has shed labor-intensive and "sun-set" manufacturing industries such as textiles, which propelled the growth of pre-1949 Shanghai as an industrial city and sustained the state-dominated manufacturing after 1949. State-owned industries declined rapidly during the 1990s through consolidation, mergers, relo-cations, early retirement, and layoffs. This major transformation of the manufacturing sector was strongly motivated and facilitated by an official policy of turning Shanghai into the kind of global city characterized by strong services and high-tech industries. Is the Shanghai government thinking and acting too narrowly in going "high-tech" and discarding "low-tech?" Is the use of the state-directed large-scale redistribution of resources across sectors the most effective way to achieve this goal? Markusen and Yu called for an occupationally oriented economic devel-opment strategy (also see Markusen 2004), an emphasis on high-tech services, and an effort to diversify the portfolio of industries and activi-ties present in the Shanghai economy. Their advocacy makes timely pol-icy sense in light of the growing concentration of foreign R&D facilities in Shanghai and hence the rising demand for professional talents, which are projected to be in shortage.

If integrating diverse and occupationally based high-tech manufac-turing and the services it represents will help Shanghai become a global city, will it lead to a global city of more balanced or specialized producer services? Focusing on airport-driven development as a new urban form and air logistics as a crucial specialized service function, John Kasarda (chapter 3) presents an extended discussion on the crucial role of aero-tropolis—the new urban form of clustered aviation-oriented businesses along the transportation corridors to and from a gateway airport—in enhancing the competitiveness of logistic hubs in the global economy. Drawing from the comparative evidence on the major U.S., European, and Asian airport cities including Hong Kong and Singapore (two cases later in the book), Kasarda shows why and how they function as "integra-tors" of intermodal transport links (among rail, road, and seaports), timely shipping of lightweight high-tech products, air logistics and e-commerce, tourism flows, and adjacent development of office campuses and entertainment facilities. Having himself been involved in the development of Pudong International Airport in the 1990s, Kasarda offers a series of practical lessons for Shanghai with regard to the improvement of logistics practices and the Customs clearance process at Pudong International Airport in light of the city's ambitious goal to become China's and the Asia–Pacific region's leading logistics, sourcing, transportation, and distribution center. The key to realizing this goal is to sharpen and solidify Shanghai's position as China's primary gateway city for connecting the global economy to its national space via an integrated transport network (see Figure 3.5 in Kasarda's chapter).

The three chapters by U.S.-based authors provide theoretical, economic, and policy perspectives on the diverse pathways for Western or Asian cities to develop highly competitive global city functions, even though they may or may not become true global cities. In different ways, these contributors offer valuable lessons for Shanghai.

FROM THE EAST TO SHANGHAI: COMPETITION, THE STATE, AND BACK TO GLOBAL CITIES

In both thematic and sequential terms, the relationship between major cities competing with one another for global city positions and functions and the resulting local political, social, and cultural consequences ties together the five chapters in Part I of this book. Whereas the first three chapters look at Shanghai from a Western (U.S.) angle, the chapters on Singapore and Hong Kong (by well-established urban scholars living in and writing about this pair of Asian global cities) provide an analytical bridge or transition from the East to the Shanghai-focused chapters in Part II.

In a new round of intercity competition, those in newly industrialized and transitional economies in Asia and beyond assert themselves vis-à-vis established global cities of advanced industrial countries as new world centers of economic and cultural prominence and power. Competition among the most powerful Asian world cities such as Singapore and Hong Kong, fueled by and in response to Shanghai's rise, has become increasingly fierce. With a strong state willing to offer financial incentives, Singapore tried to outdo Hong Kong in a race to become a world-class biotechnology center in Asia in recent years. Most recently, Singapore offered tax breaks, simpler registration, and even mandates to manage some of its own massive pool of pension savings as enticements for foreign hedge fund managers to locate there. Singapore is counting on its clean environment and efficient urban planning to shame Hong Kong's deteriorating air quality and weak government in order to lure managers and investors from Hong Kong to Singapore. Critics, however, compared Singapore's bid to its past efforts to attract targeted industries such as the Internet or biotech. It usually ends up paying top dollar, and then it turns out that its efforts lag behind those of other countries. Therefore, the analogy may still hold that Singapore is the Zurich to Hong Kong's London, or the Greenwich, Connecticut, to Hong Kong's Manhattan.[2]

Singapore, however, adopted policies and institutions and effective ways of combining them to bring about more favorable competitive outcomes for its economic development and global functions. K. C. Ho (chapter 4) uses Singapore's Economic Development Board (EDB) and other institutions as illustrative examples to provide a convincing analysis of the crucial and flexible role of effective domestic institutions in initiating and sustaining competitive economic policies for Singapore's rise to an Asian global city and its painful economic restructuring after the Asian financial crisis. The EDB has been instrumental at home and abroad in facilitating the global and regional outreach of Singaporean companies and drawing foreign investment to Singapore through its network of overseas offices. Ho also shows through the Singaporean case that the implied flexibility and reinventions needed by the cities in the global economy can induce severe strains on domestic arrangements, such as the sacrifice of social policies and benefits in order to maintain economic competitiveness. For example, the Singaporean government, with the support from labor unions, has tried to cope with its economic slowdown via such belt-tightening measures as wage cuts. Relating this issue to Shanghai, Ho stresses the lesson of balancing the delicate state-society relations, especially with regard to convincing the majority of the population to accept serious collective and personal consequences and costs from necessary economic policies and measures to make a city globally competitive.

The local consequences of global competition are complicated further by the given national context in which competing cities are embedded. The concept of the national context, however, often disappears or fades from studies of global cities in terms of the global vs. the local. Using the case of Hong Kong, Lui and Chiu (chapter 5) rediscover the "national" as the "crucial middle" by showing that the dual economic and political restructuring of Hong Kong as an Asian global city over the past two decades is best understood in light of its integration into its neighboring region and, more importantly, the national orbit of China. Lui and Chiu argue that Hong Kong evolved from an entrepôt and light manufacturing center to a powerful global and regional financial services center, while also weathering the economic downturn after the Asian financial crisis and other challenges. It did so, they maintain, by functioning as an intermediary for China's trade and investment, by acting as a channel of information to and from China, and by providing a source of finance for China's modernization. Lui and Chiu conclude that competition from Shanghai has become an impetus for Hong Kong to enhance its connectivity with the Pearl River Delta. They also highlight the paradox that the more the Hong Kong SAR Government and the business community worry about challenges from Shanghai, the more they turn to the mainland as a source of untapped resources and new economic stimuli (see Chiu and Lui, 2009).

Singapore and Hong Kong may form a triangle with Shanghai in two different but related senses of the term. In the first sense, both compete with Shanghai to different degrees in attracting or retaining the headquarters of multinational corporations, especially those operating in China (see Chen 2007). Whereas both lost a few such headquarters to Shanghai (see earlier), Hong Kong had an overall gain of all headquarters in recent years. In head-to-head competition, Hong Kong maintains an edge over Shanghai in financial services, investment banking, logistics, and supply-chain management, especially in rapidly changing product areas such as toys, gifts, and fashion. Shanghai, on the other hand, has advantages in engineering, R&D, and design due to its concentrated human talent and top-notch universities, with another advantage in the economies of scale from the critical mass of heavy industries such as petrochemicals, steel, automobiles, machines tools, and information technology. Overholt (2004) concluded that most Fortune 500 companies that are focused on China's domestic market belong in Shanghai, whereas most exporters and many sophisticated service industries belong in Hong Kong.

In the second sense, Singapore and Hong Kong each offer different but perhaps converging reference cases for Shanghai. With strong state guidance in formulating competitive strategies through the EDB (Ho, this book), Singapore confirms that Shanghai is capable of the same state-directed competition and demonstrates an effective approach to doing it. Although its government largely stayed out of its market-dominated economy, Hong Kong has been drawn more closely into the orbit of China's state-driven and globally linked market economy (Lui and Chiu, this book).

In tandem, the chapters on Singapore and Hong Kong provide a logical transition to Part II of the book. They present a variety of processes and phenomena that are comparable to the experiences of Shanghai. This not only makes the two cities appropriate comparisons to Shanghai but it also offers lessons and implications for the latter. The cases in chapters 2–5 are treated in such rich and nuanced details to appeal to the reader with interests beyond Shanghai. In complementary ways, the five chapters in Part I highlight the relative role of globalization and the state policy in reshaping economic restructuring, competitiveness, and other functions of U.S. metropolitan centers and two Asian world cities. This paves the way for the book's thematic focus on local transformations in Shanghai.

FROM GLOBAL THROUGH NATIONAL TO LOCAL: SHANGHAI'S MULTIPLE TRANSFORMATIONS

To help set the analytical backdrop for the chapters on Shanghai regarding the crucial role of the state, Fulong Wu (Chapter 6) argues that globalizing Shanghai is a strategy-based state project. He presents varied evidence on the strong and sustained involvement of the state in restructuring the local economy through policy guidance and redirection of investment across sectors, as well as unleashing and leveraging full market forces such as foreign investment and land lease. The state's push behind Shanghai's shift from the socialist productionist regime based on industrial surplus to a regime of flexible accumulation based on the service sector (Wu, this book) dovetails with the accepted conventional vision that global cities must have a strong service-oriented economy. The Shanghai government promoted the tertiary sector through downsizing the declining manufacturing industries, primarily textiles, and creating new jobs in various services, with a focus on promoting such producer services as finance, banking, and real estate. These strategies were instrumental in reorganizing the sectoral composition of the local economy (see Table I.1).

As Table I.1 shows, Shanghai shifted from a primarily industrial city to a growing service center when services as a share of both output and employment exceeded that of manufacturing for the first time in 2001. Despite the slight reversal of manufacturing and service shares in 2003, the service sector maintained its strong growth momentum as indicated by employment figures. Another aspect of the growth-based economic restructuring, driven by the state, is whether Shanghai is developing certain new capabilities in high-value-added services associated with a global city. Shanghai's finance, insurance, and real estate (FIRE) subsector grew rapidly, accounting for about one-third of the total service sector's output in 2003 (see Table I.1). As the output share of finance and insurance fluctuated and those of other services stabilized, real estate output surged through 2003, reflecting an overheated property market that forced the national

TABLE I.1

Changes in Shanghai's Economic Structure, 1978–2006 (Selected Years)

	1978	1990	1995	1997	1999	2001	2003	2006
Agriculture's Percentage of GDP (Output)	4.0	4.3	2.5	2.1	2.0	1.7	1.5	0.9
Industry's Percentage of GDP (Output)	77.4	63.8	57.3	50.1	48.4	47.6	50.1	48.5
Services' Percentage of GDP (Output)	18.6	31.9	40.2	47.8	49.5	50.7	48.4	50.6
Agriculture's Percentage of GDP (Employment)	34.3	11.1	11.9	12.7	11.4	11.6	9.1	6.2
Industry's Percentage of GDP (Employment)	44.0	59.3	54.6	49.1	46.5	41.2	39.0	37.0
Services' Percentage of GDP (Employment)	21.6	29.6	33.5	38.2	42.1	47.2	51.9	56.8
GDP per Capita (US$ and current exchange rate)	312.0	739.0	2,368.0	3,219.0	3,841.0	—	4,658.0	7,116.0
Service Sector GDP by Subsectors' Percentages[a]								
Wholesale, Retail, and Catering	45.6	24.5	27.2	24.9	22.3	21.9	21.4	18.0
Transportation, Storage, and Communications	23.7	25.9	17.1	14.9	13.6	13.7	13.9	12.8
Finance and Insurance[b]	13.8	29.5	24.8	30.0	28.9	24.7	20.6	15.7
Real Estate	0.5	1.6	9.2	9.6	10.5	12.6	15.3	13.1
Social Services	5.7	6.1	8.4	7.8	9.6	10.8	11.4	12.2

Sources: Shanghai Statistical Bureau (1998, 2002, 2004, 2007); Jizuo Yin, ed., 2001, *Institutional Reform and Social Transition, A Report of Economic Development in Shanghai 2000* (in Chinese), Shanghai: Shanghai Academy of Social Sciences Press.

Notes: [a]The percentages do not add up to 100 because of the exclusion of the health and education subsectors. [b]For 2006, the figure pertains only to finance.

and Shanghai government to intervene in 2005 and 2006. This intervention led to a moderation of the real estate sector in 2006 (Table I.1). Along the way, the share of FIRE employment in total service employment rose from 2 percent in 1997 to about 10 percent in 2003 (Shanghai Statistical Bureau 2004), which only began to narrow the gap with the typical percentages of such global financial centers as New York, London, or Hong Kong (see Sassen 2001a; Lui and Chiu, this book).

This rapid growth of the service sector aside, Shanghai projects a need for 2 million skilled professionals in financial services, trade, supply and distribution, real estate, international aviation, car manufacturing, biopharmaceuticals, new materials, and so forth by 2015. The shortage of wide-ranging professional talent indicates that not only is Shanghai some way off from becoming a world-class service center with control and command capabilities but it also may not be capable of supporting a broad-based growth of high-tech manufacturing (see Markusen and Yu, this book). This longer-term challenge calls for a different kind of state strategy that will focus more on human resource investment rather than just pouring massive financial resources into sprawling physical infrastructure.

Regardless of how the state is going to achieve a balance between "hardware" and "software" development, Wu drives home the point that the Shanghai "miracle" reflects a "dialectic tension between the waning of state capacity and the state reinventing itself in a new regulatory space. Although the launch of economic reform was initially more a response to its internal logic of removing entrenched and inefficient planning of economic activities, remaking Shanghai as a global city is instrumental for the state to justify its legitimacy in the face of globalization" (quoted in Wu, this book). Wu also reminds us of the symbiotic relations between the Chinese state and its financial capital. In Farrell's (2002, 55) words, "the Shanghai of the late 1990s and early 21st century is connected at the hip to the leadership in Beijing." Shanghai's tradition of being a launching pad for politicians in Beijing since 1949 continues (Yatsko 2001). The Shanghai-central government relationship took a drastic turn in late 2006 when Beijing removed Shanghai's Party Secretary and senior municipal government officials for being involved in a large-scale embezzlement (about US$400 million) of municipal pension funds. The rumored story about factional struggle aside, this episode exemplifies the reasserted will and prowess of the central state to rein in the powerful and autonomous Shanghai leadership, which had been pushing through ambitious megaprojects and initially refused to cool down the "hot" property market. In fact, the lucrative local real estate markets in Shanghai and other Yangtze River Delta cities lubricated the galloping municipal bureaucratic wheels but eventually resulted in the exposure of a number of corrupted mayoral- and bureau-level officials.[3]

The autonomous and aggressive local state accumulated large economic resources and used them to drive and sustain economic growth, but its role varied across different economic sectors. Focusing on the information and telecommunications sector, Zhenhua Zhou and I (chapter 7) examine the rapid, albeit uneven, growth of PC usage, fixed line and mobile telephone subscribers, Internet users, e-commerce, and data networks in Shanghai and the varied but very much stronger role of the central and local state in this growth. As the data in our chapter show, although Shanghai made huge strides in expanding the coverage or saturation rates of PCs and fixed-line and mobile phone subscribers, as well as household access to the Internet, it lags behind in developing important elements of the business information infrastructure such as company websites and e-commerce capability. Other lags in Shanghai's informatics include the institutional barriers of state-owned companies dominating the telecommunications sector and government control over access to service provision by foreign and domestic private companies (Harwit 2005). To ameliorate these lags, we point to successful strategies used by other Asian cities that helped put them on the global cutting edge of urban informatics and external connectivity.

Moving from a sectoral view to a spatial analysis of local transformations in Shanghai, Tingwei Zhang (chapter 8) provides a systematic and fine-grained comparison of the process, determinants, and outcomes of spatial and economic restructuring in three urban districts of Shanghai. In the light of administrative devolution of decision-making from the municipal level to the district level in Shanghai, Zhang's view from the ground up sheds new light on how and why the very local actors (districts in this case) became engaged directly with global forces in Shanghai. Zhang reveals the increasingly striking differences among the three districts on key indicators of land use, residential development, and economic activity. More importantly, we learn from this chapter that beyond general municipal development policies for globalizing Shanghai, history, location, economic base, and political leadership at the subcity scale intersected in complex ways to produce very uneven spatial and socioeconomic transformations of these urban districts. The most important lesson from Zhang's district-level study is that globalizing Shanghai may be a lofty goal and even successful in terms of the city's image and position in the world, but this process is inevitably accompanied by local winners (such as Huangpu and Luwan districts) and losers (such as Yangpu district).

Whereas the chapter by Zhang elevates the local in understanding Shanghai's global rise, Hanlong Lu, Yuan Ren, and I (chapter 9) provide an even stronger and sharper focus on the local by moving further down the scale hierarchy to examine community (re)building in Shanghai in response to global influence. This chapter echoes the growing research effort to understand local community change in relation to the impact of globalization by moving farther away from the classical (and dated) idea of a community as a well-bounded local system and replacing it with a new emphasis on how urban life is (re)ordered across time and space within and beyond local and national boundaries (Marcuse and van Kempen 2000a). To show that the state acted simultaneously and independently of global impact at the local level, we delineated the reform model introduced in Shanghai in 1996 as "two levels of government and three levels of management," which made the street office the most important and local level of managing and coordinating all community affairs below the two levels of municipal and district government. One street office, for example, set up four separate but complementary working committees (public administration, community development, community safety and governance, and finance and economies), which worked well together to improve the collective welfare of the broad community.

Besides community reform practices, the commodification and privatization of housing and global investment in the real estate market added a one-two punch to changing not only community governance but also identity and satisfaction with community. A survey in 1998 involving the first author of chapter 9 showed that residents in privately owned housing had a more positive evaluation of the quality of community life (see Table 9.1). This suggests that housing ownership, which represents people's major financial investment and stake, translated into a stronger identification with their community and a greater interest in local community development. According to a more recent survey (in 2001 in Pudong) involving the second and third authors of chapter 9, people with more personal global connections had a higher level of satisfaction with different aspects of community life, including community facilities and services (see Table 9.2). People with stronger global connectivity are more likely to live in luxury apartments and villas located in gated compounds and with foreigners as next-door neighbors (Chen and Sun 2007; Sun and Chen 2005; Wu and Webber 2004), and thus they become elite members of a new and privileged local community. However, this sort of community in Shanghai, with its exclusive, enclavelike feature and strong global connectivity, is already partially delocalized, or represents a localized form of the global (Sassen, this book).

The emergence of globalized local communities in Shanghai heralds the arrival of globally oriented local consumers or consumers who pursue a global lifestyle beyond luxury housing within gated communities. In Chapter 10, Jiaming Sun and I operate from the bottom of the analytical scales in Part II of the book by examining how the individual consumer in Shanghai responded to the penetration of global economic and cultural forces using data from a 2001 survey. Our most significant findings on the consumption of American fast foods (McDonald's and KFC) and brand-name clothes include: (1) 100 percent of the people living in luxury apartments and villas had fast foods; (2) young people, especially teenagers (ages 12–18) are most likely to eat American fast foods and buy foreign brand-name clothes controlling for income (see Figure 10.4 and 10.5); and (3) consumers with stronger global connections are more likely to consume global products, everything else being equal, as shown by logistic regression analysis (Table 10.1). The transformation of consumer behavior reflects a process in which the global and local meet and reinforce each other. Whereas globalization facilitates the rapid growth and broad availability of fast foods and foreign brand-name clothes in Shanghai, more differentiated personal resources, values, and lifestyle preferences along demographic and socioeconomic lines during transition to a market economy create varied consumer responses to global brand products.

This introduction, in sum, has served joint purposes. It began by presenting a striking picture of Shanghai's rise as a globalizing city in a brief historical perspective. Against its first glorious and cosmopolitan times as "the Paris of China" in the 1920s, the rise of Shanghai during the 1990s and the beginning of the twenty-first century looks "golden" and bears the most visible marks of globalization anywhere in China and probably beyond. The coupling of the speed and scale of Shanghai's rise boggles the mind even more if it is viewed against the post-1949 era during which Shanghai was suppressed by China's central government. Instead of seeing Shanghai's rise as a simple numerical outcome of the previous pent-up demand and low starting level, this book looks deeper and wider at a set of institutional, spatial, socioeconomic, and lifestyle transformations under and above the dramatically altered physical landscape of Shanghai. Moreover, avoiding the analytical trap of dialing up Shanghai's uniqueness, this introduction has fleshed out the book's broader theme of how global impact and state power influence local transformations by grafting the focused analysis of Shanghai in Part II onto a wider comparative canvass. We hope it will serve the reader well as a rough roadmap to follow in exploring the remainder of the book.

NOTES

In earlier revisions of this introduction, I benefited from the support of a Faculty Scholar Award from the Great Cities Institute at the University of Illinois at Chicago in Fall 2005. I thank Dennis Judd, Laurence Ma, Ann Markusen, Anthony Orum, and three anonymous reviewers for comments on earlier versions. Lan Wang and Hui Zhu helped locate and update the statistics in Table I.1.

1. Reports gleaned from the *South China Morning Post*'s online coverage of Asia's economy, business, and technology at www.scmp.com, July–September 2002.

2. Hugo Restall, "Financial Center Pipedreams," *Far Eastern Economic Review,* October 2006; accessed at the Asian Development Bank Institute (ADBI) Web site, www.adbi.org/e-newsline/index.html.

3. The corruption of the former Shanghai Party Secretary in late 2006 also involved the director of Shanghai's Labor and Social Security Bureau and a deputy Party secretary of Baoshan District Government. In recent years, the former deputy mayor of Suzhou in charge of construction, a former deputy mayor of Changzhou, and a deputy secretarial general of Nanjing were caught accepting huge bribes from real estate developers for running the latter's projects through the official approval process. Reported by *World Journal*, December 28, 2006, C3.

REFERENCES

Balfour, Frederik. 2007. "Shanghai Rising." *BusinessWeek* (February 19): 50–55.
Chen, Xiangming. 2005. *As Borders Bend: Transnational Spaces on the Pacific Rim.* Lanham, Md.: Rowman & Littlefield.
———. 2007. "A Tale of Two Regions in China: Rapid Economic Development and Slow Industrial Upgrading in the Pearl River and the Yangtze River Deltas." *International Journal of Comparative Sociology* 48, no. 2–3: 167–201.
Chen, Xiangming, and Jiaming Sun. 2007. "Untangling a Global–Local Nexus: Sorting Out Residential Sorting in Shanghai." *Environment and Planning A* 39, no. 10: 2324–45.
Chiu, Stephen W.K., and Tai-lok Lui. 2009. *Hong Kong: Becoming A Chinese Global City.* London: Routledge.
Dunn, Mark J. 2005. "Streamlining Shanghai Customs." *The China Business Review* (July–August): 17–20.
Farrell, Bill. 2002. "A Legend Reborn? Not Just Yet." *Topics* 32, no. 2: 54–56.
Harwit, Eric. 2005. "Telecommunications and the Internet in Shanghai: Political and Economic Factors Shaping the Network in a Chinese City." *Urban Studies* 42, no. 10: 1837–58.

Hill, Richard Child, and June Woo Kim. 2000. "Global Cities and Developmental States: New York, Tokyo, and Seoul." *Urban Studies* 37, no. 12: 2167–95.

Ho, K.C. 2000. "Competing to Be Regional Centres: A Multi-Agency, Multi-Locational Perspective." *Urban Studies* 37, no. 12: 2337–56.

Huang, Andrew. 2002. "Looking for Shangri-La." *Topics* 31, no. 10: 38–39.

Jacobs, A.J. 2006. "Embedded Localities: Employment Decline, Inner City Population Growth, and Declining Place Stratification among Japan's Mid-Size and Large Cities." *City & Community* 5, no. 3: 269–92.

Judd, Dennis R. 2003. "'Introduction': Special Issue on Globalization and the New Politics of Urban Development." *American Behavioral Scientist* 46, no. 8: 983–86.

Lambert, Mark, ed. 1996. *Containerisation International Yearbook 1996.* London: Emap Business Communications Ltd.

Lawrence, Anthony. 2002. "Hi-Tech's Promised Land." *Topics* 31, no. 10: 15–22.

Marcuse, Peter, and Ronald van Kempen. 2000a. "Introduction." In *Globalizing Cities: A New Spatial Order?* edited by Peter Marcuse and Ronald van Kempen, 1–21. Oxford and Malden, Mass.: Blackwell Publishers.

Marcuse, Peter, and Ronald van Kempen, eds., 2000b. *Globalizing Cities: A New Spatial Order?* Oxford and Malden, Mass.: Blackwell Publishers.

Markusen, Ann. 2004. "Targeting Occupations in Regional and Community Economic Development." *Journal of the American Planning Association* 70, no. 3: 253–68.

Overholt, William H. 2004. "Hong Kong or Shanghai?" *The China Business Review* (May–June): 44–47.

Ren, Xuefei. 2005. "World Cities and Global Architectural Firms: A Network Approach." Paper presented at the Social Organization of Urban Space workshop, University of Chicago, November 3.

Rosenau, James N., 1997. *Along the Domestic–Foreign Frontier: Exploring Governance in a Turbulent World.* New York: Cambridge University Press.

Sassen, Saskia. 2001a. *The Global City: New York, London, Tokyo.* 2nd ed. Princeton, N.J.: Princeton University Press.

———. 2001b. "Global Cities and Developmental States: How to Derail What Could Be an Interesting Debate: A Response to Hill and Kim." *Urban Studies* 38, no. 13: 2537–40.

———. 2006. *Territory, Authority, Rights: From Medieval to Global Assemblages.* Princeton, N.J.: Princeton University Press.

Shanghai Statistical Bureau. 1998. *Shanghai Statistical Yearbook 1998.* Beijing: China Statistics Press.

———. 2002. *Shanghai Statistical Yearbook 2002.* Beijing: China Statistics Press.

———. 2004. *Shanghai Statistical Yearbook 2004.* Beijing: China Statistics Press.

———. 2007. *Shanghai Statistical Yearbook 2007.* Beijing: China Statistics Press.

Shi, Lei, Ge Qi, and Min Yuan. 2004. *Shanghai Ren Da Zhihui (The Smart Shanghainese)* Shanghai: World Knowledge Press.

Shin, Kyoung-Ho, and Michael Timberlake. 2000. "World Cities in Asia: Cliques, Centrality, and Connectedness." *Urban Studies* 37, no. 12: 2257–85.

Smith, David A., and Michael Timberlake. 1995. "Conceptualizing and Mapping the Structure of the World System's City System." *Urban Studies* 32, no. 2: 287–302.

Sun, Jiaming, and Xiangming Chen. 2005. "Personal Global Connections and New Residential Differentiation in Shanghai." *China: An International Journal* 3, no. 2: 301–19.

Taylor, Peter J. 2004. *World City Network: A Global Urban Analysis*. London: Routledge.

Wang, Chia-Huang. 2003. "Taipei as a Global City: A Theoretical and Empirical Examination." *Urban Studies* 40, no. 2: 309–34.

Wu, Fulong, and Klaire Webber. 2004. "The Rise of "Foreign Gated Communities" in Beijing: Between Economic Globalization and Local Institutions." *Cities* 21: 203–13.

Yatsko, Pamela. 2001. *New Shanghai: The Rocky Birth of China's Legendary City*. New York: John Wiley & Sons.

Yin, Jizuo, ed. 2001. *Institutional Reform and Social Transition (in Chinese)*. Shanghai: Shanghai Academy of Social Sciences Press.

Yusuf, Shahid, and Weiping Wu. 2002. "Pathways to a World City: Shanghai Rising in an Era of Globalization." *Urban Studies* 39, no. 7: 1213–40.

PART I

GLOBAL CITIES WEST AND EAST

1. THE GLOBAL CITY PERSPECTIVE

Theoretical Implications for Shanghai

Saskia Sassen

Each phase in the long history of the world economy raises specific questions about the particular conditions that made it possible. One of the key properties of the current phase is the ascendance of information technologies and the associated increase in the mobility and liquidity of capital. There have long been cross-border economic processes—such as flows of capital, labor, goods, raw materials, and travelers. But over the last century these flows increasingly took place within the interstate system, where the key articulators were national states. The international economic system was ensconced largely in this interstate system. This has changed rather dramatically since the 1980s as a result of privatization, deregulation, the opening up of national economies to foreign firms, and the growing participation of national economic actors in global markets.

It is in this context that we see a rescaling of the strategic territories that articulate the new system. With the partial unbundling, or at least weakening, of the nation as a spatial unit due to privatization and deregulation and the associated strengthening of globalization come conditions for the ascendance of other spatial units or scales. Among these are the subnational, notably cities and regions; cross-border regions encompassing two or more subnational entities; and supranational entities, that is, global electronic markets and free trade blocs. The dynamics and processes that are territorialized at these diverse scales can in principle be regional, national, or global. I locate the emergence of global cities in this context and against this range of instantiations of strategic scales and spatial units.

In the case of global cities, the dynamics and processes that get territorialized are global as well.

ELEMENTS IN A NEW CONCEPTUAL ARCHITECTURE

The globalization of economic activity entails a new type of organizational structure. To capture this theoretically and empirically requires, correspondingly, a new type of conceptual architecture. Constructs such as the global city and the global city–region are, in my reading, important elements in this new conceptual architecture.[1] The activity of naming these elements is part of the conceptual work. There are other closely linked terms that could conceivably have been used, such as world cities,[2] "supervilles" (Braudel 1984), and informational city (Castells 1989, 1996). Thus choosing how to name a configuration has its own substantive rationality.

When I first chose to use global city (1984), I did so knowingly—it was an attempt to name a difference: the specificity of the global as it gets structured in cities in the contemporary period. I did not choose the obvious alternative, world city, because it had precisely the opposite attribute: it referred to a type of city that we have seen over the centuries (e.g., Braudel 1984; Hall 1966; see also Gugler 2004; Short 2005), and most probably also in much earlier periods in Asia (Abu-Lughod 1989) or in European colonial centers (King 1990) than in the West. In this regard it could be said that most of today's major global cities are also world cities, but there may well be some global cities today that are not world cities in the full, rich sense of that term. This is partly an empirical question; further, as the global economy expands and incorporates additional cities into the various networks, it is quite possible that the answer to this particular question will vary (see also Abu-Lughod 1999; Amen et al. 2006; Koval et al. 2006; Orum and Chen 2003; Paddison 2001; Sachar 1990; Short and Kim 1999; Taylor et al. 2006). Thus the fact that Miami has developed global city functions beginning in the late 1980s (Nijman 1996) does not make it a world city in that older sense of the term; nor does the absence (at least until very recently) of global city functions in Kolkata (Calcutta) diminish its status as a historically and culturally rich world city.

Depending on the object of study or purpose of the inquiry, either term might be more suitable. If the concern is with today's structuring of cities as key spaces in the lumpy geography produced by global capitalism, then global city is the appropriate term—its specificity is its specialized advantage.

Cities in the process of becoming global cities are referred to herein as globalizing cities, such as Shanghai, which is the central focus of this book.

THE GLOBAL CITY MODEL:
ORGANIZING HYPOTHESES

There are seven hypotheses through which I organized the data and the theorization of the global city model (Sassen 2001). I will discuss each of them briefly as a way of producing a more precise representation and will draw implications for Shanghai as appropriate.

- First, the more dispersed a firm's operations across different countries, the more complex and strategic its central functions—that is, the work of managing, coordinating, servicing, and financing a firm's network of operations. Multiple countries mean multiple accounting and legal systems, business cultures, and so on, all conditions that raise the complexity and level of specialization of central corporate functions.
- Second, the more complex, specialized, and particularized these central functions become, the more likely at least part of them will be subcontracted by headquarters of global firms to specialized corporate service firms. In other words, headquarters are increasingly likely to buy a share of their central functions from specialized accounting, legal, insurance, publicity, public relations, programming, telecommunications, and other such service firms. Thus, although even as recently as the 1980s the key site for the production of these central headquarter functions was the headquarters of a firm, today there is a second key site: the specialized service firms contracted by headquarters to produce some of these central functions or components of them.
- Third, it is increasingly these specialized service firms, which are engaged in the most complex and globalized markets, rather than headquarters, that are subject to agglomeration economies. The complexity of the services they need to produce, the uncertainty of the markets they are involved with either directly or through the headquarters for which they are producing the services, and the growing importance of speed in all these transactions, all contribute to new types of agglomeration economies.
- Fourth, derived from the third, is that the more headquarters outsource their most complex and unstandardized functions,

particularly those subject to uncertain and changing markets and to speed, the freer they are to opt for any location because the work actually done in the headquarters is not subject to agglomeration economies. This hypothesis was developed in response to a very common notion that the number of headquarters is what specifies a global city. Empirical analysis may still indicate that, in many countries, the leading business center is also the main center of concentration for headquarters, but this is likely due to an absence of alternative locational options.

- Fifth, because specialized service firms need to provide an increasingly global service, they strengthen cross-border intercity transactions and networks. The growth of global markets for finance and specialized services, the need for transnational servicing networks due to sharp increases in international investment, the reduced role of the government in the regulation of international economic activity, and the corresponding ascendance of other institutional arenas, notably global markets and corporate headquarters—all point to the existence of a growing number of highly specialized transnational networks that bring together particular groupings of cities. One implication of this is that the economic fortunes of these cities become increasingly disconnected from their broader hinterlands or even their national economies.

- Sixth, the larger the concentration of high-income professionals and high-profit specialized service firms, the sharper the degree of spatial and socioeconomic inequality evident in these cities. The strategic role of these specialized services raises the value of top-level professionals and their numbers. Further, talent can matter enormously for the quality of these strategic outputs, and given the importance of speed, proven talent is an added value and con-tributes to rapid increases in salaries and profits in the sector as firms raid each other of their respective top professionals.

- Seventh, as a result of the dynamics described in hypothesis six, there is a growing informalization of economic activities that are in demand in global cities that lack the profit rates that would allow them to compete with the high profit–making firms at the top of the system. It also signals that the growth of advanced economic sectors in today's global cities contributed to the expansion of a new type of informal economy, one very much a part of advanced global capitalism.

The first three hypotheses may have more limited relevance and applicability to Shanghai, which has not yet developed the concentrated level of and networked transactions among advanced service firms that exist in New York or London. However, it is evident that Shanghai is moving in this direction because its overall service sector continues to expand relative to manufacturing (see Table I.1 in Chen, introduction, this book). The other four hypotheses bear differing degrees of pertinence to Shanghai, although they need to be more rigorously evaluated in the latter's context. Shanghai has gained more appeal and salience as China's top corporate headquarters city (Beijing may be a close second), especially in research and development (R&D). Fifty-five multinational companies set up regional headquarters in Shanghai after 2003, leading to increased membership in the city's American Chamber of Commerce. There was an average annual addition of thirty multinational R&D centers in Shanghai from 2002 to 2005. The total number of R&D facilities of multinationals in Shanghai is expected to grow from around 150 in 2005 to around 200 by the end of 2008 (Chen 2007). Although this is due to a lack of alternative and competitive locations in China (hypothesis four), Shanghai's rise as a top headquarters city has not led to its disconnection from the regional hinterland as predicted by hypothesis five (see Chen and Orum, conclusion, this book). Increased socioeconomic inequality is also evident in Shanghai during its recent period of high growth: Shanghai's Gini index rose from 0.37 in 1994 to 0.45 in 2001 (on global inequality, see also generally Alderson, Beckfield, and Nielsen 2007; Kerbo 2006). This increase in inequality in Shanghai results from its own specific conditions, partly fed by the bifurcation of the service sector (hypothesis six) and partly fed by a vast low-wage manufacturing and construction boom. Some of this larger income disparity is also the result of the growing informal economy (hypothesis seven), which absorbs a large number of laid-off state-sector factory workers into low-paying service jobs (see Lu, Ren, and Chen, this book).

WORLDWIDE NETWORKS AND CENTRAL COMMAND FUNCTIONS

The geography of globalization contains a dynamic of both dispersal and centralization. The massive trend toward the spatial dispersal of economic activities at the metropolitan, national, and global level associated with globalization has contributed to a demand for new forms of territorial centralization of top-level management and control functions. This raises the question of why they should benefit from agglomeration economies, especially because globalized economic sectors tend to be intensive users of the new information and telecommunications technologies and increasingly produce a partly digitized output, such as financial instruments and specialized services (for an exhaustive review of the many different trends, see Daniels and Bryson 2007). One component of the answer is the growing evidence that business networks are crucial to maximize the utilities firms can extract from technical networks (Ernst 2005; Garcia 2002). Such business networks were also crucial for other, earlier communication technologies and in domains other than the economic (e.g., Glasius, Kaldor, and Anheier 2002; Howard and Jones 2004). Business networks benefit from agglomeration economies and hence thrive in cities, even today when simultaneous global communication is possible (Graham 2002, 2004). The key variable contributing to the spatial concentration of central functions and associated agglomeration economies is the extent to which this dispersal occurs under conditions of concentration in control, ownership, and profit appropriation (Sassen 2001, chapters 2 and 5). Global firms operate in multiple countries but want to maintain centralized control and appropriation of profits; it is this combination that raises the level of complexity of their central corporate functions.

This dynamic of simultaneous geographic dispersal and concentration is, in my analysis, one of the key elements in the organizational architecture of the global economic system. Let me first give some empirical examples and then examine some of the implications of globalization and the new technologies on cities, including Shanghai.

The rapid growth of affiliates illustrates the dynamic of simultaneous geographic dispersal and concentration of a firm's operations (see Sassen 2006 for a detailed empirical elaboration). Firms with large numbers of geographically dispersed factories and service outlets face massive needs for central coordination and servicing, especially when their affiliates involve foreign countries with different legal and accounting systems. By 1999 well over half a million affiliates outside their home countries accounted for US$11 trillion in sales, a very significant figure if we consider that global trade stood at US$8 trillion. By 2003, the number of affiliates had doubled, reaching almost one million. China attracted the largest number of foreign affiliates (see Table 1.1), again pointing to the fact that economic globalization takes place through rather specific geographies. This trend is consistent with the growing number of multinationals setting up Chinese or Asian regional headquarter offices in Shanghai (Chen, introduction).

TABLE 1.1

Numbers of Parent Transnational Corporations and Foreign Affiliates, by Region and Country, 1990–2008 (Selected Countries and Years)

All and Selected Developed Countries	Year	Parent Corporations Based in Countries	Foreign Affiliates Located in Countries	All and Selected Developing Countries	Year	Parent Corporations Based in Countries	Foreign Affiliates Located in Countries
All Developed Countries	1990	33,500	81,800	All Developing Countries	1990	2,700	71,300
	1996	43,442	96,620		1996	9,323	230,696
	2003	45,007	102,560		2003	14,192	580,638
	2008[a]	56,448	366,628		2008[a]	20,586	413,446
Australia	1992	1,306	695	Brazil	1992	566	7,110
	1997	485	2,371		1995	797	6,322
	2001	682	2,352		1998	1,225	8,050
	2006	1,380	1,991		2007	201	3,712
Canada	1991	1,308	5,874	China	1989	379	15,966
	1996	1,695	4,541		1997	379	145,000
	1999	1,439	3,725		2002	359	424,196
	—	—	—		2005	3,429	280,000
Germany	1990	6,984	11,821	Hong Kong, China	1991	500	2,828
	1996	7,569	11,445		1997	500	5,067
	2002	6,609	9,268		2001	948	9,132
	2006	5,935	9,631		2007	1,167	9,712

(Continues)

TABLE 1.1
(Continued)

All and Selected Developed Countries	Year	Parent Corporations Based in Countries	Foreign Affiliates Located in Countries	All and Selected Developing Countries	Year	Parent Corporations Based in Countries	Foreign Affiliates Located in Countries
Japan	1992	3,529	3,150	Philippines	—	—	—
	1996	4,231	3,014		1987	—	1,952
	2001	3,371	3,870		1995	—	14,802
	2006	4,663	4,500		2004	—	311
United Kingdom	1991	1,500	2,900	Korea	1991	1,049	3,671
	1996	1,059	2,609		1996	4,806	3,878
	2003	2,607	13,176		2002	7,460	12,909
	—	—	—		2007	7,460	14,689
United States	1990	3,000	14,900	East and Central Europe	1990	400	21,800
	1995	3,379	18,901		1996	842	121,601
	2000	3,235	15,712		2003	2,313	243,750
	2005	2,360	13,667		2008[a]	1,783	14,820

Source: Based on UNTAD, *World Investment Report* (1998, 4, 4; 2004, 273, 274; 2008, 211).

Note: [a]Based on the latest data available for this year.

Another instance today of this negotiation between global cross-border dynamics and territorially specific sites is that of the global financial markets. The orders of magnitude in these transactions have risen sharply, as illustrated by the US$192 trillion in 2002, US$290 trillion in 2005, and US$640 trillion in 2008 before the September 2008 financial crisis for traded derivatives, a major component of the global economy. It dwarfs the value of global trade, which stood at, respectively, US$8 trillion in 2002, US$12 trillion in 2005, and US$13.8 trillion in 2007 (UNCTAD 2008). These transactions are partly embedded in electronic systems that make possible the instantaneous transmission of money and information around the globe. Much attention has gone to this capacity for instantaneous transmission of new technologies. But the other half of the story is the extent to which the global financial markets are located in an expanding network of financial centers. The degrees of concentration internationally and within countries are unexpectedly high for an increasingly globalized and digitized economic sector. Indeed, well over half of the global capital market is concentrated in the global North (see Table 1.2). A second trend pointing toward strong concentration dynamics is that the leading financial centers today concentrate a greater share of their own national financial activity than even ten years ago. For example, Frankfurt today has gained share over the other six regional financial centers in Germany, and so has Paris over the other French financial centers, in a pattern that repeats itself across countries in the North and in the South. This is a subject I discuss empirically in a later section.

One of the components of the global capital market is stock markets. The late 1980s and early 1990s saw the addition of markets, such as Buenos Aires, Sao Paulo, Mexico City, Bangkok, Taipei, and Moscow, and growing numbers of nonnational firms listed in most of these markets. Shanghai entered the world of financial exchanges in the early 1990s. The total volume of traded stocks on the Shanghai Stock Exchange rose from US$100 million in 1991 to US$360 billion in 2003 (World Federation of Exchanges 2007; see also Shanghai Statistical Bureau 2004, 220), although its tiny share of global market capitalization dropped from 2002 to 2004 (Table 1.2). When individual small investors entered the market en masse, the Shanghai market saw the beginning of a rather spectacular boom, reaching US$917 billion by the end of 2006 (World Federation of Exchanges 2007). Although much was said about Shanghai replacing Hong Kong as China's leading financial center, it is now clear that Shanghai has emerged as a predominantly national market, whereas Hong Kong remains a major international exchange (see Lui and Chiu, this

TABLE 1.2

Select Stock Exchanges Domestic Market Capitalization, 1990–2008[a] (in US$ million)

	1990	2000	2002	2004	2005	2006	2007	2008
Bombay Stock Exchange	n/a	n/a	130,390.18	386,321.10	553,073.74	818,878.58	1,819,100.50	1,472,768
Bursa Malaysia	47,868.80	113,155.30	122,892.35	181,623.79	180,517.54	235,580.90	325,290.30	317,996.10
Hong Kong Exchanges	83,385.90	623,397.70	463,054.92	861,462.94	1,054,999.32	1,714,953.25	2,654,416.10	2,208,643.50
Korea Exchange[b]	110,301.10	148,361.20	216,116.59	389,473.36	718,010.71	834,404.28	1,122,606.30	957,388.90
National Stock Exchange India	n/a	n/a	112,453.86	363,276.02	515,972.48	774,115.60	1,660,096.80	1,345,543.50
Shanghai Stock Exchange	n/a	n/a	306,443.58	314,315.71	286,190.31	917,507.53	3,694,348.00	3,134,719.30
Tokyo Stock Exchange	2,928,533.70	3,157,221.80	206,9299.13	3,557,674.42	4,572,901.03	4,614,068.83	4,330,921.70	4,128,950.50
London Stock Exchange	850,011.80	2,612,230.20	1,856,194.41	2,865,243.18	3,058,182.41	3,794,310.29	3,851,705.90	3,449,909.60
Euronext	n/a	2,271,727.50	1,538,684.38	2,441,261.38	2,706,803.49	3,708,150.05	4,222,679.80	3,728,153.30

Source: World Federation of Exchanges Annual Reports.

Notes: [a]The value is the total for domestic companies and foreign companies that do not list elsewhere. It is the comprehensive value of the market at the end of the calendar year listed. [b]Korea Exchange 2005 data include also Kosdaq after the integration of Korea Exchange.

book) with a far larger capitalization of US$1.7 trillion by the end of 2006, twice as large as Shanghai's (World Federation of Exchanges 2007). By January 2008, Shanghai had almost doubled its capitalization to US$3.1 trillion, well above Hong Kong's US$2.2 trillion even though the latter has 1,231 listed companies (in comparison to Shanghai's 860) and is far more international in nature (World Federation of Exchanges 2008). In the recent past Hong Kong drew the most lucrative listings of China's domestic companies, which were unsatisfied with Shanghai's sluggish capital markets, but this is now changing. At the same time, the Shanghai Stock Exchange's 130-percent rise in total traded value and 250-percent rise in new accounts in 2006 prompted the central government and its affiliated analysts to warn against the market overheating and the bubble bursting.[3] This deep worry came alive on February 28, 2007, when the Shanghai Stock Market composite index fell 8.8 percent just one day after breaking record highs. The sell-off triggered a global market downturn, with the Dow Jones industrial average losing 416 points, or 3.29 percent, the biggest single-day point drop since September 11, 2001. This was the first time that the New York and other global stock markets were driven by Shanghai and China. This sharp fall in Shanghai's exchange came after the Chinese government approved a special task force to clamp down on illegal activities, such as speculative buying of Chinese stocks with borrowed money, that had fueled the rapid rise in value of Shanghai's exchange. Although this strong government intervention might have been necessary to reduce overspeculation and euphoria, it raised a major concern for both corporate and individual investors, who see regulatory barriers as hindering the expansion of major financial markets in the global South. Another factor through which finance affects cities is through the current crisis in the residential mortgage capital market, a subject I have analyzed elsewhere (Sassen 2009).

The specific forms assumed by globalization over the last decade have created particular organizational requirements. The emergence of global markets for finance, the growth of investment as a major type of international transaction, the installation of industrial zones designated for export–production, and the rapid growth in the number of affiliates of global firms have contributed to the expansion in command functions and in the demand for specialized services for firms.[4]

By central functions I mean not only top level headquarters but also all the top level financial, legal, accounting, managerial, executive, and planning functions necessary to run a corporate organization operating in more than one country and, increasingly, in several countries. These central functions are partly embedded in headquarters but also, in good part, in the corporate services complex—the network of financial, legal, accounting, advertising, and other such firms that handle the complexities of operating in more than one national legal system, accounting system, advertising culture, and so on, and do so under conditions of rapid innovations in all these fields. Such services have become so specialized and complex that headquarters increasingly buy them from specialized firms rather than produce them in-house. These firms, which contribute to producing central functions for the management and coordination of global economic systems, are disproportionately concentrated in the highly developed countries—particularly, though not exclusively, in global cities. But because such concentrations of functions represent a strategic factor in the organization of the global economy, as the latter expands we see these same conditions in a growing number of global cities of the South (GaWC; Gugler 2004; Marcuse and van Kempen 2000; Parnreiter 2002; Schiffer 2002; Short 2005; Taylor 2004).[5]

In brief, global markets and firms require central places where the work of globalization gets done. Finance and advanced corporate services are industries producing the organizational commodities necessary for the implementation and management of global economic systems. Cities are preferred sites for the production of these services, particularly the most innovative, speculative, and internationalized service sectors. These patterns of spatial concentration are further strengthened by the fact that firms specializing in global finance and advanced corporate services require a vast physical infrastructure containing strategic nodes with hyperconcentration of facilities; it is necessary to distinguish between the capacity for global transmission/communication and the material conditions that make this possible. Finally, even the most advanced information industries have production processes that are at least partly place-bound because of the combination of resources required even when the outputs are hypermobile.

Theoretically this addresses two key issues in current debates and scholarship. One of these is the complex articulation between capital fixity and capital mobility, and the other is the position of cities in a global economy. Elsewhere (2001, chapter 2, 2008, chapters 5 and 7) I have developed the thesis that capital mobility cannot be reduced simply to that which moves or the technologies that facilitate movement. Rather, multiple components of what we traditionally define as capital fixity are actually components of capital mobility. This conceptualization allows us to reposition the role of cities in an increasingly globalizing world. Cities contain many of the critical resources that enable firms and markets to maintain global operations.[6] The mobility of capital, whether in the form of investments, trade, or through overseas affiliations, needs to be managed, serviced, and coordinated. These activities are often rather place-bound, yet they are key components of capital mobility. Finally, states—place-bound institutional orders—play an often crucial role in producing regulatory environments that facilitate the implementation of cross-border operations for national and foreign firms, investors, and markets (Sassen 2008, chapter 5).

A focus on cities makes it possible to recognize the anchoring of multiple cross-border dynamics in a network of places, particularly global cities or those with global city functions. This in turn anchors various features of globalization in the specific conditions and histories of these cities, in their variable articulations with their national economies, and with various world economies across time and place (e.g., Abrahamson 2004; Abu-Lughod 1999; Allen, Massey, and Pryke 1999; Amen, Archer, and Bosman 2006; Brenner and Keil 2006; Cochrane, Peck, and Tickell 1996; Gugler 2004; Koval et al. 2006; Krause and Petro 2003; Lloyd 2005; Lo and Marcotullio 2000; Lo and Yeung 1996; Rutherford 2004; Santos, de Souza and Silveira 1994; Yeung 2000). This optic on globalization contributes to identifying a complex organizational architecture that cuts across borders and is partly deterritorialized and partly spatially concentrated in cities (Chen 2005; Friedmann 2005; Sum 1999). Further, it creates an enormous research agenda, in which every particular national or urban economy has its specific and partly inherited modes of articulating with current global circuits. Once we have more information about this variance we may also be able to establish whether the deep economic history of a city partly shapes its position in the global hierarchy and, in turn, what difference such a position makes to the city's dynamism and the various ways in which it might do so. In the case of Shanghai, deep historical analysis of its development is crucial to assessing whether it can escape or deviate from its past while also becoming a distinctive global city (see Chen and Orum, conclusion).

IMPACTS OF NEW COMMUNICATION TECHNOLOGIES ON CENTRALITY

Cities have historically provided national economies, polities, and societies with something we can think of as centrality. In terms of their economic function, cities provide agglomeration economies, massive concentrations of information on the latest developments, and a marketplace. In principle, the new information and communication technologies (ICT) have the technical capacities to alter, and indeed eliminate, the role of centrality and hence of cities as key economic spaces.

The new ICT have not eliminated the importance of massive concentrations of material resources but have rather reconfigured the interaction of capital fixity and hypermobility. The complex management of this interaction has given some cities a new competitive advantage (Sassen 2001, 2006). The vast new economic topography that is being implemented through electronic space is one moment, or one fragment, of an even vaster economic chain that is in good part embedded in nonelectronic spaces (Garcia 2002; Graham 2004; Harvey 2007). There is today no fully virtualized firm or economic sector (Ernst 2005). As I discussed earlier, even finance, the most digitized, dematerialized, and globalized of all activities has a topography that weaves back and forth between actual and digital spaces. To different extents in different types of sectors and different types of organizations, a firm's tasks now are distributed across these two kinds of spaces.

The combination of the new capabilities for mobility along with patterns of concentration and operational features of the cutting edge sectors of advanced economies suggests that spatial concentration remains a key feature of these sectors. But it is not simply a continuation of older patterns of spatial concentration. Today there is no longer a simple or straightforward relation between centrality and such geographic entities as the downtown or the central business district (CBD). In the past, and up to quite recently in fact, centrality was synonymous with the downtown or the CBD. The new technologies and organizational forms have altered the spatial correlates of centrality (e.g., Chen 2005).[7]

Given the differential impacts of the capabilities of the new information technologies on specific types of firms and sectors of the economy, the spatial correlates of the "center" can assume several geographic forms, likely to be operating simultaneously at the macro level. Thus the center can be the CBD, as it still is largely for some of the leading sectors, notably finance, or an alternative form of CBD, such as Silicon Valley. Yet even as the CBD in major international business centers remains a strategic site for the leading industries, it is one profoundly reconfigured by technological and economic change (Ciccolella and Mignaqui 2002; Fainstein 2001; Marcuse and van Kempen 2000; Ren 2008; Schiffer 2002) and by long-term immigration (e.g., Laguerre 2000). Further, there are often sharp differences in the patterns assumed by this reconfiguring of the central city in different parts of the world (Marcuse and van Kempen 2000).

The center can extend into a metropolitan area in the form of a grid of nodes of intense business activity, a pattern well illustrated by recent developments in cities as diverse as Buenos Aires (Ciccolella and Mignaqui 2002), Paris (Landrieu et al. 1998; Veltz 1996), Shanghai (Gu and Tang 2002; Ren 2008), or Los Angeles (Dear 2004; Scott 2004). One might ask whether a spatial organization characterized by dense strategic nodes spread over a broader region constitutes a new form of organization of the territory of the "center," rather than, as in the more conventional view, an instance of suburbanization or geographic dispersal. Insofar as these various nodes are articulated through digital networks and state of the art conventional transport, they can represent a new geographic correlate of the most advanced type of "center." The places that fall outside this high-connectivity grid, however, remain suburban, or may become peripheralized. This regional grid of nodes represents, in my analysis, a reconstitution of the concept of region, one based not on narrowly geographic or merely administrative boundaries but on the character of activities and its pertinent infrastructures (see, e.g., RPA 2007). This partly digital, regional grid is likely to be embedded in conventional forms of communications and transport infrastructures, notably mobile telecommunications and web-based networks, as well as rapid rail and highways connecting to airports. In the case of Shanghai, where the build-up of more conventional transport and telecommunications infrastructures such as highways and mobile telecommunications has been rapid, more sophisticated service infrastructures such as airport logistics and e-commerce have not evolved accordingly. (see Kasarda, this book; Zhou and Chen, this book).

Ironically perhaps, conventional infrastructure can maximize the economic benefits derived from telematics. I think this is an important issue that has been lost somewhat in discussions about the neutralization of geography through telematics. Taylor and his colleagues (see generally GaWC) have made the most significant contributions in terms of empirical research and the development of a system of measures, but other contributions can also be found (Alderson and Beckfield 2004; Smith and Timberlake 2002; Taylor 2005). The most powerful of these new geographies of centrality at the interurban level binds the major international financial and business centers: New York, London, Tokyo, Paris, Frankfurt, Zurich, Amsterdam, Sydney, Hong Kong, and Toronto, among others. But this geography now also includes Shanghai, Singapore, Sao Paulo, Mexico City, and many others. The intensity of transactions among these cities, particularly through the financial markets, trade in services, and investment, has increased sharply, and so have the orders of magnitude involved.

Finally, we see emergent regional hierarchies, as illustrated by the growth corridors in East Asia (Chen 2005) and Southeast Asia (Lo and Yeung 1996), the case of Sao Paulo in the Mercosur free-trade area (Schiffer 2002), and by the relation between the participating entities in the Iran–Dubai corridor (Parsa and Keivani 2002).

In addition to their impact on the spatial correlates of centrality, the new ICT are expected to reduce inequality between cities and inside cities. There is an expectation expressed in much of the literature regarding these technologies that they will override older hierarchies and spatial inequalities through the universalizing of connectivity that they represent. The available evidence suggests that this is not quite the case (Ernst 2005; Garcia 2002). Whether it is the network of financial centers and foreign direct investment patterns or the more specific spatial organization of diverse global cities, the new ICT have not reduced inequality of resources among different types of firms or spatial inequalities within cities (Castells 1996; Conzen and Greene 2007; Graham 2004; Graham and Marvin 2001; Koval et al. 2006)—even in the face of massive upgrading and the building of state-of-the-art infrastructure in a growing number of cities worldwide. In fact, it has only accentuated urban spatial fragmentation between resource rich spaces such as the financial centers— whether in New York, Sao Paulo, or Shanghai (see Zhou and Chen, this book).

Further, the pronounced orientation to the world markets evident in many of these cities raises questions about the articulation with their nation-states, their regions, and the larger economic and social structure in such cities, respectively. Cities typically have been deeply embedded in the economies of their region, indeed often reflecting the characteristics of the latter; and they remain so today. But cities that are strategic sites in the global economy tend, in part, to disconnect from their region, especially if they are largely financial and specialized service exporters, such as New York and London. This conflicts with a key proposition in traditional scholarship about urban systems, namely, that these systems promote the territorial integration of regional and national economies. There has been a sharpening inequality in the concentration of strategic resources and activities between each of these cities and others in the same country. For example, Mexico City today concentrates a higher share of some types of economic activity and value productivity than it did in the past, but to see this requires a very particularized set of analyses, as Parnreiter (2002) shows us.

As illustrated by Shanghai and the surrounding Yangtze River Delta region, there are novel ways in which global cities become articulated with new kinds of regional economies. This is often linked to the development of new types of manufacturing and sometimes linked to older industrial histories, as is evident in cities as diverse as Chicago, Shanghai, and Sao Paulo. Their pasts as heavy manufacturing regions matters, but not simply in ways that are a continuation of these older histories. It is important to capture these developments through new types of analytical instruments for a more nuanced understanding of intraregional and interregional spatial inequalities (see Chen and Orum, conclusion, this book).

THE GLOBAL CITY AS A NEXUS FOR NEW POLITICOCULTURAL ALIGNMENTS

The incorporation of cities into a new cross-border geography of centrality also signals the likely emergence of a parallel political geography. Major cities have emerged as a strategic site not only for global capital but also for the transnationalization of labor (Mahler 1995; Smith and Guarnizo 2001), the formation of translocal communities and identities (Bartlett 2007; Farrer 2007; Laguerre 2000), and new types of global multisited politics (Buechler 2007; Lustiger-Thaler and Dubet 2004; Sassen 2008, chapters 6 and 7). In this regard cities are a site for new types of political operations and for a whole range of new "cultural," subjective, and other operations (Abu-Lughod 1994; Berner and Korff 1995; Drainville 2004; Featherstone and Lash 1999; Hagedorn 2006; Lloyd 2005; Sennett 1992). The centrality of place in a context of global processes makes possible a transnational economic and political opening for the formation of new claims and hence of new actors; possibly, such politics can succeed in the constituting of entitlements, notably those pertaining to claims of rights to place. At the limit, this could be an opening for new forms of "citizenship" (e.g., Holston 1996; Isin 2000; Bartlett 2007).

The emphasis on the transnational and hypermobile character of capital has contributed to a sense of powerlessness among local actors, a sense of the futility of resistance. But an analysis that emphasizes place suggests that the new global grid of strategic sites is a terrain for politics and engagement. The loss of power at the national level produces the possibility for new forms of power and politics at the subnational and local levels. In Shanghai, administrative decentralization, coupled with community reform, has empowered local communities in self-governance, even though they have taken on more financial burden in providing social services (see Lu, Ren, and Chen, this book; see also Henderson 2005).

One way of thinking about the local political implications of strategic space in global cities is within the context of the formation of new claims on that space. The global city, in particular, has emerged as a site for such new claims—those made by global capital, which uses the global city as an "organizational commodity," but also those articulated by disadvantaged sectors of the urban population, frequently as internationalized a presence in global cities as is capital. The "denationalizing" of urban space and the emergence of competing claims by both transnational and translocal actors raises the question: To whom does the city really belong?

The global city and the network of global cities is a space that is both place-centered, that is, embedded in particular and strategic locations, and transterritorial, because it connects sites that are not geographically proximate, yet are intensely connected to each other. If we consider that global cities concentrate both the leading sectors of global capital and a growing share of disadvantaged populations—immigrants, many disadvantaged women, people of color generally, and, in the megacities of developing countries, masses of shanty dwellers—then we can see that cities have become a strategic terrain for a whole series of conflicts and contradictions.

THE LIMITS OF TOPOGRAPHIC REPRESENTATIONS OF THE GLOBAL CITY

Understanding a city or a metropolitan region in terms of built topography is increasingly inadequate when global and digital forces are part of the urban condition. What we might call the topographic moment is a critical and large component of the representation of cities. But it cannot incorporate the fact of globalization and digitization as part of the representation of the urban. Nor can it critically engage today's dominant accounts about globalization and digitization, accounts that evict place and materiality even though the former are deeply imbricated with the material and the local and hence with that topographic moment.

The global city model contains as one of its key analytic modes a bridging between these very diverse dimensions: it captures the possibility that particular components of a city's topography can be spatializations of global/digital dynamics and formations (Sassen 2008, chapter 7). Such particular topographic components are thereby reconceptualized as sites in one or several multisited circuits or networks. Such spatializations destabilize the meaning of the local or the sited and thereby of the topographic understanding of cities. This applies in particular to global cities, but partly also to other cities (e.g. cities with significant foreign firms or factories, or global civil society organizations). Once this spatialization of various global and digital components is made legible, the richness of topographic analysis can add to our understanding of this process. The challenge is to locate and specify the existence of such spatializations and their variability.

This brings up a second set of issues: how topographic representations of the as-built environment of cities tend to emphasize the distinctiveness of the various socioeconomic sectors, such as the differences between poor and rich neighborhoods, commercial and manufacturing districts, and so on. Although valid, this type of representation becomes particularly partial when, as is happening today, a growing share of advanced economic sectors also employ significant numbers of very low-wage workers and subcontract to firms that do not appear to belong in the advanced corporate sector. Similarly, the growth of high-income professional households has generated a whole new demand for low-wage household workers, connecting expensive residential areas with poorer ones and linking these professional households to global care–chains that attract many of the cleaners, nannies, and nurses that migrate to global cities from poorer countries. These and other such processes that are particularly evident in global cities produce multiple interconnections among parts of the city that topographically appear to have little in common.

In Shanghai, work and residential landscapes have become more visibly fragmented as a result of globally linked sectors and jobs, the influx of mostly poor rural migrants, the government's plan to reduce older kinds of high-density housing in the center of the city, and the promotion of more diverse and globally oriented lifestyles. One critical strategy has been for the government and/or real estate developers to offer compensation to entice residents of older types of central city housing to vacate their homes so that their units can be replaced with new commercial towers and luxury apartment buildings. Some residents refuse to move to new and cheaper apartments in outlying areas because they do not like the inconvenience of long commutes to and from downtown Shanghai, where they can find employment as house cleaners in high-income households. This results in politicized urban space. Rural migrant workers who work as security guards and gardeners for gated communities in Shanghai can only afford to rent peasant houses on the city's far fringes. Yet another diversifying dynamic is the trend among residents in luxury apartments and villas to consume U.S.-style "fast food" and brand-name clothing (see Sun and Chen, this book).

One consequence of these dynamics, particularly in global cities, is that much of what we might still experience as the "local" (an office building, a house, or an institution in our neighborhood or downtown, or a poor community on the city's edges linked into an electronic activist network) actually is something I would think of as a "microenvironment with global span" insofar as it is deeply internetworked (Sassen 2008, chapter 7). Such a microenvironment is in many senses a localized entity, something that can be experienced as local, immediate, and proximate and hence captured in topographic representations. But it is also part of global digital networks, which give it an immediate, far-flung span—a feature that cannot be captured through topography. To continue to think of this as simply local is neither very useful nor is it adequate (see Lu, Ren, and Chen, this book).

What then is the meaning of locality under these conditions? The new networked advanced corporate sectors in global cities and the new globally linked, even if local, civil society organizations, each in their own way occupy a strategic, partly deterritorialized, geography that cuts across borders and connects a variety of points on the globe. Its local insertion accounts for only a (variable) fraction of its total operations, and its boundaries are neither those of the city within which it is partly located, nor those of the local area where it is sited.

SUMMARY AND IMPLICATIONS

An examination of globalization through the concept of the global city introduces a strong emphasis on strategic organizational components of the global economy rather than the broader and more diffuse homogenizing dynamics we associate with the globalization of consumer markets. Such a focus brings an emphasis first on the actual work of managing, servicing, and financing a global economy. Second, a focus on the city when studying globalization will tend to bring to the fore the growing inequalities between highly provisioned and profoundly disadvantaged sectors and spaces of the city, and therefore introduces yet another formulation of questions regarding power and inequality.

Third, the concept of the global city places a strong emphasis on the networked economy because of the nature of the industries that tend to be located therein: finance and specialized services, the new multimedia sectors, and telecommunications services. These industries are characterized by cross-border networks and specialized divisions of functions among cities rather than international competition per se. In the case of global finance and the leading specialized services catering to global firms and markets— legal, accounting, credit rating, telecommunications—it is clear that we are dealing with a cross-border system, one that is embedded in a series of cities, each possibly part of a different country. It is, therefore, a *de facto* global system, and Shanghai is becoming a part of it. But a focus on global cities also brings attention to the fact that disadvantaged and resource-poor civil society organizations can become similarly globally linked.

Global cities around the world are the terrain whereupon a multiplicity of globalization processes assume concrete, localized forms and induce local transformations. These localized forms and local transformations are, in good part, what defines globalization. Recovering any given place means recovering the multiplicity of global presences and local transformations with in this landscape. The large city of today has emerged as a strategic site for a whole range of new types of operations—political, economic, and cultural. It is a prominent nexus where the transformation of old practices and formation of new claims, involving both the powerful and the disadvantaged, unfold and take hold. To help establish an in-depth examination of this dynamic within the distinctive context of Shanghai, the other chapters of part I of this book provide additional comparative perspectives and implications from the United States and Asian experiences.

NOTES

1. Here Arrighi's analysis is of interest (1994) because it posits the recurrence of certain organizational patterns in different phases of the capitalist world economy, but they are at higher orders of complexity and expanded scope and timed to follow or precede particular configurations of the world economy.

2. Originally attributed to Goethe, the term was relaunched in the work of Peter Hall (1966) and more recently respecified by John Friedmann (Friedmann and Goetz 1982). See also Stren (1996).

3. Reported by *China Economic Review* online at www.chinaeconomicreview.com/subscriber/newsdetail/8528.html, accessed on February 2, 2007. Also see Kathleen Kingsbury, "China Braces for a Bubble." *Time,* February 12, 2007, 48–49.

4. A central proposition here, developed at length in my work, is that we cannot take the existence of a global economic system as a given but rather need to examine the particular ways in which the conditions for economic globalization are produced. The recovery of place and production also implies that global processes can be studied in great empirical detail.

5. We are seeing the formation of a distinct economic complex situated in an expanding network of global cities. This complex has a valorization dynamic that distinguishes it from other economic complexes whose valorization dynamic is far more articulated with the public economic functions of the state, the quintessential example being Fordist manufacturing. Global markets in finance and advanced services partly operate through a "regulatory" umbrella that is not state-centered but market-centered. This in turn brings up a question of control linked to the currently inadequate capacities to govern transactions in electronic space (Sassen 2008, chapter 5; 2009).

6. There are multiple specifications to this argument. For instance, and going in the opposite direction, the development of financial instruments that represent

fixed real estate repositions the pertinent buildings in various systems of circulation, including global ones. In so doing, the meaning of capital fixity is partly transformed, and the fixed capital also becomes a site for circulation. For a fuller elaboration see Sassen (2001, chapter 2; 2009).

7. Several of the organizing hypotheses in the global city model concern the conditions for the continuity of centrality in advanced economic systems in the face of major new organizational forms and technologies that maximize the possibility for geographic dispersal.

REFERENCES

Abrahamson, Mark. 2004. *Global Cities*. Oxford: Oxford University Press.

Abu-Lughod, Janet L. 1989. *Before European Hegemony: The World System A.D. 1250–1350*. New York: Oxford University Press.

———. 1994. *From Urban Village to "East Village": The Battle for New York's Lower East Side*. Cambridge: Blackwell.

———. 1999. *New York, Los Angeles, Chicago: America's Global Cities*. Minneapolis: University of Minnesota Press.

Alderson, Arthur S., and Jason Beckfield. 2004. "Power and Position in the World City System." *American Journal of Sociology* 109, no. 4: 811–51.

Alderson, Arthur S., Jason Beckfield, and François Nielsen. 2005. "Exactly How Has Income Inequality Changed? Patterns of Distributional Change in Core Societies." *Journal of Comparative Sociology* 46: 405–23.

Allen, J., D. Massey, and M. Pryke, eds. 1999. *Unsettling Cities*. New York: Routledge.

Amen, Mark M., Kevin Archer, and M. Martin Bosman, eds. 2006. *Relocating Global Cities: From the Center to the Margins*. New York: Rowman & Littlefield.

Arrighi, Giovanni. 1994. *The Long Twentieth Century*. New York: Verso.

Bartlett, Anne. 2007. "The City and the Self: The Emergence of New Political Subjects in London." In *Deciphering the Global: Its Spaces, Scales and Subjects*, edited by Saskia Sassen, 221–241. New York and London: Routledge.

Berner, E., and Korff, R. 1995. "Globalization and Local Resistance: The Creation of Localities in Manila and Bangkok." *International Journal of Urban and Regional Research* 19, no. 2: 34–52.

Brenner, Neil, and Roger Keil, eds. 2006. *The Global Cities Reader*. New York and London: Routledge.

Braudel, Fernand. 1984. *The Perspective of the World, Vol. III*. London: Collins.

Buechler, Simone. 2007. "Deciphering the Local in a Global Neoliberal Age: Three Favelas in Sao Paulo, Brazil." In *Deciphering the Global: Its Spaces, Scales, and Subjects*, edited by Saskia Sassen, 97–116. New York and London: Routledge.

Castells, Manuel. 1989. *The Informational City: Information Technology, Economic Restructuring, and the Urban-Regional Process*. Oxford, UK: Basil Blackwell.

———. 1996. *The Networked Society*. Oxford, UK: Blackwell.

Chen, Xiangming. 2005. *As Borders Bend: Transnational Spaces on the Pacific Rim.* Lanham, Md.: Rowman & Littlefield.

————. 2007. "A Tale of Two Regions in China: Rapid Economic Development and Slow Industrial Upgrading in the Pearl River and the Yangtze River Deltas." *International Journal of Comparative Sociology* 48, no. 2: 79–113.

Cicollela, Pablo, and Iliana Mignaqui. 2002. "The Spatial Reorganization of Buenos Aires." In *Global Networks/Linked Cities,* edited by Saskia Sassen, 309–26. New York and London: Routledge.

Cochrane, Allan, Jamie Peck, and Adam Tickell. 1996. "Manchester Plays Games: Exploring the Local Politics of Globalization." *Urban Studies* 33, no. 80: 1319–36.

Conzen, Michael, and Richard Greene, eds. 2007. "The LA and Chicago Schools: A Debate." Special issue of *Progressive Geography* (forthcoming).

Daniels, Peter W., and John R. Bryson. 2007. "Sustaining Business and Professional Services in a Second City Region: The Case of Birmingham, UK." *The Service Industries Journal* 25, no. 4: 642–58.

Dear, Michael. 2004. "Los Angeles as a Model for Comparative Urbanism." *Geographische Rundschau* 5, no. 1: 78–94.

Drainville, Andre. 2004. *Contesting Globalization: Space and Place in the World Economy.* London: Routledge.

Ernst, Dieter. 2005. "The New Mobility of Knowledge: Digital Information Systems and Global Flagship Networks." In *Digital Formations: IT and New Architectures in the Global Realm,* edited by Robert Latham and Saskia Sassen, 89–114. Princeton, N.J.: Princeton University Press.

Fainstein, Susan. 2001. *The City Builders.* Lawrence: Kansas University Press.

Farrer, Gracia Liu. 2007. "Producing Global Economies from Below: Chinese Immigrant Transnational Entrepreneurship in Japan." In *Deciphering the Global: Its Spaces, Scales and Subjects,* edited by Saskia Sassen, 179–99. New York and London: Routledge.

Featherstone, Mike, and Scott Lash, eds. 1999. *Spaces of Culture: City, Nation, World.* London: Sage.

Friedmann, John. 2005. *China's Urban Transition.* Minneapolis: University of Minnesota Press.

Friedmann, John, and Goetz Wolff. 1982. *World City Formation: An Agenda for Research and Action.* Los Angeles: Graduate School of Architecture and Urban Planning, University of California, Los Angeles.

Garcia, D. Linda. 2002. "The Architecture of Global Networking Technologies." In *Global Networks/Linked Cities,* edited by Saskia Sassen, 39–69. New York and London: Routledge.

GaWC. (continuously updated). *Globalization and World Cities—Study Group and Network.* www.lboro.ac.uk/gawc/.

Glasius, Marlies, Mary Kaldor, and Helmut Anheier, eds. 2002. *Global Civil Society Yearbook 2002.* London: Oxford University Press.

Graham, Stephen. 2002. "Communication Grids: Cities and Infrastructure." In *Global Networks/Linked Cities,* edited by Saskia Sassen, 71–91. London and New York: Routledge.

————, ed. 2004. *The Cybercities Reader.* London: Routledge.

Graham, Stephen, and Simon Marvin. 2001. *Splintering Urbanism: Networked Infrastructures, Technological Mobilities, and the Urban Condition.* New York and London: Routledge.

Gu, Felicity Rose, and Zilai Tang. 2002. "Shanghai: Reconnecting to the Global Economy." In *Global Networks/Linked Cities,* edited by Saskia Sassen, 273–307. London and New York: Routledge.

Gugler, Joseph. 2004. *World Cities beyond the West.* Cambridge, UK: Cambridge University Press.

Hagedorn, John, ed. 2006. *Gangs in the Global City: Exploring Alternatives to Traditional Criminology.* Chicago: University of Illinois at Chicago.

Hall, Peter. 1966. *The World Cities.* New York: McGraw-Hill.

Harvey, Rachel. 2007. "The Sub-National Constitution of Global Markets." In *Deciphering the Global: Its Spaces, Scales and Subjects,* edited by Saskia Sassen, 201–218. New York and London: Routledge.

Henderson, Jeffrey. 2005. "Governing Growth and Inequality: The Continuing Relevance of Strategic Economic Planning." In *Towards a Critical Globalization Studies,* edited by Richard Appelbaum and W. Robinson, 227–36. New York: Routledge.

Holston, James, ed. 1996. *Public Culture*: Special issue—"Cities and Citizenship," 8 no. 2.

Howard, Philip N., and Steve Jones, eds. 2004. *Society Online: The Internet in Context.* London: Sage.

Isin, Engin F., ed. 2000. *Democracy, Citizenship, and the Global City.* London and New York: Routledge.

Kerbo, Harold R. 2006. *World Poverty: Global Inequality and the Modern World System.* Boston: McGraw-Hill.

King, A.D. 1990. *Urbanism, Colonialism, and the World Economy: Culture and Spatial Foundations of the World Urban System.* London and New York: Routledge.

Koval, John P., Larry Bennett, Michael I.J. Bennett, Fassil Demissie, Roberta Garner, and Kiljoong Kim. 2006. *The New Chicago: A Social and Cultural Analysis.* Philadelphia: Temple University Press.

Krause, Linda, and Patrice Petro, eds. 2003. *Global Cities: Cinema, Architecture, and Urbanism in a Digital Age.* New Brunswick, N.J., and London: Rutgers University Press.

Laguerre, Michel S. 2000. *The Global Ethnopolis: Chinatown, Japantown, and Manilatown in American Society.* London: Macmillan.

Landrieu, Josse, Nicole May, Dirige Par, Therese Spector, and Pierre Veltz, eds. 1998. *La Ville Exclatee.* La Tour d'Aigues: Editiones de l'Aube.

Lloyd, Richard. 2005. *NeoBohemia: Art and Bohemia in the Postindustrial City.* London and New York: Routledge.

Lo, Fu-chen, and P.J. Marcotullio. 2000. "Globalization and Urban Transformations in the Asia-Pacific Region: A Review." *Urban Studies* 37, no. 1: 77–111.

Lo, Fu-chen, and Yue-man Yeung, eds. 1996. *Emerging World Cities in Pacific Asia.* Tokyo and New York: United Nations University Press.

Lustiger-Thaler, Henri, and François Dubet, eds. 2004. *Current Sociology*: Special Issue—"Social Movements in a Global World," 52, no. 4.

Mahler, Sarah. 1995. *American Dreaming: Immigrant Life on the Margins.* Princeton, N.J.: Princeton University Press.

Marcuse, Peter, and Ronald van Kempen, eds. 2000. *Globalizing Cities: A New Spatial Order?* Oxford: Blackwell.

Nijman, Jan. 1996. "Breaking the Rules: Miami in the Urban Hierarchy." *Urban Geography* 17, no. 1: 5–22.

Orum, Anthony M., and Xianming Chen. 2003. *The World of Cities: Places in Comparative and Historical Perspective.* Oxford: Blackwell Publishers.

Paddison, Ronan, ed. 2001. "Introduction." In *Handbook of Urban Studies,* edited by Ronan Paddison, 1–13. London: Sage.

Parnreiter, Christof. 2002. "The Making of a Global City: Mexico City." In *Global Networks/Linked Cities,* edited by Saskia Sassen, 145–82. New York and London: Routledge.

Parsa, Ali, and Ramin Keivani. 2002. "The Hormurz Corridor: Building a Cross-Border Region between Iran and the United Arab Emirates." In *Global Networks/Linked Cities,* edited by Saskia Sassen, 183–207. London and New York: Routledge.

Regional Planning Association (RPA). 2007. *Economic Megaregions.* Princeton, N.J.: Policy Research Institute for the Region, Woodrow Wilson School of Public and International Affairs, Princeton University.

Ren, Xuefei. 2008. "Forward to the Past: Historical Preservation in Globalizing Shanghai." *City and Community* 7, no. 1: 23–43.

Rutherford, Kenneth R. 2004. *A Tale of Two Global Cities: Comparing the Territories of Telecommunications Developments in Paris and London.* Aldershot, UK: Ashgate.

Sachar, Arie. 1990. "The Global Economy and World Cities." In *The World Economy and the Spatial Organization of Power,* edited by Arie Sachar and Sture Oberg, 149–60. Aldershot, England: Avebury.

Santos, Milton, Maria Adelia Aparecida de Souza, and Maria Laura Silveira. 1994. *Território: Globalização e Fragmentação.* Sao Paulo: Editora Hucitec.

Sassen, Saskia. 1984. "The New Labor Demand in Global Cities." In *Cities in Transformation,* edited by Michael P. Smith, 139–71. Beverly Hills, Calif.: Sage.

———. 2001. *The Global City: New York, London, Tokyo.* 2nd ed. Princeton, N.J.: Princeton University Press.

————. 2006. *Cities in a World Economy*. 3rd ed. Thousand Oaks, Calif.: Pine Forge/Sage.

————. 2008. *Territory, Authority, Rights: From Medieval to Global Assemblages*. Princeton, N.J.: Princeton University Press.

————. 2009. "When Local Housing Becomes an Electronic Instrument: The Global Circulation of Mortgages." *International Journal of Urban and Regional Research* (forthcoming).

Schiffer, Sueli Ramos. 2002. "Sao Paulo: Articulating a Cross-Border Region." In *Global Networks/Linked Cities*, edited by Saskia Sassen, 209–36. New York and London: Routledge.

Scott, Allen J. 2004. "A Perspective of Economic Geography." *Journal of Economic Geography* 4, no. 5: 479–99.

Sennett, Richard. 1992. *The Conscience of the Eye: The Design and Social Life of Cities*. New York: W.W. Norton.

Shanghai Statistical Bureau. 2004. *Shanghai Statistical Yearbook 2004*. Beijing: China Statistics Press.

Short, John Rennie. 2005. *Global Metropolitanism*. London: Routledge.

Short, John Rennie, and Yeong-Hyun Kim. 1999. *Globalization and the City*. Essex: Addison Wesley Longman.

Smith, Michael P., and Luis Guarnizo. 2001. *Transnationalism from Below*. New Brunswick, N.J.: Transaction.

Smith, David A., and Michael Timberlake. 2002. "Hierarchies of Dominance among World Cities: A Network Approach." In *Global Networks/Linked Cities*, edited by Saskia Sassen, 117–41. New York and London: Routledge.

Stren, Richard. 1996. "The Studies of Cities: Popular Perceptions, Academic Disciplines, and Emerging Agendas." In *Preparing for the Urban Future: Global Pressures and Local Forces*, edited by Michael A. Cohen, Blair A. Ruble, Joseph S. Tulchin, and Allison M. Garland. Washington, D.C.: Woodrow Wilson Center Press (distributed by Johns Hopkins University Press).

Sum, Ngai-Ling. 1999. "Rethinking Globalisation: Re-articulating the Spatial Scale and Temporal Horizons of Trans-border Spaces." In *Globalization and the Asia-Pacific: Contested Territories*, edited by Kris Olds, et al., 129–45. London: Routledge.

Taylor, Peter J. 2004. *World City Network: A Global Urban Analysis*. London: Routledge.

————. 2005. "New Political Geographies: Global Civil Society and Global Governance through World City Networks." *Political Geography* 24, no. 4: 703–30.

Taylor, Peter J., D.R.F. Walker, and J.V. Beaverstock. 2002. "Firms and Their Global Service Networks." In *Global Networks/Linked Cities*, edited by Saskia Sassen, 93–116. New York and London: Routledge.

Taylor, Peter J., Ben Derudder, Pieter Saey, Frank Witlox, eds. 2006. *Cities in Globalization: Practices, Policies and Theories*. New York and London: Routledge.

Torres, Rodolfo D., Jonathan Xavier Inda, and Louis F. Miron. 1999. *Race, Identity, and Citizenship*. Oxford: Blackwell.

UNCTAD Handbook of Statistics. 2008. "1.1: Values and Shares of Merchandise Exports and Imports." UNCTAD. http://stats.unctad.org/Handbook/TableViewer/tableView.aspx?ReportId=1902.

Veltz, P. 1996. *Mondialisation Villes et Territoires: L'Economie d'Archipel*. Paris: Presses Universitaires de France.

World Federation of Exchanges. 2007. "Latest Statistics: YTD Monthly." www.world-exchanges.org/statistics/ytd-monthly.

———. 2008. "Latest Statistics: YTD Monthly." www.world-exchanges.org/statistics/ytd-monthly.

Yeung, Yue-man. 2000. *Globalization and Networked Societies*. Honolulu: University of Hawaii Press.

2. HIGH-TECH ACTIVITY AND URBAN ECONOMIC DEVELOPMENT IN THE UNITED STATES

Where Should the Bar Be Set for Shanghai?

Ann R. Markusen and Pingkang Yu

Since the early 1980s, researchers have been struck by the dynamism of new industries—dubbed "high-tech"—and their apparent roles in driving differential regional growth rates. Older American industrial and financial cities such as New York and Chicago, growing slowly and subject to considerable deindustrialization, no longer seem capable of performing as "seedbeds of innovation" (Markusen and McCurdy 1989), whereas places such as Silicon Valley and Route 128 outside Boston have become famous as prototypical new industrial regions (Saxenian 1994). Although some of the purported drivers of high-tech location, including university research and development activity, are not borne out by clear evidence (Markusen, Hall, and Glasmeier 1986), economic development policies at the state and local level have become preoccupied with fashioning strategies that will attract, retain, and "home-grow" high-tech industries and firms.

How can we determine how high-tech a city is? Our view is that technology intensity is best captured by the scientific and technical composition of the workforce in an industry (Markusen, Hall, and Glasmeier 1986; Chapple et al. 2004). Our choice of science-and-technology occupations (S&T), a human capital-based measure, reflects a growing interest in skilled labor, rather than resources or physical capital, as a driver of economic development (Markusen 2004; Markusen and Schrock 2006; Mather 1999). Our measure and approach raises a timely question for Shanghai: where should the bar be set in focusing on developing high-tech manufacturing as a strategy for achieving status as a global city? In narrowly chasing certain high-tech industries, such as in establishing semiconductor plants in Pudong, Shanghai may neglect the more basic and comprehensive value of upgrading human capital development in its traditionally strong manufacturing sectors and in its new business services. Using U.S.-based analysis and findings, we identify some policy lessons for Shanghai as it seeks to better position its high-tech manufacturing in building a global city.

USING OCCUPATIONS TO IDENTIFY HIGH-TECH INDUSTRIES

In a recent study (Chapple et al. 2004), we refined the widely used science and engineering metric to include managers having scientific and engineering backgrounds, as well as certain groups of computer professionals—a group representing what we term science and technology occupations. We then ranked all manufacturing and service industries at the three-digit SIC level by the shares of their national workforce that are engaged in the S&T occupations. We explicitly incorporated services, because we reject the notion that manufacturing is a more important driver of employment growth than services.

Conforming to popular conceptions, computer services and electronics are identified as high-tech by this method, but so are a number of sectors not included in many other high-tech definitions: missile and aerospace technologies; pharmaceuticals; engineering and architectural services; medical instrument sevices; management and public relations; and research, testing and evaluation services. Some of these are among the fastest-growing of all high-tech industries. For instance, employment in sectors such as pharmaceuticals; engineering and architectural services; research, testing, and evaluation services; and management and public relations all grew faster nationally during the 1990s than did electronics employment and many of the other industries more popularly perceived as high-tech.

HIGH-TECH METROPOLIS

Using these definitions, we then ranked as high-tech the thirty U.S. metropolitan areas that added the greatest number of net new jobs across all sectors during the period 1991–1999. In our rankings, the Chicago and Washington, D.C. metropolitan areas hosted the largest numbers of employees in high-tech industries as of 1997 (Table 2.1). Both are home

TABLE 2.1

Highest Job-Adding Metropolitan Statistical Areas/Primary Metropolitan Statistical Areas (MSA/PMSA) Ranked by Total High-tech Jobs, 1997; Absolute Job Growth, 1991–99; High-tech Job Share, 1997; and High-tech Specialization, 1997

MSA/PMSA	High-tech Industry Jobs, 1997 (000)	Total Job Growth, 1991–99 (000)		High-tech Job Share, 1997 (%)		High-tech Specialization, 1997	
		Job Growth	Rank	Job Share	Rank	Specialization Index	Rank
Chicago	347.1	528.0	2	12.4	16	1.25	25
Washington, D.C.	321.6	337.3	6	20.3	4	2.19	2
San Jose	289.1	163.0	29	41.3	1	1.56	14
Boston	281.5	262.6	14	20.9	3	1.3	23
New York	250.3	277.6	13	10.1	21	1.85	5
Philadelphia	222.5	216.0	18	13.1	13	1.26	24
Dallas	197.9	484.5	4	16.4	9	1.54	15
Seattle	174.9	257.8	15	21.1	2	2.23	1
Minneapolis–St. Paul	162.6	318.5	7	15.3	11	1.22	26
Houston	162.5	392.9	5	12.2	17	1.49	17
Orange County	152.4	201.5	20	18.4	6	1.2	27
Atlanta	151.1	642.4	1	10.2	20	1.64	8
Detroit	138.8	295.7	9	8.8	25	1.67	7
Phoenix	116.0	515.5	3	13.0	15	1.46	19
San Diego	112.7	187.6	24	16.4	8	1.19	28
Denver	94.5	286.3	11	14.5	12	1.61	12
Portland, Ore.	77.7	218.8	17	13.0	14	1.37	22
Austin	75.7	230.5	16	19.7	5	1.98	3

(Continues)

TABLE 2.1
(Continued)

MSA/PMSA	High-tech Industry Jobs, 1997 (000)	Total Job Growth, 1991–99 (000)		High-tech Job Share, 1997 (%)		High-tech Specialization, 1997	
		Job Growth	Rank	Job Share	Rank	Specialization Index	Rank
Tampa-St. Petersburg	73.2	299.0	8	8.8	24	1.4	21
Raleigh-Durham	69.0	195.4	23	16.8	7	1.44	20
Kansas City	61.8	183.4	25	9.4	22	1.5	16
Charlotte	61.3	200.0	21	10.3	19	1.56	13
Salt Lake City	60.6	196.7	22	16.2	10	1.18	29
Fort Worth	54.6	171.1	26	10.9	18	1.68	6
Columbus, Ohio	53.7	157.6	30	9.1	23	1.48	18
Orlando	43.6	280.4	12	7.6	26	1.61	11
Riverside-San Bernardino	32.7	214.8	19	6.1	27	1.16	30
San Antonio	28.1	170.4	27	6.1	28	1.64	9
Nashville	27.4	164.7	28	5.7	29	1.64	10
Las Vegas	23.1	292.1	10	4.9	30	1.85	4

Source: 1997 Economic Census and Bureau of Labor Statistics, Current Employment Series.

Note: Higher specialization index scores reflect a greater concentration of high-tech employment in certain industries; lower scores indicate broader distribution among high-tech industries. The coefficient of variation measures the spread of a set of data as a proportion of its mean. It provides a measure of relative variation and is scale-free, so it is particularly useful in making comparisons between different cities. For each metropolitan area, the specialization index (coefficient of variation) is calculated as the ratio of the standard deviation of all high-tech sectors' employment divided by the mean.

to high-tech industry establishments with more than 300,000 jobs, out-performing Silicon Valley, which earns third place; Boston is fourth.

Our findings refute the argument that the American Sunbelt is the clear winner in high-tech business. In addition to Chicago and the four other East Coast cities in the top ten, Detroit also ranks among the top twenty with more high-tech industry jobs are not, as some have argued, than Phoenix, San Diego, Denver, Portland, or Austin, respectively. Moreover, high-tech jobs are not, as some have argued, concentrated on "the coasts." The midcontinental cities of Detroit, Chicago, Minneapolis/St. Paul, Austin, Phoenix, and Denver all rank within the top twenty.

The more mature industrial cities do well in the study because they are not penalized for being diversified. Some studies of high-tech regions (e.g., DeVol 1999) rely on the percent of the regional workforce employed in high-tech industries. Using such a metric, relatively young cities that postdate the Industrial Revolution, such as Phoenix or Austin, appear very high-tech, because they lack more mature manufacturing functions in their economies and thus do not represent this in their total employment. The evidence strongly suggests that cities such as Chicago, Boston, New York, and Philadelphia are exhibiting an ability to supplement their more mature manufacturing and financial sectors with dynamic new activities, adding more net new high-tech jobs than many of what have popularly been considered the emerging high-tech centers.

These findings bear lessons for Shanghai, China's premier industrial city, similar in this regard to American cities such as New York, Boston, and Chicago. Shanghai, too, is going through a process of restructuring, in which manufacturers, particularly those dealing in textiles, are moving to lower-cost locations as the service sector expands. We believe that an occupational approach to identifying Chinese high-tech sectors—both manufacturing and services—will yield a list of sectors in which Shanghai possesses a strong competitive advantage. It is also important to understand that a number of service sectors are exporting their activities, and are essential to the viability of China's manufacturing activities.

METROPOLITAN DIVERSIFICATION AND RESILIENCY

We discovered a relatively broad range of differences in the degrees of specialization and diversification among the cities we studied in the United States. Washington, D.C., Seattle, Austin, and New York are among the most specialized of the high-tech metropolitan areas, whereas Boston, Chicago, Minneapolis/St. Paul, and San Diego are among the most diversified (Table 2.1). Diversification is unrelated to a metropolitan area's regional location, relative "age," or absolute size.

Of the top ten high-tech cities, four are highly specialized. High-tech jobs in Washington, D.C., are heavily concentrated in computer services; research, development, and testing services; engineering and architectural services; and management/public relations. New York specializes in financial services, insurance, research and engineering services, and management/public relations. Both Silicon Valley and Seattle specialize in high-tech manufacturing. Detroit's well-known specialization in transportation equipment is apparent not because autos are high-tech (they don't qualify, despite the presence of automotive engineers) but because Detroit has large numbers of people working with engines and turbines, computer services, engineering and architectural services, and management and public relations, many of them auto-related. Although China's major industrial cities, too, are likely specialized in a similar fashion, Shanghai stands out more as an increasingly dominant auto production center that is developing a Detroit-like concentration of auto-related manufacturing and service employment.

Some metropolitan areas possess economies rich in high-tech manufacturing and poor in high-tech services. Silicon Valley, Seattle, and Austin top this list, with high-tech manufacturing–to–high-tech service ratios that are at least 2.5 times the national average. Interestingly, other western and southern U.S. metropolitan areas also dominate the list of manufacturing-specialized high-tech areas. Yet other metropolitan areas from these regions are high-tech manufacturing–poor—including Houston, Atlanta, San Antonio, and Las Vegas. With the exception of the Twin Cities, the northeastern–midwestern metropolitan areas fall at or below the national ratio of high-tech manufacturing to services, revealing their strong high-tech service base.

The nature of high-tech activity across metropolitan areas differentially positions them for the future. Recessions place great stress both on incipient, youthful industries and on mature ones ripe for restructuring. Accordingly, metropolitan areas that are more high-tech diversified may find themselves better positioned to weather a downturn than those that are highly specialized. Among the latter, employment trends will be highly sensitive to the performance of these core industries. Seattle's overall performance, for instance, is heavily tied to the aerospace industry; New York's is tied to finance, marketing, and management; and Silicon Valley's is tied to electronics and computing. In the U.S. recession of 2001, each of these cities was more vulnerable to unemployment and displacement than were the more diversified metropolitan economies such as Chicago, Boston, and Minneapolis/St. Paul.

IMPLICATIONS FOR SHANGHAI AND CHINESE CITIES

The American experience with high-tech development offers important lessons for Chinese cities such as Shanghai. As the unquestioned industrial and financial capital of China, Shanghai is poised to play significant roles in the remaking of the national economy. But, as a relatively mature city, it also faces challenges of its own, as older manufacturing sectors move to lower-cost locations. Shanghai, however, has options. It could suffer the slow-growth fate of other older industrial cities around the world (e.g., Rio de Janeiro) or become a highly specialized finance and service center—and thus vulnerable to cyclical swings and structural changes as is New York City. Or it could attempt to remake itself into a high-tech region in its own right.

If Shanghai leaders find this third option attractive, the American experience will be instructive. We caution against too narrowly defining high-tech, arguing for a human capital and skills-based criterion for identifying high-tech activity. Equating high-tech with electronics and computing narrows the field in damaging ways, for other fields, from aircraft to biotechnology to business services, may also be comprised of high-skill activities and offer promising growth futures.

We will now reflect on three sets of implications from our high-tech redefinition study for Chinese economic development policymakers. First, in light of the increasing importance of human capital as a driver of economic development, an occupation-oriented development policy should be formulated to supplement traditional industrial targeting practices. Second, increased attention should be paid to promoting high-tech services, not merely to manufacturing. Third, redoubled efforts should be made to promote the diversification of Shanghai's high-tech industries, strengthening the whole urban economy.

TARGETING OCCUPATIONS AS WELL AS INDUSTRIES

For the past three decades, economic development planners have been identifying and targeting selected industries in communities based on their export potential. This practice rests on the view that some industries offer greater wealth-creating prospects than others because of existing or potentially higher productivity and lower cost advantages offered by the local economy as opposed to other locations. Since the 1980s, the meteoric success of electronics and computing has encouraged localities to compete for firms and plants in these sectors. The spectacle of Silicon Valley has captured the imaginations of many policymakers around the globe, and thousands of visitors have flocked to the Valley to try to discern its secrets and replicate them. In fact, few places will ever be able to match the "first-mover" advantages of Silicon Valley or benefit from the enormous and continued government military spending that has underwritten much of its research and purchased many of its leading-edge products (Gray et al. 1999).

But technology content is not confined to electronics and computing. Many other sectors demand high-tech talent and rely on it for innovation: pharmaceuticals, biotechnology, aerospace, telecommunications, architecture and engineering, computer software, and many more. We use an occupational definition to identify high-tech sectors, because we believe that human skill—not a particular set of firms or plants—is the most important asset of an urban economy. Technology-skilled workers are increasingly mobile between firms, and it is their presence in the city itself and their commitment to it rather than to particular firms that gives large high-tech cities their edge (Markusen 1996).

We are now taking this emphasis further by exploring an alternative to focusing on firms and industries in economic development practice: envisioning metropolitan regions as ensembles of occupations rather than of industries (Markusen and Barbour 2003). In parallel studies of economic development (Markusen 2004; Markusen and Schrock 2006), we laid out a series of rationales for using occupations as a lens to view the specialization and potential of a regional economy. A brief recapitulation will suffice here (see Markusen and Barbour 2003 for a fuller treatment).

In this conceptualization, a metropolitan economy is comprised predominantly of people in their roles as decision-makers and workers. They are starting up and closing down firms, buying and using resources, building plants and equipment, hiring others, and working to generate marketable goods and services. In this conception, we visualize and characterize economies by "what workers do, not what they make" (Thompson and Thompson 1985).

As analysts, we can draw abstract maps of regional economies based primarily on occupation rather than industry. Each occupation is distinguished by its particular skills, educational requirements, and functional tasks. Individual workers are key decision-makers in an occupational framework, because they decide whether to acquire certain skills and how to deploy them, in light of their options in their respective labor markets (another conceptualization). But other decision-makers are also important within this framework, particularly—those who supply skills and training, including schools, colleges, and private-sector firms.

Through the occupational lens, we perceive Silicon Valley as a place perpetually poised to emerge as a regional hub of technology managers, venture capitalists, aeronautical and electrical engineers, inspectors and testers, and commercial artists. The occupational lens, then, helps us identify the relatively unique pools of talent that a region possesses. Not all such regional occupational specializations can be neatly mapped onto a single set of industries. Some are dispersed across a broad range of sectors, and this trend appears to be modestly increasing (Markusen and Schrock 2006).

Approaching economic development as an occupational rather than an industrial phenomenon offers alternative paths for economic developers. For example, when an industry is in structural decline because production is cheaper elsewhere, or because substitutes are destroying its market, working with occupational groups is an alternative to simply trying to prevent plant closings.

Because of their evolved industry orientation, economic development practitioners in the past few decades have worked extensively with firms, industries, and business associations, which are increasingly perceived as customers. In contrast, a practice reoriented around occupations would pursue occupational and occupation-shaping partners. Prominent among these would be membership associations formed along occupational lines, ranging from trade and craft unions (e.g., of electricians, machinists, writers, musicians, operating engineers, nurses, actors, or janitors) to professional associations (e.g., of mechanical engineers, economists, doctors, or accountants). Strong ties would also be forged with institutions and organizations that recruit, educate, and provide training services to workers.

The occupational frame gives priority to labor rather than to physical capital as the key to regional development. An occupation-oriented economic development strategy would make significant investments in human capital not just through the general educational system, but also through a specialized workforce training system matching the skill development services offered to workers with employers' needs. As one of China's higher education centers, Shanghai has a good general educational system that fosters one of the nation's most educated workforces. In implementing an occupation-focused development strategy, its leaders should therefore consider establishing a specialized workforce training system to provide workers with the special skills demanded by employers (Schrock et al. 2002). The training system should consist of partnerships involving industries or occupations that bring together government, nonprofit organizations, labor, and businesses in order to identify the common needs of business and workers and to leverage the training done privately and academically through the use of targeted governmental and nonprofit programs. Although the recent boom of executive MBA programs at Shanghai's top business schools is necessary, and has already paid its way by strengthening the middle and senior management ranks, more targeted training for skilled manufacturing workers and managerial training for technical engineers lag behind and are imperative to achieve broader knowledge upgrading in Shanghai's competitive industries.

PROMOTING HIGH-TECH SERVICES RATHER THAN MANUFACTURING

Worldwide, employment in services has been growing faster than in manufacturing. This is in large part a function of tremendous gains in manufacturing productivity compared with relatively poor gains in services. Some business services are growing precisely because they enable manufacturers to work more efficiently. In countries where planned economies were once in control, economic development planners often ignore services at their peril—although Shanghai has come a long way quite rapidly in developing and strengthening its services from their initial low starting point (see Chen, introduction, this book).

In the United States, high-tech employment has grown disproportionately in the service sector (Table 2.2). Science and technology occupational concentrations correspondingly rose much more rapidly in services than in manufacturing sectors.

Those metropolitan areas in the U.S. that excelled in adding high-tech jobs are relatively specialized in high-tech services rather than in

TABLE 2.2

Science and Technology (S&T) Occupational Employment in Services and Manufacturing, the United States, 1989 and 1998

	Share of Total S&T 1989	Share of Total S&T 1998	S&T Employment Growth 1989–98 (%)	Employment Growth 1989–98 (%)
Manufacturing	36.6	25.5	−4.1	−3.2
HT Manufacturing	26.1	17.0	−10.5	−10.1
Services	28.0	41.0	100.5	32.2
HT Services	22.9	35.1	110.5	51.6

Source: Bureau of Labor Statistics, *National Industry-Occupation Time Series Matrix,* 1989, 1998.

manufacturing. Eight out of the top ten high-tech job–adding metropolitan areas possess more jobs in high-tech services than in high-tech manufacturing (see Table 2.1). Silicon Valley and Seattle, with their large manufacturing sectors, are the exceptions. Moreover, Silicon Valley also relies heavily on adjacent San Francisco for services.

The U.S. job generation record of high-tech services compared with manufacturing suggests that Chinese economic development planners should include services when formulating high-tech strategy. To date, Chinese initiatives in high-tech urban development, such as establishing high-tech industrial parks, narrowly focus on a small pool of high-tech manufacturing sectors. In light of its pride of place in the Yangtze River Delta economic region, Shanghai could enhance its high-tech service role vis-à-vis its hinterland. Outer smaller industrial cities such as Suzhou, Wuxi, Changzhou, and Nantong rely heavily on Shanghai for services, and a strong high-tech service sector in Shanghai would help to propel these cities toward innovative adoption. In recent years, large foreign investments in electronics and computer equipment plants have favored lower-cost locations in the near cities and exurbs of Shanghai, a development that underscores Shanghai's potential as a service center. Although services' share of Shanghai's overall employment rose rapidly from 21.6 percent in 1978 to 55.6 percent in 2005 (Table I.1 in Chen, introduction), it remains far lower than in other major global cities.

High-tech services are closely aligned with producer services. All the high-tech service sectors identified in our high-tech redefinition study are producer service sectors.[1] Over the past three decades, producer services have experienced rapid growth, the result of increasingly complex and specialized systems of production (Sassen, this book). One of the key functions of producer services is to introduce external expertise into manufacturing activity (Beyers and Lindahl 1996). In addition, a recent study of high-tech producer services reveals its role in fostering innovation through the embedded entrepreneurship and technical expertise of skilled workers in high-tech service firms (Schrock 2003). From Shanghai and other Chinese cities emancipated from the planned economy, high-tech producer service sectors could fuel the nation's growth dynamic by introducing advanced technology to many industries and generating entrepreneurial opportunities. Shanghai is uniquely positioned to benefit from this type of activity, which may account for its surge in the number of R&D centers of multinational corporations in recent years (see Sassen, this book).

The challenges facing high-tech service sectors in China are a function of the country's remaining socialist economic institutional practices, which are slowly disintegrating in the face of marketizing reforms. State-owned and operated production units are subject to centralized coordination, the economic plan, and an exclusive element—the state work unit. The central economic plan discourages competition within the system, thus restraining the incentives for specialization. The state work unit reduces the demand for external expertise by internalizing all possible professional and information services. The producer service sectors remain underdeveloped in this system and have only recently begun emerging in conjunction with reform efforts and the external stimulus of global firms that have set up local producer service facilities in Shanghai.

Another hindrance for high-tech producer services is the deficient legal protection of intellectual property. People and firms in knowledge-intensive sectors are frequent creators, users, and distributors of intellectual products. The protection of the value of these products is prerequisite for business. Although a number of laws and administrative regulations protecting intellectual property have been enacted in China since 1985, enforcement is inadequate. China's accession to the World Trade Organization creates pressure on the Chinese government to improve intellectual property protection, which it must do to satisfy the Agreement on Trade-Related Aspects of Intellectual Property Rights (TRIPS). China's ability to advance beyond a low-wage manufacturing stage will depend upon its ability to foster a producer services sector.

PROMOTING ECONOMIC DIVERSIFICATION

The findings of our study suggest that high-tech cities are not penalized but rewarded for being diversified. Highly diversified cities such as Chicago top the high-tech job-adding list, outdoing high-tech service cities such as New York or high-tech manufacturing cities such as Silicon Valley. In addition, our findings suggest that a city's high-tech job–adding capacity has little to do with its degree of technology dependency. The high-tech star Silicon Valley is not exhibiting a stronger capacity for adding high-tech jobs than mature industrial cities such as Chicago and New York, although its overall specialization rate in high-tech is triple the national average. Chicago and New York, by way of contrast, are not high-tech–specialized at all (see Table 2.3).

Shanghai, in our view, resembles Chicago more than New York or Silicon Valley. A second-tier city located within San Francisco's metro economy, Silicon Valley specializes in an array of high-tech manufacturing sectors, including electronics, computing, and aerospace, and hosts

Table 2.3

High-Tech Industries by Location Quotient: Chicago, New York, and San Jose Primary
Metropolitan Statistical Areas (PMSA) in Comparison

SIC	Description	Chicago, Ill. PMSA	New York, N.Y. PMSA	San Jose, Calif. PMSA
1310	Crude Petroleum And Natural Gas	0.00	0.00	0.00
1480	Nonmetallic Minerals Services, Except Fuels	0.00	0.00	0.00
2110	Cigarettes	0.00	0.00	0.00
2810	Industrial Inorganic Chemicals	0.69	0.05	0.00
2820	Plastics Materials And Synthetic Resins, Synthetic	0.89	0.02	0.00
2830	Drugs	2.32	1.08	0.84
2860	Industrial Organic Chemicals	0.51	0.26	0.00
3480	Ordnance And Accessories, Except Vehicles And	0.00	0.05	0.00
3510	Engines And Turbines	0.50	0.00	0.32
3550	Special Industry Machinery, Except Metalworking	0.97	0.00	2.68
3570	Computer And Office Equipment	0.42	0.14	14.31
3660	Communications Equipment	2.14	0.15	13.20
3670	Electronic Components And Accessories	0.90	0.11	11.52
3720	Aircraft And Parts	0.07	0.12	0.00
3760	Guided Missiles And Space Vehicles And Parts	0.00	0.00	22.87
3810	Search, Detection, Navigation, Guidance,	0.50	0.04	1.99
3820	Laboratory Apparatus And Analytical, Optical,	0.99	0.14	7.24
3840	Surgical, Medical, And Dental Instruments And	1.01	0.19	4.00
3860	Photographic Equipment And Supplies	0.43	0.10	0.00
4820	Telegraph And Other Message Communications	0.00	0.00	0.00
4890	Communications Services, Not Elsewhere	0.10	0.48	0.00
4930	Combination Electric And Gas, And Other Utility	1.03	1.57	0.00
6010	Central Reserve Depository Institutions	0.94	3.13	0.10
6310	Life Insurances	1.06	2.18	0.11
6710	Holding Offices	0.00	0.00	0.00
7370	Computer Programming, Data Processing, And	1.18	0.93	3.56
8710	Engineering, Architectural, And Surveying	0.84	0.73	1.72
8730	Research, Development, And Testing Services	1.39	1.17	3.17
8740	Management And Public Relations Services	1.69	1.85	0.86
8990	Other Business Services	0.50	1.08	0.76
	Total HT Sector Employment	0.92	0.75	3.07

Source: 1997 Economic Census.

significant branch plants of large national and foreign firms (Gray et al. 1999). It is much like Suzhou in terms of location, scale, and industries, especially since Singapore built its only industrial park in China therein. This is borne out by Suzhou's recent growth, not only in more sophisticated manufacturing but also in the R&D activities of companies such as Samsung (Chen 2007). New York is strong in financial and management services, but its mature manufacturing sectors have largely departed (Table 2.3).

Shanghai can avoid the fate of New York in the coming decades by modeling itself more after Chicago. Chicago has a diversified economic base with strength in services, and it has an ability to upgrade and retain its manufacturing as well. Shanghai is the premier industrial (as well as service) center in China, just as Chicago is in the United States. Its size and diversity positions it well to attract and retain a broad mix of high-tech activities. The mix should include high-tech services sectors such as data processing, engineering services, and management consulting that will help introduce foreign technologies into Chinese manufacturing. Such a mix would enable Shanghai to protect itself against potential cyclical downturns, structural decline in particular sectors, and disappointing results in innovative sectors (such as the recent telecommunications bust in the United States). Diversification will also strengthen the evolutionary import-replacing trajectory common to large, fast-growing cities.

Diversification has yielded substantial benefits for other regions. Taiwan, for example, once relied on labor-intensive manufacturing. But, after successfully incorporating many Japanese and American technologies into electronics and semiconductor lines, Taiwan has become one of the world's major producers of computer equipment and electronics. This is attributable at least in part to the Taiwanese government's efforts in promoting economic diversity from the 1960s onward. Singapore offers another pertinent example of sustained economic dynamism through a mix of government-directed diversification and overseas expansion (see Ho, this book).

Diversification strategies require a careful assessment of a city's comparative advantages; unique strengths could be a platform for creating Shanghai's international specializations. The Dutch cut flower industry, for example, employs a unique set of house growing techniques and creates high levels of wealth for Dutch workers and farmers. Another example is Israeli agriculture; and the early Japanese success with small, fuel-efficient cars in the international market is, a case study illustrating how scarcity of resources (e.g., air quality, petroleum) can drive innovation in a particular country. Shanghai planners should take stock of the human capital and know-how of the region to identify opportunities for new, successful products and services.

To diversify Shanghai's economy, economic planners of the municipal and central governments should seek to eliminate barriers to local competition. Vigorous competition among local rivals creates persistent competitive advantage in an industry (Porter 1990). Japan is the premier example of this; in every leading product area, including automobiles and semiconductors, it hosts more than ten firms competing for the small domestic market. Domestic champions are thus primed to assert world leadership. For contemporary local industries to survive the influx of foreign rivals, firms must be able to strengthen themselves through local competition, something discouraged in the planned economy. But pro-competitive policies should not be applied abruptly, as in the former Soviet Union; instead, they should be phased in over time, accompanied with tax, land-use, technical assistance, and workforce training that will help managers learn how to compete in a very different market, ensuring a superior distribution of wealth and assets as well as preventing corruption. Although barriers to competition in Shanghai remain high because of the dominance of giant state corporations in selected industries such as automotives, steel, and petrochemicals—and because of the continued existence of corruption—the local penetration of global manufacturers and the growing competition among small private firms in consumer goods industries tend to weaken these barriers.

Diversification and long-term prosperity will be easier to achieve with further market-oriented economic reforms. The Chinese economy is much more diversified now than it was at the beginning of the reforms. But the government still bars the entry of domestic private firms into many sectors, including telecommunications, airlines, petroleum chemistry, steel and iron, and news. It also tightly regulates private firms operating another dozen sectors, including those dealing with automobile manufacturing, electronic appliances, and travel. In addition, China's stiff governmental approval system required before founding a firm has arbitrary and often very high registration capital requirements that deter many entrepreneurial endeavors. Technology alone cannot ensure latecomers prosperity, as was demonstrated by the failure of the westernization movement in China one-and-a-half centuries ago, and by the failure of Soviet Union's planned economy (Yang 2001).

Taiwan's developmental path is a good model for China. China's sectoral distribution in 1993 was similar to Taiwan's in 1965 (Jian 1996). In the 1950s, Taiwan had a heavy proportion of state investments in most industries. In the 1960s, the government began its market liberalization process by enacting the Regulations for the Encouragement of Investment (REI). As a result, the proportion of the output of state-run enterprises over the total industrial production value declined from 57 percent in 1952 to 21 percent in 1980 and further, to 18 percent, in 1990. This process, which occurred relatively slowly and gradually for Taiwanese enterprises and workers, has unfolded rapidly in Shanghai (see Chen, introduction).

CONCLUSION

We have compared Shanghai's prospects with lessons drawn from American high-tech experience over a period of forty years. Although Shanghai is unique, and faces a more competitive and integrated world economy than have most nations in the past, its trajectory is readily shapeable by the kinds of economic development and related policies that the government of the city and the nation will undertake over the coming decades. We have called for an occupationally oriented economic development strategy, an emphasis on high-tech services, and an effort to diversify the portfolio of industries and activities that are present in the Shanghai economy. We believe that Shanghai is admirably positioned to play major regional, national, and international roles in the economy, and that it has the potential to leaven its daily bread with high-tech activities that will generate growth and stability far into the future.

To achieve these goals, we recommend a portfolio of policies that includes the following: To facilitate more high-tech service activity, Shanghai should introduce land-use planning changes that will counteract the scarcity of buildings and space. It should also extend business assistance to service sector firms (foreign as well as domestic) and entrepreneurs rather, than confining it to manufacturing. The city should use tax-based and other incentives to attract foreign firms to Shanghai, with particular attention to how they fit into the city's new diversified portfolio. It should create venture capital funds and incubator facilities to nurture new startups and small, promising high-tech businesses. The business and labor market information infrastructure should be improved.

These economic development, fiscal, and land-use initiatives can be supplemented by changes in the regulatory and educational systems. High-tech manufacturing and services will benefit from the creation of streamlined, pro-innovation regulatory standards, the elimination of discrimination against domestic private investments, and sponsorship of independent testing product certification and rating services. Finally, and equally important, Shanghai should adopt a human capital strategy that targets key occupations, building a workforce training system that matches the skill development of workers to employers' needs and to the longer-term flexibility and evolutionary needs of the economy.

NOTE

1. They are computer programming and data processing services (SIC 737), engineering, architectural, and surveying services (SIC 871), research, development, and testing services (SIC 873), management and public relations services (SIC 874), and other business services (SIC 899). Here the definition of services refers to the sectors falling into the services category in the SIC classification, and thus does not include communication, finance, and insurance.

REFERENCES

Beyers, William B., and David P. Lindahl. 1996. "Explaining the Demand for Producer Services: Is Cost-driven Externalization the Major Factor?" *Papers in Regional Science* 75, no. 3: 351–74.

Chapple, Karen, Ann Markusen, Gregory Schrock, Dai Yamamoto, and Pingkang Yu. 2004. "Gauging Metropolitan 'High Tech' and 'I-Tech' Activity." *Economic Development Quarterly* 18, no. 1: 10–29.

Chen, Xiangming. 2007. "A Tale of Two Regions in China: Rapid Economic Development and Slow Industrial Upgrading in the Pearl River and the Yangtze River Deltas." *International Journal of Comparative Sociology* 48, nos. 2–3: 167–201.

DeVol, Ross. 1999. *America's High-technology Economy: Growth, Development, and Risks for Metropolitan Areas.* Santa Monica, Calif.: Milken Institute.

Gray, Mia, Elyse Golob, Ann Markusen, and Sam Ock Park. 1999. "The Four Faces of Silicon Valley." In *Second Tier Cities: Rapid Growth beyond the Metropolis,* edited by Ann Markusen, Yong Sook Lee, and Sean DiGiovanna, 291–310. Minneapolis: University of Minnesota Press.

Jian, Tianlun. 1996. "Priority of Privatization in Economic Reforms: China and Taiwan Compared with Russia." Development Discussion Paper #566, the Harvard Institute for International Development. www.cid.harvard.edu/hiid/566abs.html.

Markusen, Ann. 1996. "Sticky Places in Slippery Space: A Typology of Industrial Districts." *Economic Geography* 27, no. 3: 293–313.

———. 2004. "Targeting Occupations in Regional and Community Economic Development." *Journal of the American Planning Association* 70, no. 3: 253–68.

Markusen, Ann, and Elisa Barbour. 2003. *California's Occupational Advantage.* San Francisco: Public Policy Institute of California. www.hhh.umn.edu/ projects/prie/pub.html.

Markusen, Ann, and Karen McCurdy. 1989. "Chicago's Defense-Based High Technology: A Case Study of the 'Seedbeds of Innovation' Hypothesis." *Economic Development Quarterly* 3, no. 1: 15–31.

Markusen, Ann, and Gregory Schrock. 2006. "The Distinctive City: Divergent Patterns in Growth, Hierarchy, and Specialisation." *Urban Studies* 43, no. 8: 1301–23.

Markusen, Ann, Peter Hall, and Amy Glasmeier. 1986. *High-tech America: The What, How, Where, and Why of the Sunrise Industries.* Boston and London: Allen & Unwin.

Mather, Vijay. 1999. "Human Capital-based Strategy for Regional Economic Development." *Economic Development Quarterly* 13, no. 3: 203–16.

Porter, Michael E. 1990. *The Competitive Advantage of Nations.* New York: Free Press.

Saxenian, Annalee. 1994. *Regional Advantage: Culture and Competition in Silicon Valley and Route 128.* Cambridge, Mass.: Harvard University Press.

Schrock, Greg. 2003. "Innovation and High-technology Producer Services: Evidence from Twin Cities Firms." Working paper. Minneapolis: Humphrey Institute of Public Affairs, University of Minnesota.

Schrock, Greg, David Hudson, Pingkang Yu, Janice LaFloe, and Nate Dorr. 2002. "Regional Leadership in Economic and Workforce Development: Implications for Twin Cities Economic Development and West Central Initiative." Minneapolis: State and Local Policy Program, University of Minnesota.

Thompson, Wilbur, and Philip Thompson. 1985. "From Industries to Occupations: Rethinking Local Economic Development." *Economic Development Commentary* 9: 12–18.

Yang, Xiaokai. 2001. "China's Entry to the WTO." *China Economic Review* 11, no. 4: 437–42.

3. AVIATION INFRASTRUCTURE, COMPETITIVENESS, AND AEROTROPOLIS DEVELOPMENT IN THE GLOBAL ECONOMY

MAKING SHANGHAI CHINA'S TRUE GATEWAY CITY

John D. Kasarda

Shanghai, like all major cities, is competing in an increasingly fast-paced, networked world that is formed by a catalytic convergence of digitization, globalization, aviation, and time-based competition. The combined thrust of these forces is creating a new economic geography, with international gateway airports driving and shaping business location and urban development in the twenty-first century as much as highways did in the twentieth century, railroads in the nineteenth century, and seaports in the eighteenth century. Today, gateway airports have become key nodes in global production and enterprise systems and engines of local economic development, attracting air commerce linked businesses of all types to their environs. These include, among others, time-sensitive manufacturing and distribution; e-commerce fulfillment centers; third-party logistics firms; hotel, entertainment, and exhibition complexes; and office buildings that house regional corporate headquarters and air-travel intensive professionals such as consultants, auditors, and high-tech industry executives.

As more and more aviation-oriented businesses cluster near such airports and along transportation corridors radiating from them, a new urban form is emerging, the *aerotropolis*, stretching up to twenty-five kilometers outward from the airport. With the airport and its immediate area serving as a multimodal transportation and commercial nexus, strings and clusters of aviation-oriented business parks, logistics parks, industrial parks, distribution centers, information and communications technology (ICT) complexes, and wholesale merchandise marts are forming along connecting transportation corridors.

All this is happening because of the competitive advantages gateway airports provide to cities and businesses in the new speed-driven, globally networked economy. After discussing the macro forces underlying these advantages, key structural and functional attributes of the aerotropolis are described as well as its planning and development principles. Examples of emerging aerotropolises around the world are presented and implications drawn for the role Shanghai Pudong International Airport can play in making Shanghai more competitive while bringing business investment, job creation, and economic development to China's interior provinces.

THE IMPERATIVES OF SPEED AND AGILITY

In *Powershift*, futurist Alvin Toffler (1990) argued that by the beginning of the twenty-first century one indisputable law would determine competitive success: survival of the fastest. In Toffler's view, producing high-quality goods at competitive prices would still be necessary but no longer sufficient for commercial success. Speed and agility would take center stage, as industry increasingly emphasized accelerated development cycles; international sourcing and sales; flexible, customized production; and rapid delivery.

How right he was. Today's most successful companies are using advanced information technology and high-speed transportation to source parts globally, minimize inventories, and provide fast and flexible responses to unique customers' needs, nationally and worldwide. (The global supply-chain model of Dell Computer, which pioneered this process in the early 1990s, is illustrated in Figure 3.1.) They seek international partners, just-in-time suppliers, sophisticated distributors, and third-party logistics service providers. By combining flexible production and high-speed transportation systems with information systems that connect companies simultaneously to their suppliers, distributors, and customers, firms can often postpone manufacturing until customers

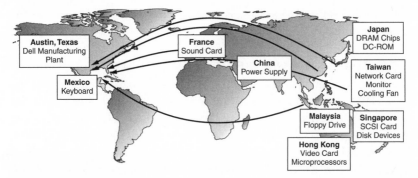

FIGURE 3.1
Global Supply Chain–Dell Computer
Source: Abbey, Douglas D., David E. Twist, and Leo J. Koonman. 2001. "The Need for Speed: Impact on Supply Chain Real Estate." *ULI on the Future.* Washington, D.C.: Urban Land Institute.

place specific orders. This reduces inventory, uncertainty, and cycle times while allowing customization of products, which creates additional value.

Mandating such changes are rapid and relentless worldwide technological, political, and economic transformations. Modern transportation, telecommunications, and goods-producing technologies have spread throughout the globe. Trade policies are being liberalized and new markets opened. China and other socialist countries have entered the global capitalist marketplace with vigor. Huge wage differences between advanced industrial and developing countries have resulted in much wider geographic dispersion of component manufacturing sites, places of assembly, and distribution. With rising workforce skills and rapid cross-border technology transfer, what were previously known as Third World countries in Asia and Latin America have achieved much higher levels of output and now produce sophisticated goods and services.

International customers (including those in developing countries, which many believe are the best long-term markets) have also become far more sophisticated and demanding. They have available an unparalleled variety of products from all over the world. They are able to assess and identify value and are therefore highly selective in purchasing. They expect quality, reliability, and competitive pricing. They also want customization of the products they buy, and they want these customized products right away, not in two to six months. For many purchases, not even two to six weeks is fast enough.

E-COMMERCE AND ORDER FULFILLMENT

The rise of e-commerce further heightened time-based competition. As late as 1995, sales through the Internet were essentially nonexistent. By 1999, U.S. Internet-based business-to-consumer (B2C) sales had grown to nearly US$7 billion. According to Forrester Research (2005), approximately 70 percent of online purchases are shipped by expedited delivery. Despite the death of thousands of dot-coms between 2000 and 2002, it is near consensus among economic and business forecasters that e-commerce will flourish in the future. Recent statistics bear this out; online retail sales in the United States alone were US$172 billion in 2005 and are expected to grow to US$329 billion in 2010, according to Forrester Research. Many of the products that Forrester sees as growing in online popularity are likely to be shipped by air, such as health and beauty products and consumer electronics. Even the U.S. Postal Service (USPS) is benefiting from the boom in B2C shipments. Some have said that e-mail and online bill paying would hurt the USPS, but e-commerce has helped it achieve five straight years of strong profits between 2003 and 2007.

Business-to-business (B2B) transactions have also skyrocketed in popularity—supply-chain transactions where materials and components are ordered through the Internet and shipped to next-stage producers. Manufacturers already are able to electronically access an international network of suppliers in order to acquire the best-quality materials and parts at the lowest price. The introduction of e-marketplaces (auctions, aggregators, bid systems, and exchanges) is greatly expanding B2B e-commerce. According to eMarketer (2004), B2B e-commerce, which stood at US$551 billion in 2003, was expected to reach over US$1.3 trillion in 2008. (For the rapid growth of e-commerce in China and Shanghai, see Zhou and Chen, this book.)

The expansion of the B2C e-commerce and other direct-to-customer Internet orders has placed a particular premium on speed and reliability in the delivery process. Unfortunately, as many B2C U.S. e-tailers discovered during the early years of e-commerce, as valuable as the Internet is in generating sales, the Web cannot move a box. Order fulfillment frequently broke down, and the WWW—world wide wait—cost e-tailers plenty.

To meet the imperatives of speed and reliability in order fulfillment, e-commerce distribution centers were built near gateway airports with extensive flight networks, a location trend that appears to be accelerating. This is especially the case at major air express hubs such as Memphis International (FedEx) and Louisville (UPS) in the United States. Both FedEx and UPS have also expanded rapidly in China, the latter focusing on Shanghai as its key Asia hub. Air express hubs actually extend the business day for e-commerce fulfillment by allowing drop-offs for next day delivery as late as 11:00 PM. Dozens of e-tailers have thus already located their fulfillment centers near Memphis International Airport, including barnesandnoble.com, Hewlittpackard.com, Nike.com, Disneyshopping.com, and Williams-sonoma.com, to leverage the FedEx air express network.

Complementing airport-linked e-commerce fulfillment centers are flow-through facilities for perishables (either in the physical or economic sense), just-in-time supply-chain and emergency parts provision centers, and reverse logistics facilities for the repair and upgrade of high-tech products such as computers and cell phones. The clustering of such time-critical goods facilities around airports (often within air logistics parks) is stimulating further expansion of air cargo, air express, less-than-load (LTL) trucking, freight forwarders, and third party logistics providers along major arteries leading into and out of gateway airports (Kasarda 1998/1999).

Speedy, reliable delivery of products over long distances has become so critical to the new economy that air commerce is quickly becoming its logistical backbone. Almost 40 percent of the value of world trade now goes by air, and the percentage is steadily rising (Colography Group 2003). Air cargo is expected to triple between 2005 and 2025 with international air-express shipments increasing fivefold during this period (Boeing Company 2006). In the United States, the total value of air freight imports and exports grew three-and-one-half-fold between 1990 and 2006 and totaled US$2.0 billion per day (U.S. Department of Commerce 2007).

Already, air cargo and air express are the preferred modes of shipping of higher value to weight B2B transactions in microelectronics, automobile electronic components, aircraft parts, mobile telephones, fashion clothing, pharmaceuticals, optics and small precision manufacturing equipment, as well as many perishables such as seafood and fresh cut flowers. Even lower value to weight B2B product distribution such as apparel, footwear, and toys are becoming time sensitive and increasingly shipped by air. As just one example, Nike chose a site near the FedEx hub in Memphis as the location for its only apparel distribution center and one of its two footwear distribution centers. If a major athletic shoe retail chain such as Foot Locker is offering a special on a new Nike product and sales are running high, its stores can make replacement orders at closing time and have them filled via air express and in stock by the time the stores open the next morning.

The rapidly growing importance of air commerce in global trade is illustrated by global trade statistics, which show that the value of U.S. air exports surpassed values shipped by vessel in 2006, with air cargo growth rates substantially exceeding vessel (waterborne) export growth rates. In Asia, Europe, and South America the trends are the same. For example, between 1990 and 2006, the value of Japan's exports by air to the United States grew by 126 percent compared to a growth of 51 percent in the value of its exports for vessels. During the same period, Germany's value of air exports rose by 268 percent compared to a 183 percent rise by vessel, and the value of Brazil's exports to the United States by air grew by 250 percent compared to growth of 230 percent by vessel (U.S. Department of Commerce 2007).

Although China currently lags behind most advanced manufacturing nations in the percentage of its trade moving by air, its growth rate in air commerce has been spectacular. China–United States merchandise trade data presented in Table 3.1 illustrates that between 1990 and 2006, China's imports by air from the United States grew by 2,557 percent (from US$698 million to US$18.5 billion), and its exports via air to the United States grew by 4,604 percent (from US$1.4 billion to just under US$68 billion). Detailed breakdowns of the merchandise trade data by four-digit industrial categories showed that microelectronic and digitized parts and products such as integrated circuits, magnetic and optical readers, and accessories for office and data processing equipment accounted for over 40 percent of the value of China's air imports from the United States in 2006 as well as over 40 percent of the value of its air exports (U.S. Department of Commerce 2007). Such figures represent logistical shifts to air commerce–based supply chains in response to the speed imperative for microelectronics and many other new economy (high value to weight ratio) manufacturing sectors.

AIRPORTS AS OFFICE, COMMERCIAL, AND KNOWLEDGE-WORKER MAGNETS

As the world's service economy also shifts into fast-forward, airports are becoming magnets for not only time-sensitive goods-processing and distribution facilities but also regional corporate headquarters, trade representative offices, and professional associations that require officers and staff to undertake frequent long-distance travel. Airport access is likewise a powerful attraction to information-intensive industries such as consulting, advertising, legal and financial services, data processing, and

TABLE 3.1

Total Trade between China and the United States by Air and Vessel, 1990, 1997, and 2006 (in US$ million)

	Exports (from China to the United States)		
	1990	1997	2006
Total Value	15,048	61,495	278,323
Air Value	1,439	7,679	67,698
Vessel Value	13,609	53,817	210,625
Growth	1990–1997	1997–2006	1990–2006
Total Value	309%	3,523%	1,750%
Air Value	434%	782%	4,604%
Vessel Value	296%	291%	1,448%
	Imports (into China from the United States)		
	1990	1997	2006
Total Value	4,191	10,858	49,056
Air Value	698	2,850	18,550
Vessel Value	3,493	8,009	30,506
Growth	1990–1997	1997–2006	1990–2006
Total Value	159%	352%	1,070%
Air Value	308%	551%	2,557%
Vessel Value	129%	281%	773%

Source: United States Department of Commerce (2007).

accounting and auditing, which often send out professionals to distant customers' sites or bring in their clients by air. Business travelers benefit considerably from access to hub airports, which offer greater choice of flights and destinations, more frequent service, more flexibility in rescheduling, and generally lower travel-related costs (for example, hub airports make it easier to avoid the time and expense of overnight stays). For global cities with the networked and dense concentration of producer services professionals (see Sassen, this book), airport access and connectivity is crucial for speedy and flexible travel.

The accessibility and travel flexibility that hub airports offer have become essential to attracting business meetings and conventions, trade shows, and merchandise marts. Two U.S. mega facilities—Infomart and Dallas Market Center, both of which are located on the I-35 corridor between Love Field Airport and the Dallas–Ft. Worth International

Airport—offer good examples of the latter attraction. Infomart is a huge, ultracontemporary merchandise display building for ICT companies. Dallas Market Center—a cluster of six large buildings that contain nearly seven million square feet of display space for fashion clothing and home merchandise—is the world's largest wholesale merchandise mart. Hundreds of thousands of buyers and vendors fly into Dallas annually to conduct business at Infomart and Dallas Market Center.

Knowledge networks and air travel networks are also increasingly overlapping and reinforcing each other. With intellectual capital supplanting physical capital as the primary factor in wealth creation, time has taken on heightened importance for today's knowledge workers. So has the mobility of these workers over long distances. Research has shown that high-tech professional workers, for example, travel by air at least 60 percent more frequently than most other professionals (Erie et al. 1999).

Some observers have suggested that advances in Internet access, videoconferencing, and other distributed communications technologies will diminish the need for air travel. The evidence indicates that telecommunications advances often promote additional air travel by substantially expanding long-distance business and personal networking. Indeed, innovations in telecommunications technology have generated spatial mobility at least since the days of Alexander Graham Bell—whose first words over his newly invented telephone were, if you recall, "Watson, come here, I need you." Face-to-face interaction remains crucial for trusted professional networking in global cities regardless of the omnipresence of information and telecommunication devices (Sassen 2001, this book).

Others have suggested that prolonged global downturns exacerbated by catastrophic events, such as the New York World Trade Center attack of September 11, 2001, will permanently diminish air commerce in general and business travel by air in particular. This does not seem likely because the business imperatives giving rise to the growth of air commerce and business travel (speed, mobility, and global access) are increasing in importance. By 2006, air commerce and air travel fully recovered from their 2001–2003 cyclical dip to reach record levels despite skyrocketing jet fuel prices. World passenger traffic, which stood at 4.2 billion in 2006, is expected to reach nearly 9 billion annually by 2020.

HIGH-TECH AND URBAN ECONOMIC IMPACTS

Nowhere are these impacts felt more than in the centerpiece of the new economy—the high-tech sector. With this sector's supply chains and employees increasingly geared to speed, mobility, and global access, the availability of frequent and extensive air service has become essential to the location of many ICT firms and other high-tech facilities. In the United States, clusters of ICT and high-tech companies are thus locating along major airport corridors, such as the Washington, D.C., Dulles Airport access corridor in northern Virginia and the expressways leading into and out of Chicago's O'Hare International Airport. Dulles's and O'Hare's experiences are being replicated across the United States and throughout the world with centrality in aviation networks becoming a primary predictor of an area's high-tech job growth (Markusen and Yu, this book). Easier access to Pudong International Airport is a good reason for high-tech manufacturers to cluster in Zhangjiang High-tech Park (see Chen, introduction, this book).

Apropos this logistical centrality, Kenneth Button and Roger Stough (1998) conducted a comprehensive study of the impact of hub airports on employment growth in high-tech fields. Their multiple-regression analysis (which controlled for other factors that may affect high-tech job growth) covered all 321 U.S. metropolitan statistical areas (MSA) and generated convincing results. Button and Stough showed that the presence of a hub airport in an MSA increases the number of high-tech jobs in the area by over 12,000, and their multiple-regression model explained over 64 percent of the variation among metropolitan areas in the high-tech employment growth. Additional analysis revealed that the causal link between job growth and air network centrality flowed from extensiveness of connections to the creation of high-tech employment and not vice versa. This finding corroborates a prior study that documented that airports have pervasive effects on overall metropolitan employment growth and that the causal relationship flows from centrality in air networks to employment growth (Irwin and Kasarda 1991).

Numerous other studies from the United States and around the world document the remarkable impact of gateway airports on urban economies. Following is just a sample:

- Los Angeles International Airport (LAX) is responsible for over 400,000 jobs in the five-county Los Angeles region; 80 percent of which are in LA County, where one in twenty jobs was found to be tied to LAX. The airport currently generates US$61 billion in regional economic activity, which translates to $7 million per hour.
- In the Philippines, Subic Bay Freeport is rapidly expanding around a former U.S. naval air base that was converted to commercial use in 1993. Since FedEx located its Asia/Pacific hub at

Subic Bay in 1994, over 150 firms—employing 40,000 workers—have located there, generating almost US$2.5 billion in investment. Between 1995 and 2000 the annual value of exports from Subic Bay jumped from US$24 million in to US$559 million. In late 1998, Acer opened its largest personal computer assembly facility in the world at Subic Bay; the facility relies heavily on air freight for its supply-chain management.

• Over 70 percent of the international firms in the region surrounding Amsterdam's Schiphol Airport cited their dependence on the airport as a primary reason for their location. The airport alone accounts for 1.9 percent of The Netherlands' GNP with forecasts indicating that by 2015, it will generate 2.8 percent—approximately US$14 billion.

The impact of airport-induced job growth on land use in the vicinity of airports is likewise substantial. An analysis of employment growth in the suburban rings of U.S. metropolitan areas showed that areas within four miles of airports added jobs two to five times faster than the overall job-growth rate of the suburban ring within which the airport was located (Weisbrod, Reed, and Neuwirth 1993).

THE RISE OF THE AEROTROPOLIS

Emerging corridors, clusters, and spines of airport-linked businesses are giving rise to a new urban form—the aerotropolis—stretching as far as twenty-five kilometers from gateway airports (Kasarda 2000a, 2000b, 2000c, 2001, www.aerotropolis.com). The airports function as the multimodal convergent nucleus and commercial nexus of this diffuse airport-integrated urban complex, analogous to the function the central business district (CBD) plays in the traditional metropolis (see Figure 3.2 for a generic illustration). Indeed, under the rubric of Airport Cities, some of these airports have assumed the same roles of metropolitan CBDs by becoming regional intermodal surface transportation nodes and major employment, shopping, meeting, and entertainment destinations in their own right (see Güller and Güller 2001.)

An excellent example is Amsterdam's Schiphol. Its grounds employ 58,000 people daily—more than the 50,000 resident criteria to attain metropolitan central city status in the United States. Two major motorways link the airport to downtown Amsterdam and the broader urban area. A modern train station, directly under the air terminal, efficiently connects travelers to the city center, the rest of the

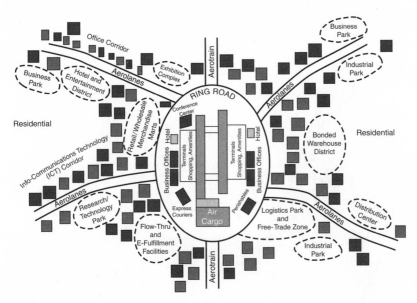

FIGURE 3.2
Aerotropolis Schematic

Netherlands, and much of Western Europe. Schiphol's passenger terminal, incorporating modern retail mall design elements, contains expansive, well-appointed shopping and entertainment arcades accessible both to travelers and to the general public. Before going through customs, passengers walk through streetscapes of designer shops, boutiques, restaurants, authentic Dutch coffee corners, Internet cafes, and even a gourmet supermarket. This area also includes restaurants of all varieties, banks, and business centers, and once through customs one finds private rooms for a sauna and massage, a casino, and even a branch of the Rijksmuseum where passengers can view Dutch Masters' paintings. By combining terminal design with modern mall design, Schiphol has substantially increased its revenues through rents and passenger purchases.

Directly across from Schiphol's passenger terminal is the World Trade Centre, which houses meeting and commercial facilities and regional headquarters of such firms as Thomson-CFS and Unilever. Two five-star hotels adjoin this complex. Within a ten-minute walk is another complex of high quality office buildings housing aviation-related business and internationally oriented companies in financial and commercial services. The commercial value of this property is reflected in its office rents,

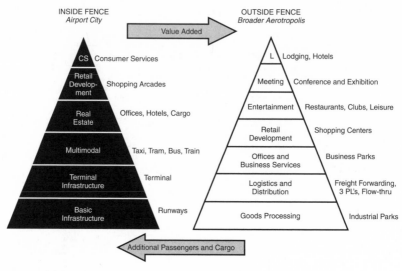

FIGURE 3.3
Amsterdam-Schiphol Airport City-Aerotropolis Synergies
Source: Schiphol Group and John D. Kasarda

which command a solid premium in the Amsterdam area. Research by the international real estate firm DTZ Zadelhoff showed office rentals in the immediate airport area in 2006 were averaging 365 Euros (US$504) per square meter per year, compared to 270 in the Amsterdam city center and 215 in other Amsterdam suburban areas. Between 1997 and 2001, lease rates of prime space at Schiphol rose by 65 percent and strong demand has continued to the present. Only six minutes via expressway or commuter train from Schiphol is Amsterdam Zuidas (Amsterdam's new second CBD), where over ten million square feet of office space has been occupied by air travel oriented businesses, including the world headquarters of ABN Amro and ING banks. Figure 3.3 illustrates the synergies between Schiphol's Airport City and its broader aerotropolis.

AEROTROPOLIS DEVELOPMENT AND PLANNING PRINCIPLES

Reflecting the new economy's demands for networking, speed, and reliability, the aerotropolis is optimized by corridor and cluster development, wide lanes, and fast movements. In other words, form follows function.

Although aerotropolises have so far evolved largely spontaneously—with previous nearby development often creating arterial bottlenecks—in the future they will be improved through strategic infrastructure planning. For example (as illustrated in Figure 3.2), dedicated expressway links (aerolanes) and high-speed rail (aerotrains) will efficiently connect airports to nearby and more distant business and residential clusters: for instance, the train connecting Shanghai's Pudong International Airport to the city has the world's highest speed. Special truck-only lanes will be added to airport expressways, and highway interchanges will be improved to reduce congestion. Seamlessly connected multimodal infrastructure will accelerate intermodal transfers of goods and people, improving transport system effectiveness and further influencing nearby land values, business locations, and resulting urban form. Advanced information processing technologies and multimedia telecommunications systems served by high-density fiber-optic rings and satellite uplinks and downlinks will instantly connect companies in the aerotropolis to their suppliers, distributors, customers, and branch offices and partners around the globe.

The metric for determining land value and particular business locations will be time–cost access to the airport. Firms of various types will bid against each other for airport accessibility predicated on the utility each gives to the related combination of time and cost of moving people and products to and from the airport and the extensiveness of the airport's flight networks to regional and global markets. Land values, lease rates, and commercial use will no longer be measured by traditional bid–rent functions that decline linearly with spatial distance from the primary node (here the airport) but by speed to the airport from alternative sites via connecting highway and high-speed rail arteries.

To many, this new land use and structure will appear simply as additional sprawl along main airport transportation corridors. Yet the aerotropolis is actually a highly reticulated system based on time–cost access gradients radiating outward from the airport. In short, the three A's (accessibility, accessibility, accessibility) are replacing the three L's (location, location, location) as the most important business location and commercial real estate organizing principles. Of course, accessibility and location are closely related.

Those in the air cargo industry know that the competitive battle is won on the ground—not in the air—with multimodal surface connections being key. This is why most of the world's leading air cargo airports also have excellent on-site or nearby intermodal interfaces. Many of the largest centers (e.g., Amsterdam, Hong Kong, Incheon, Memphis, Miami, Shanghai, and Singapore) are quadramodal, possessing efficient access to all four transportation modes (air, highway, rail, and water).

Commercial growth surrounding Southern California's LA/Ontario Airport—an emerging aerotropolis that cornerstones a major logistics complex forty-five kilometers east of Los Angeles—offers an excellent contemporary illustration of such quadramodality. The airport is at the nexus of major east–west and north–south interstate highways I-10 and I-15, respectively, with the Burlington Northern–Santa Fe intermodal rail yard nearby. The ports of Los Angeles–Long Beach are connected to the airport by interstate highways and rail lines. Over 75 million square feet of logistics and distribution space were added between 2000 and 2006 adjacent to the airport and along Interstates 10 and 15 radiating out from it, led by e-commerce fulfillment and distribution facilities with one million or more square feet in floor space for companies such as Staples and Home Shopping Network. Class A office space, retail, and entertainment/recreation complexes are following in the airport area and are making Ontario a full-fledged aerotropolis.

Aerotropolises are also emerging in distinct patterns around new international airports in Asia. One example is Lantau Island, where the relatively new Hong Kong International Airport is spawning highly visible business and commercial clusters directly linked to the airport. Ten million square feet of commercial land is being developed adjacent to the main passenger terminal. This area, known as Hong Kong SkyCity, opened in 2006 and contains offices and upscale retail, a large hotel, and a golf course, which will eventually be developed as a business park (see Figure 3.4). In addition, a 2 million–square foot international exhibition center for meetings, trade shows, and trade representative offices has opened, featuring a cross-border ferry terminal.

The Walt Disney Company has located its third international theme park (Hong Kong Disneyland, which opened in 2006) on Lantau Island to take advantage of the international airport and its high-speed dedicated rail (aerotrain) and expressway (aerolane) links to Kowloon and Hong Kong. This siting decision is not unlike those Disney made earlier for Tokyo Disneyland, near Narita International Airport, and EuroDisney, near Paris's Charles de Gaulle Airport. Hong Kong International Airport's urban impact will eventually include southern China via high-speed ferries and cargo water shuttles, efficiently connecting fourteen nearby Pearl River Delta manufacturing and commercial centers on the mainland to the airport. Lantau's quadramodality (aerolanes, aerotrain, airplanes, and sea/air links) will be integrated and enhanced through twenty-first century–designed mixed-use passenger/commercial terminals, business centers, and logistics parks at or near the airport.

FIGURE 3.4
Hong Kong SkyCity Master Plan
Source: Skidmore, Owings, and Merrill LLP

Perhaps the most efficient and aesthetic airport city that is evolving into a full aerotropolis is Singapore's Changi. At its landside core, the passenger terminals house memorable arcades designed around thematic retail, restaurant, and entertainment center concepts. Open twenty-four hours per day, Changi's arcades also include lounges, business centers, transit hotels, fitness centers, saunas, and local area networks (LAN) providing computer-equipped passengers with free wireless access to the Internet. Changi's wide, uncongested aerolane to downtown Singapore is complemented by an aerotrain going to the city center from under the passenger terminals. An air logistics park adjacent to the airport is designed to further improve Singapore's rapid fulfillment functions and allow third-party logistics providers (3PLs) to offer distant customers highly customized products with minimum response time. Virtually every major 3PL in the world is active in and around Changi.

IMPLICATIONS FOR SHANGHAI

The idea of aerotropolis development is not new to China. In fact, during the mid to late 1990s an effort (with which the author was involved) was made to design and develop the land surrounding the new Zhuhai airport in the Pearl River Delta according to a number of aerotropolis principles as described above. Development never took place for a variety of reasons.

First, intense competition from Hong Kong International Airport, the new Macau International Airport (which was less than thirty kilometers away), and other Pearl River Delta airports absorbed almost all passenger and cargo traffic from the Delta. Second, Zhuhai was never able to acquire international flights and become a gateway. Third, though linked by hovercraft and ferry to Hong Kong (about a sixty-minute trip), Zhuhai was considered too distant from other primary cities and production centers in the Delta, mainly Guangzhou, Shenzhen, and Huizhou. Fourth, the People's Republic of China central government in Beijing became disenchanted with Zhuhai's expensive "build it and they will come" high-risk approach and eventually withdrew its support. The result was a costly, grossly underutilized airport with a magnificent terminal, the longest runway in China, and well-designed surface transportation links, but only limited domestic traffic, no international traffic, and virtually no surrounding commercial development. The engine that would power Zhuhai's aerotropolis development had no aviation or commercial fuel. In 2006, Hong Kong International Airport took majority ownership of Zhuhai with plans to develop it as a cargo and maintenance, repair, and overhaul (MRO) complex.

The opposite is the case with Shanghai, where commercial development during the past fifteen years is the envy of the world. Shanghai, in fact, is making solid progress toward its lofty ambitions of becoming a global city and being counted among the world's leading twenty-first century transportation and commercial nodes (Leman 2002). The city is providing the advanced telecommunications and modern aviation and port infrastructure along with state-of-the-art connecting surface transportation infrastructure to facilitate these outcomes by achieving interrelated development goals.

Shanghai's near-term goal is to become China's high-tech center, overtaking Beijing and Tianjin (McDaniels and Zhao 2001). One specialized manufacturing sector where this has already occurred is in the production of integrated circuits (computer chips). Led by a series of huge foreign investments at its Zhangjiang High-tech Park in Pudong, Shanghai's chip output accounted for 60 percent of China's total in 2002 (Yong 2002). Five of the world's top ten integrated circuit producers had facilities in the park in 2006. By the end of 2006, the park housed over sixty-five enterprises centered on integrated circuits (IC), including two of the world's largest: Semiconductor Manufacturing International, which invested US$1.5 billion in a fabrication facility in 2003, and Grace Semiconductor Manufacturing Corporation, which completed its US$1.6 billion facility in late 2002. In 2006 the park produced over US$1.4 billion in IC and other electronic components. Other locations in the Shanghai area are also quickly jumping on the IC bandwagon.

Since the vast majority of IC exports and their component imports move by air, we may expect to see the air value of Shanghai's and China's exports and imports climb sharply during the coming decade. As a result, more and more global supply chain charts of computer manufacturing and other microelectronics firms, such as that displayed for Dell Computer in Figure 3.1, have been using Shanghai as a key sourcing node and will enhance it further in the future. For example, the Taiwanese firm of Compal employs 13,000 workers at a notebook factory in Kunshan near Shanghai to make Dell PCs, which are shipped out from Shanghai (Einhorn 2005).

The municipality likewise has set a second goal of becoming the largest and most important trade and exhibition center in the Asia–Pacific region, displaying and merchandising high-tech and other products from around the world. Exhibition centers and merchandise marts are being constructed near the city center and Pudong International Airport as well as along expressways radiating from them. Shanghai's apex in this arena is anticipated in 2010 when 70 million tourists are expected to travel to Shanghai for its 2010 World Expo. Of these visitors, 15–20 million are expected to arrive by air. Shanghai's exhibition and trade centers will be complemented by expansive family entertainment theme parks, including those that may be developed by Disney and Universal Studios from the United States. Although Shanghai's one day automobile drive market exceeds 100 million people (among the highest in the world), substantial numbers of visitors to these major theme parks will no doubt come by air.

A third municipal goal is to become the Asia–Pacific center for multinational regional corporate headquarters. The current mayor has set the city's sights on having at least 700 foreign firms establish their regional headquarters in Shanghai by 2015 (see Chen, introduction; Sassen, this book). As the city center expands outward with large office complexes, the Pudong International Airport area will become doubly attractive with its international and domestic aviation access and its roughly eight-minute connectivity to the city center via the new superspeed magnetic levitation (maglev) train, which became commercially operational in 2004 and extended its hours of service in 2006. With shorter-range people-movers (i.e., monorails) connecting Pudong International Airport to nearby business parks, executives and professionals can move quickly and efficiently between the airport-linked office parks and those in the city center.

It is important to remember that a key aerotropolis principle is time–cost accessibility, not spatial distance. Time–cost access gradients replace traditional bid–rent distance decay functions in this new urban location model. Access and resulting locational utility in the aerotropolis model is measured both in terms of (1) the movement time locally to the airport and (2) the airport's connectivity to national and global markets in terms of number of destinations served and flight frequency to those destinations. Relatively few cities in the world possess such rapid simultaneous local, national, and international accessibility potential for multinational corporate executives and other air travel-intensive professionals than does Shanghai.

Shanghai's fourth commercial goal is to become China's and the broader Asia–Pacific region's leading logistics, transportation, and distribution center. In the more open logistics sector, not to be outdone by the likes of DHL, UPS, and FedEx, which are all expanding their business, German-based logistics provider Dachser has recently joined the race, building on the foothold established through its Hong Kong–domiciled Dachser Far East operation, by setting up a wholly foreign-owned enterprise (WFOE) in Shanghai to oversee north China operations.

For Shanghai, achieving this fourth goal will greatly facilitate success in achieving the first three commercial goals. Here the city may be labeled as "halfway home and a long way to go." Since 1990, Shanghai has made massive investments and improvements in its logistics, transportation, and trade infrastructure. These include the modernized and substantially expanded Waiquoqiao container port, a major new fifty-berth container port developed on Yangshan Island to serve fourth and fifth generation megavessels, the new Pudong International Airport, expansive new local highways, bridges and tunnels, and the US$1.4 billion maglev train connecting Pudong Airport with the city center and other key commercial nodes, where passengers are whisked between the Airport and central Pudong at up to 430 kilometers per hour (270 miles per hour). Major investments in ICT infrastructure, including broadband, high-speed multifunction networks, fiber optic loops, and integrated information pipelines for data exchange have all been completed (see Zhou and Chen, this book). Shanghai's quadramodality (air, vessel, rail, and highway) and ICT infrastructure are being integrated to accelerate people and product flows across all modes. Considering that the huge volumes of low-value exports to the United States (toys and shoes bound for Walmart's shelves) still travel by containerized sea shipping, port development may be crucial in Shanghai. Not surprisingly, with the opening of Yangshan deepwater port in December 2005, Shanghai is poised to surpass Hong Kong and Singapore as the world's largest port by 2010.

Apropos airport-linked commercial development, the city is in its embryonic stage, with remarkable opportunities available. Pudong International Airport has yet to be adequately leveraged. This airport was opened in October 1999 to supplement Shanghai's aging Hongqino Airport and serve as the city's aviation infrastructure for twenty-first century growth. For the first three years, conflicting policies and haggling over division of flights between the two airports by Shanghai's Aviation Authority (which oversees both airports) led to suboptimization and underutilization of each. For example, both airports handled international flights, whereas domestic feeder routes were poorly integrated, reducing airline transit efficiencies and passenger and cargo volumes at each airport. This problem was finally resolved in 2002 when the Airport Authority mandated that by the end of that year, virtually all international flights would be at Pudong and that Pudong airport would also receive priority in integrated domestic connections.

With the international gateway issue settled, the city undertook a 10 billion yuan (about US$1.2 billion) expansion of Pudong International Airport, including a second runway, which opened in March 2005, and a second terminal that became operational in March 2008. Pudong is planned to eventually have four runways capable of handling 80 million passengers annually by 2015, compared to 27 million handled in 2006. Should Shanghai's commercial growth continue at its torrid pace, there is sound reason to believe that such capacity will eventually be required.

Shanghai's two airport system may well be needed in the long term, but for the near term (say the next five to ten years) questions must be raised about the efficiency of operating two major airports given Pudong's planned capacity expansion and Shanghai's projected overall passenger and cargo volumes. An objective study should be conducted of the merits of having a single airport (i.e., Pudong International) with all domestic and international flights consolidated and integrated there until its capacity constraints are reached. In addition to scale economies and interline revenues that would be achieved, moving transiting domestic origin and destination passenger and cargo across town between airports is costly, time-consuming, and inefficient—going against the fundamental speed and agility competitive principles noted previously. Added surface traffic between airports (which are at opposite ends of the city) is environmentally unfriendly as well.

There is another reason for consolidation. This is to achieve a hub and spoke system that quickly and efficiently links China's inland provincial cities to regional and global markets through the Pudong gateway. As discussed previously, accessibility, not location, is key to competitive siting of many twenty-first century industries, especially those that are part of time-sensitive supply chains.

One of the primary reasons that modern industries such as microelectronics, pharmaceuticals, and digitized automobile and aerospace components have not dispersed to China's interior provinces is that the time required to receive and ship parts, components, and finished goods to and from them far exceeds acceptable parameters. With frequent daily flights between interior cities and Pudong, their accessibility disadvantage could be substantially reduced. Through additional upgraded surface transportation linkages to the inland airports, as illustrated in Figure 3.5, industries located up to three hours traveling time from the interior airport

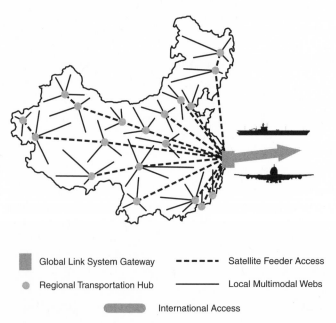

Global Link System Gateway   - - - - -   Satellite Feeder Access

Regional Transportation Hub   ————   Local Multimodal Webs

International Access

FIGURE 3.5
Illustrative Global Link System for China with Shanghai Hub and Local Multimodal Webs

could often complete a full day's production, truck it to the interior airport and be connected through Pudong to international markets within twenty-four to forty-eight hours.

Creating aviation accessibility for China's interior provinces to international and distant domestic markets via the consolidated Pudong hub may be the best way to attract modern, high-value industries to the interior provinces and achieve national government policies to stem migration to coastal cities, raise wages, and reduce growing income inequality between China's interior and coastal areas. In addition to helping attain these goals, this global-link system could make China more competitive overall by allowing its firms to produce products at lower costs in the interior than the developed coastal urban areas, benefiting them the same way western-based industries benefit by sourcing from China, despite additional transportation time and costs they assume compared to producing domestically. Consistent with this multimodal global-link model, it may be fruitful for China to look at itself as a spatially dispersed supply chain system based on comparative advantages of places (wages, worker skills, material availability, etc.). To be optimized, such a system will require a far better countrywide logistics and transportation system than that which exists today. Let me elaborate briefly.

Shanghai's logistics practices (and those throughout China) lag substantially behind those of most competitor cities and nations. Studies suggest that logistics costs for Chinese businesses, on average, constitute over 21 percent of the GDP compared to 8.6 percent for the United States (ARC Advisory Group 2006). State-run monopolies in the transportation and cargo handling sectors as well as "state favored" private firms in these sectors often operate with inefficient, cumbersome procedures and antiquated equipment. Lacking any real competition, there is little incentive for them to introduce innovative practices and new technologies, putting a drag on supply chains and impeding the competitiveness of the firms they are serving. Excess inventory must be maintained, boosting costs, while customer response times are much slower than they need be. As just one example, two state-owned enterprises are licensed to process virtually all air cargo ground handling at Pudong Airport. As a result of this government "duopoly" handling prices are considerably higher than they should be and performance is low by international airport standards (American Chamber of Commerce in Shanghai 2002). This further illustrates the importance of removing the lack of competition legacy of the planned and state-controlled economy, as called for by Markusen and Yu in the preceding chapter.

China's customs clearance process has been another Achilles heel for multinational manufacturing firms depending on speed, agility, and time-definite delivery. According to the Global Alliance for Trade Efficiency: China Working Group (Gillis 2002), customs practices in Shanghai and elsewhere in China have far to go to improve (1) transparency of regulations, policies, and practices; (2) consistency in valuation of imported merchandise; (3) coordination among various government agencies involved in the import and export process; (4) electronic data interchange and electronic documentation; and (5) introduction of "risk management" techniques that focus on specific types of shipments rather than wholesale inspection of virtually all.

In fairness, Shanghai's government is well aware of these problems. It has offered APEC and WTO useful experiments in customs process modernization at its ports as well as express customs clearance (including a separate air express facility) at Pudong Airport through the Shanghai Model Port project jointly funded by the U.S. and Chinese governments (Mullen 2001). Nonetheless, many time-sensitive importers and shippers in China believe that Chek Lap Kok (the new Hong Kong International Airport) maintains a huge advantage in customs processes and air cargo ground handling, and that this will continue to hamper Shanghai's competitiveness with the greater Hong Kong area. International aviation connectivity is also a relative disadvantage for Shanghai compared to Hong Kong. Hong Kong has maintained a substantial lead in international flights with Chek Lap Kok serving 150 foreign markets in 2007, compared to some seventy foreign destinations by Shanghai's Pudong. This gap will have to be closed considerably if Shanghai is to compete as a global city.

Shanghai may hold a long-term trump card with its superior domestic aviation connectivity. International airlines (especially air cargo airlines) tend to be reactive to passenger and/or cargo loads, expanding service where demand is high and rising. Should airport consolidation occur in Shanghai and an integrated domestic hub and spoke system be implemented through Shanghai Pudong as described previously, international service would likely also increase considerably.

Because international air rights are tied to complex bilateral negotiations between nations, Shanghai will have to lobby through Beijing to attain additional international frequencies. If the city is really serious about becoming the nation's high-tech manufacturing center and leader in global distribution, it could go far toward achieving this ambition by offering an open skies policy for all-freight aircraft. International air cargo and air express service providers would likely flock to Pudong, providing

Shanghai with unmatched global access for rapid shipping and receiving of high-tech and other high value to weight products. Aerotropolis development would accelerate with clusters of international third-party logistics providers (3PLs), high-tech manufacturing parks, e-commerce fulfillment complexes, and high velocity flow thru distribution centers near Pudong International Airport and modern highways radiating outward from it. Some of these developments, such as the open skies policy, would definitely need central government approval, and the recent effort of Beijing to rein in ambitious Shanghai, especially its hot real estate market, as symbolized by sacking the latter's Party secretary represents constraints on the development of large-scale projects (see Chen, introduction; Wu, this book).

Even without an open skies agreement, Shanghai Pudong's passenger and air cargo enplanements will grow significantly in the decade ahead. This will stimulate substantial logistics and commercial real estate development around the airport and along connecting surface transportation corridors. The real question, then, is whether this commercial development will occur intelligently through aesthetically planned clusters optimally located for economic efficiency and environmental sustainability, or will it develop in the spontaneous, haphazard, unsightly, and economically inefficient manner that characterizes much airport-driven commercial development in the West?

REFERENCES

Abbey, Douglas D., David E. Twist, and Leo J. Koonman. 2001. "The Need for Speed: Impact on Supply Chain Real Estate." In *Future* (A publication of the Urban Land Institute), 4–19. Washington, D.C.: Urban Land Institute.

American Chamber of Commerce in Shanghai. *2002 Position Papers*. Shanghai: American Chamber of Commerce.

ARC Advisory Group. 2006. *State of Logistics in China*. Dedham, Mass.: ARC Advisory Group.

Boeing Company. 2006. *World Air Cargo Forecast 2005–2006*. Seattle, Wash.: Boeing Company.

Button, Kenneth, and Roger Stough. 1998. *The Benefits of Being a Hub Airport City*. Fairfax, Va.: Institute of Public Policy, George Mason University.

Colography Group. 2003. *World Cargo Traffic Flow Model*. Atlanta, Ga.: The Colography Group.

Einhorn, Bruce. 2005. "Why Taiwan Matters?" *BusinessWeek* (May 16): 76–81.

Erie, Steven P., John D. Kasarda, Andrew McKenzie, and Michael A. Molloy. 1999. *A New Orange County Airport at El Toro: Catalyst for High-wage, High-tech Economic Development*. Irvine, Calif.: Orange County Business Council.

eMarketer. 2004. *B2B E-Commerce Spending in the U.S., 1998–2008.* New York, N.Y.: eMarketer.

Forrester Research. 2005. *US eCommerce: 2005 to 2010.* Cambridge, Mass.: Forrester Research.

Gillis, Chris. 2002. "Gate Opens in China, Industry Group Intends to Help China Customs to Meet WTO Obligations." *American Shipper* (November): 28–32.

Gűller, Mathis, and Michael Gűller. 2001. *From Airport to Airport City.* Barcelona, Spain: Airports Regions Conference.

Irwin, Michael D., and John D. Kasarda. 1991. "Air Passenger Linkages and Employment Growth in U.S. Metropolitan Areas." *American Sociological Review* 56, no. 4: 524–37.

Kasarda, John D. 1998/1999. "Time-based Competition and Industrial Location in the Fast Century." *Real Estate Issues,* Winter, 24–29.

———. 2000a. "Aerotropolis: Airport-Driven Urban Development." *Cities in the 21st Century.* Washington, D.C.: Urban Land Institute.

———. 2000/2001b. "Logistics and the Rise of Aerotropolis." *Real Estate Issues,* Winter, 43–48.

———. 2000c. "Planning the Aerotropolis." *Airport World* 5, no. 5: 52–54.

———. 2001. "From Airport City to Aerotropolis." *Airport World* 6, no. 4: 42–47.

Leman, Edward. 2002. "Can Shanghai Compete as a Global City?" *The China Business Review* (September–October): 7–15.

McDaniels, Iain, and Sophie Zhao. 2001. "APEC in China: Shanghai Snapshot." *The China Business Review* (September–October): 42–45.

Mullen, Michael C. 2001. "The Shanghai Model Port Project." *The China Business Review* (September–October): 22–26.

Sassen, Saskia. 2001. *The Global City.* Princeton, N.J.: Princeton University Press.

Toffler, Alvin. 1990. *Powershift: Knowledge, Wealth, and Violence at the Edge of the 21st Century.* New York: Bantam Books.

United States Department of Commerce. 2007. *U.S. Merchandise Trade Data.* Machine-readable files. Washington, D.C.: U.S. Census Bureau, Economics and Statistics Administration.

Weisbrod, Glen E., John S. Reed, and Roanne Neuwirth. 1993. "Airport Area Economic Development Model." Paper presented at the PTRC International Transport Conference, Manchester, England.

Yong, Zhang. 2002. "City Takes Bite of Chip Industry." *China Daily,* July 31 (Factiva database).

4. COMPETITIVE URBAN ECONOMIC POLICIES IN GLOBAL CITIES

Shanghai through the Lens of Singapore

K. C. Ho

> The fact of inter-urban competition and urban entrepreneurialism has opened up the urban spaces of advanced capitalist countries to all kinds of new patterns of development, even when the net effect has been the serial reproduction of science parks, gentrification, world trading centers, cultural and entertainment centers, large-scale interior shopping malls with postmodern accoutrements, and the like. (Harvey 2000 [1989])

Harvey's observation, written almost twenty years ago, indicates one impact of globalization, the rise of intercity competition and its effect on the landscapes of competing cities. With economic globalization, cities are driven to become more competitive in developing strategies to attract both capital and skilled labor. The literature has covered the place marketing and development strategies that were attempted (e.g., Hubbard and Hall 1998; Olds 1995) as well as the consequences in terms of the state's regulation and treatment of different groups (e.g., Body-Gendrot 2000; Holston and Appadurai 1999; Mayer 1999). In the development literature, apart from the very large body on the developmental state in East Asia, there have been a series of studies on the role of subnational units and their role in local economic development (e.g., Clarke and Gaile 1998; Fry 1990;

Soldatos 1990). If place promotion by a postsocialist entrepreneurial state defines and drives Shanghai's competition with other top cities in Asia and beyond (see Wu 2000, 2003), how does this differ from distinctive strategies adopted by capitalist developmental states in East Asia to push and promote their global cities' continued competitiveness? Singapore offers an interesting comparative lesson that illustrates the need to tailor organizational arrangements and practices to a changing economic environment, and this need for reshaping institutional environments has important socioeconomic implications for Shanghai.

There is evidence that competition is most intense at the level of global cities, where the aspirations of city managers and national leaders to project an economic role for major national cities beyond their natural hinterlands require a sustained effort at attracting a range of advanced financial and business services, whose cumulative presence creates what Sassen (2001, 11) terms global control capability. Governments also place high priority on attracting research and development activities. And although Castells and Hall (1994, 11, 144–92) track new spatial forms of technologically advanced complexes, they also recognize the role of cities as centers of advanced manufacturing. Both sets of activities yield high economic dividends to locations that house them, in terms of both high-paying occupations and their linkages to other services and production activities. Because both sets of activities are also likely to move to new centers, which may offer better access to markets, stronger infrastructure, and better skilled labor, there is a need to have in place a set of strategies and policies that retain valuable activities and at the same time attract new ones. The global city is therefore a sum total of such activities, whose cumulative presence enables the city to exert the command and control function as a node in the global economy.

This chapter is an attempt to understand the sociopolitical environment in which competitive strategies can be developed and sustained in Singapore with Shanghai as potential recipient of beneficial lessons. My intention here is not to repeat the link between competition and spatial outcomes but to develop a broader understanding of the *process* of building competitiveness through the involvement of different institutional actors and in some cases the transformation of their functions. This chapter is not an attempt to look at policies, which are more ephemeral, but at the organizations that provide a more permanent structure that can build capacity through its ability to monitor, assess, and initiate action. Examining a fifty-year period of development in Singapore will allow us to draw out the factors that determine the institutional basis for resilience and reinvention and provide some comparative implications for Shanghai.

DEVELOPING AND ENFORCING COMPETITIVE URBAN ECONOMIC POLICIES

Economic policies can only be sustained if domestic institutions support such efforts. This requires an examination of the type of institutions that are implicated in such policies.

Singapore's initial foray into manufacturing was in terms of the development of the city-state as a location for multinational companies producing for Western markets. Planning and economic management centered on the development of incentives to attract overseas investments and on the creation of infrastructure and industrial environment. In contrast to the laissez-faire management style of the colonial state, urban development in the postcolonial phase was characterized by heavy state intervention in the form of direct state-led programs guided by agencies created specifically to handle these tasks.

A significant move in Singapore's economic history was the creation of the Economic Development Board (EDB) in 1961, which was empowered to promote industrialization through its ability to finance projects as well as provide land for such projects. The initial economic strategy was one of import substitution with Malaysia as a common market. But when Singapore and Malaysia were separated in 1965 and this strategy became immediately obsolete, a massive corporate restructuring exercise was initiated in 1968, and the industrial land division of the EDB became the Jurong Town Corporation (JTC), whereas the financing arm took on a new independent identity as the Development Bank of Singapore. Schein (1996, 65–66) argued that this breakup was necessary not only because of the new emphasis on industrial promotion because of changing political circumstances but also because EDB had become too powerful and diverse, and there was increasing potentials for conflicts of interests between its functions.

With this new division, Jurong Town Corporation worked to develop industrial estates. Its efforts were supported by two other organizations, the Urban Redevelopment Authority (URA) to manage the central area of Singapore and the Housing and Development Board to build public housing and resettle households affected by redevelopment.

The actions of these agencies were supported by legal reforms, primarily the Lands Acquisitions Act of 1966, which gave authorities the right to acquire land in the interests of national development and phased out rent control, which spurred new construction. The key instruments in the state's economic development effort were industrial development schemes operating in tandem with urban redevelopment and public housing.

The easing of congestion and the change from residential to commercial uses in the central area started gathering momentum with the second phase of the building program (1966–1970). The second-phase projects were located in the outer city limits and therefore moved the residential population farther away from the central area. Later developments in the second-phase projects also came with retail and recreational amenities, thus easing retail demands on the central area (Liu 1985, 13). The public housing program, which moved residential and retail activities out of the central area, opened up vast tracts of land for redevelopment.

Left with the singular task of industrial promotion, EDB started its own internal change by placing greater emphasis on attracting foreign capital. The arrangement prior to 1966 was an informal arrangement that relied on honorary representatives. This system was obviously very inefficient partly because it depended on where these representatives were located and also because of the fact that the representatives were not doing this full-time. The growth of newly dedicated offices began in 1966 in response to where the perceived opportunities were. For example, the Frankfurt office was in response to growing interest by German companies in opportunities in Singapore (Economic Development Board 1970, 37). A second office was added in Osaka in 1976 when EDB surmised that Japanese investments were likely to outstrip U.S. and European investments. By the same token, although not stated in the EDB reports, declining potential probably led to a string of closures listed in the notes to Figure 4.1. The other important point to note was the practice of placing senior EDB officials in overseas offices to allow for better coordination and strategic decisions.

Thus, by the 1980s, the Economic Development Board had, through the expansion of dedicated offices in fourteen key cities, developed an economic intelligence network that was capable of working with overseas clients with the intention of attracting investments to Singapore. The 1990s saw only two new offices established, both in Asia, in Jakarta, Indonesia, and in Suzhou near Shanghai, China. The more significant

TABLE 4.1

Location and Evolution of Singaporean Investment Promotion Agencies

United States	Europe	Asia
New York (1966)	Stockholm (1967)	Tokyo (1969)
San Francisco (1968)	London (1969)	Osaka (1976)
Venture Capital (1992)	Int'l Manpower (1994)	Jakarta (1992)
Biotechnology (1992)	Frankfurt (1970)	Shanghai (2002)
Int'l Manpower (1994)	Paris (1985)	Beijing (2002)
Chicago (1969)	Milan (1985)	Mumbai (2004)
Los Angeles (1977)		Guangzhou (2006)
Boston (1981)		
Washington (1985)		
Dallas (1985)		

Source: Estimates from *Economic Development Board Annual Reports, Straits Times,* and *Business Times.*

Notes: Before 1966, EDB Overseas Operations were managed by a number of honorary representatives in Melbourne, Seattle, Honolulu, and Bangkok. The following offices no long exist: Zurich (1971), Houston (1974), Nagoya (1985), Stuttgart (1989), Taipei (1993) Suzhou (1996), Hong Kong (1966).

move during this period was the placement of directors in charge of special tasks in San Francisco and London. More recent developments include the closure in 2006 of the Hong Kong office, which was one of the first offices started by the EDB. The reason as reported in the *Business Times* report (February 25, 2003) was "the better deployment of the Board's resources for its China operations." This was after the opening of several offices in major Chinese cities—Beijing (in 2002), Shanghai (in 2002), and Guangzhou (in 2006).[1] This move suggests the growing economic distance of Hong Kong from China's economy. India's ascendance in the global economy resulted in the opening of the Mumbai office in 2006 to tap into the growing potential of Indian companies (*Straits Times,* February 10, 2004).

The promotional efforts of the EDB, along with the work done by JTC and URA, placed Singapore in a position to benefit from the internationalization of production in the 1970s. Multinational corporations looking for a base in Asia found in Singapore political stability, efficient infrastructure, and planned industrial estates, which are also among the most attractive and competitive features of Shanghai today. The policy of locating light nonpolluting industries at the periphery of housing estates allowed industrial activities to tap into the large residential base. By 1972 there were already nine industrial estates within public housing estates, and workers in these estates accounted for about 22 percent of the manufacturing workforce (Pang and Khoo 1975, 242, 246). Since the early 1990s, Shanghai has been among the most successful cities in China in using well-developed industrial zones in and around the city proper to host a large number of manufacturing and service facilities set up by multinational corporations.

Singapore's efforts resulted in the spectacular rates of industrial development in the 1970s. As mentioned earlier, Mirza (1986, 6) estimated that in 1975, an astonishing 48.6 percent of foreign direct investment flowing into Asia ended up in Singapore. If we take the manufacturing share of GDP as an indication of the growth of manufacturing, then this increased from 11.4 percent in 1961 to 20.4 percent in 1970, reaching a peak of 29 percent in 1980. In terms of manufacturing employment share, this grew from 4.2 percent in 1957 to 22 percent in 1970 and 30.1 percent in 1980. Thus, from these sets of indicators, Singapore has, in the span of about twenty-five years, moved from a center of commerce to a manufacturing-dominated economy.

Such efforts regarding the development of an organizational structure dedicated to economic development have important implications for Shanghai. Specifically, can the city develop its own range of specialist economic development agencies whose role is to facilitate the insertion of the city into the global economy? The notion of a division of labor among specialist agencies is important, as important as the need to ensure proper coordination among these organizations. The move of the EDB office from Hong Kong to Beijing and Shanghai in order to be closer to the rapidly growing economy is also a significant lesson. The cities are, in John Friedmann's (1986) words, significant nodes in the articulation of the global economy because they act as "basing points" for global capital, and thus the city's economic fortunes are closely tied to that of its subregion, and the abandonment of Hong Kong by the EDB for Shanghai and Beijing in some sense marks the more difficult economic path that Hong Kong has to take in the years to come.

Being competitive involves a process of economic restructuring, where old industries move out and new industries need to be grown and attracted. In this process, the institutional players become transformed or get replaced.

The Singapore economy not only shifted from commerce to manufacturing but within the manufacturing sector there have also been a

TABLE 4.2

Key Industries in Singapore's Manufacturing History (Industry Share of Total Manufacturing Output)

Industry	1961	1970	1980	1990	2000	2005
1961–1970						
Food, beverages, tobacco	40.6	18.3	6.6	4.0	2.1	2.2
Wood products	7.5	5.4	3.1	1.2	0.1	0.1
Paper products, printing	10.3	3.5	2.6	3.6	0.5	0.4
1971–1980						
Textiles, garments, footwear, and leather	2.5	5.2	4.5	3.1	0.8	0.4
Petroleum products	0.2	31.4	36.4	15.9	12.3	19.4
1981–2000						
Electronic components	3.4	7.3	16.9	39.1	51.8	35.9
2000–2005						
Chemicals, pharmaceuticals	3.4	2.9	2.9	6.9	10.2	19.8
Total manufacturing output (S$ billion)[a]	0.511	3.89	31.66	71.33	158.77	207.62

Sources: Singapore, Department of Statistics, *Census of Industrial Production* (1985, 18);
Singapore, Department of Statistics, *Economic and Social Statistics* (1960–1982, 80–81);
Singapore, Department of Statistics, *Yearbook of Statistics* (1994, 108–9; 2001, 98; 2006, 100).
Notes: Until 1970, electric appliances were classified together with electronic components.
[a] 1 US$ = 1.5 Singapore dollar (S$) (Sep. 2007).

number of shifts in terms of different industries. Table 4.2 shows the shifts in industrial concentration in the last fifty years. The concentration in the 1960s was in the basic food and raw material processing industries, a legacy of an earlier period when manufacturing consisted of basic processing of agricultural products. The first wave of foreign direct investments was in textiles and garments, of which most were Hong Kong companies, and in petroleum and transport equipment, by large multinational corporations. The most dramatic increases came from the electronics industry during the late 1970s throughout the 1980s and the 1990s. After 2000, the chemical and pharmaceutical industry became a major contributor. In a similar but later sequence, Shanghai's manufacturing sector shifted from a dominant textile base through the 1980s to an increasingly strong presence of electronics in the 1990s (Chen, introduction, 2007).

As a result of earlier success, Singapore's costs have been increasing along with other East Asian economies. Just slightly more than one decade of rapid economic growth in the 1970s created pressures for economic restructuring. Both land prices and wages have continued their steady increase, adding to the cost of doing business in Singapore. The presence of consistent balance of payment surpluses, growing reserves, plus the policy of keeping the Singapore dollar stable in order to develop the financial sector has caused a steady appreciation of the currency, affecting external orders and lowering foreign exchange earnings. This is coupled with the growing competition posed by newly industrializing countries, especially China, that provide challenges in more labor-intensive activities. One sign of the restructuring of the economy is the slow decline in importance of the manufacturing sector, as rising costs create incentives for plant relocation to cheaper production locations (Ho 1994). The gross domestic product share of the manufacturing sector hovered around 29 percent between 1980 and 1990, and in the 1990s, the GDP (at current prices) share of manufacturing actually declined slightly by several percentage points to around 25 percent. The contribution of the manufacturing sector remained at around this level after 2000 (Department of Statistics 1990, 87; 2000, 63; 2006, 61).

The EDB continued its role, most notably building on the existing strengths in the electronic industry and attracting more technology intensive segments and building the chemical and pharmaceutical industries in the 1990s. During this period, there developed an interesting shift in strategy in the form of the regionalization plan and the associated transformation of the Jurong Town Corporation in managing this strategy.

The growth triangle concept developed in 1989 involves incorporating Singapore's two immediate neighbors, the state of Johor (Malaysia) and the Riau Islands (Indonesia), into an economic zone within which developments among the three partners are differentiated according to each region's comparative advantage (Ng and Wong 1991). The significant wage cost (and skill) and land cost differentials in Batam, Johor, and Singapore create incentives to conceive of the three places as a single subregion, where companies can base their different activities (managerial, administrative, production, etc.) in close proximity and still enjoy the benefits of lower costs and access to skilled labor and well-developed amenities.

Although the success of the growth triangle concept is still unclear, especially with the continued economic uncertainties in Indonesia, it seems clear that Singapore, as a city-state that is facing severe land and labor constraints, has to develop a strategy that goes beyond its shores as a means of maintaining the growth of its domestic industries. Such a hinterland strategy requires relegating the more land-labor–intensive phase to this hinterland, with either the firm maintaining administrative control and other service operations from the city or with the more sophisticated production operations kept in the city. In this division of labor, Singapore exports its technical planning and project management expertise, and central local partners handle the regulatory environment, land allocation, and labor sourcing process. This model was in fact developed in Batam, Indonesia, with the Batamindo project and has now been exported to a wider region, with varying degrees of success.

The capitalist logic of starting production in a low-wage country but in a highly efficient environment that guarantees quick startup and minimal disruptions will continue to appeal to many multinationals, and this has in fact been the operating principle for JTC moving overseas in the various ventures. However, developing and managing industrial parks in other countries is not without its attendant problems, especially when political cultures and regulations in host environments vary vastly from one country to another.[2]

Similar to Singapore's functional relations with its neighbors, but in an intranational regional context, Shanghai has shed some of its labor-intensive industries to the surrounding cities in the Yangtze River Delta region under the pressure of its rising land and labor costs. At the same time, Shanghai faces a new dilemma: trying to keep enough manufacturing jobs to keep unemployment low while upgrading to more technology- and knowledge-intensive manufacturing and strengthening the service sector (Chen 2007).

Even though there have been mixed successes associated with the regionalization strategies of Singapore and Shanghai, Singapore launched a science and technology initiative in 1991 as a new attempt to create a more permanent advantage in manufacturing by fostering the development of industrial research and product development.

As detailed in the two National Technology Plans (National Science and Technology Board 1991, 1996), this initiative was developed at several levels. Similar to the creation of statutory boards in the 1960s to spearhead key industrial responsibilities, the government formed the National Science and Technology Board (NSTB)[3] and tasked it with the mission of identifying and promoting key areas of research and development in order to enhance economic competitiveness. Alongside this key institution was the development of a number of research centers and institutes. The NSTB adopted two major indicators in order to benchmark its efforts against other nations and to chart progress over time. This was the share of GDP devoted to research and development and the proportion of research scientists and engineers (RSE) per 10,000 workers (see Markusen and Yu, this book, regarding using a similar measure of high-tech development in U.S. metropolitan areas). The first technology plan set targets of 2 percent of GDP spending and 40 RSE per 10,000 to be achieved by 1995. By 1994, research and development spending still fell short of the target at 1.12 percent, although the RSE target was achieved at 41.9 RSE per 10,000.

Hang (1999), who served as Deputy Chairman of the NSTB and Deputy Vice Chancellor of the National University of Singapore (NUS) in charge of research, technology transfer, and strategic planning argued that the new target of 65 RSE per 10,000 by the year 2000 set by the NSTB (1999, 11) was not going to be sufficient. Because Singapore is a small country the absolute number of RSE derived from this target would not be enough to sustain a viable research and development program, and he noted that smaller nations such as Israel have set targets as high as 130 (Hang 1999, 29). On both research and development (R&D) spending as well as RSE per 10,000 workers, Singapore has lagged behind not only the industrially advanced nations in the West and Japan but also its East Asian neighbors of Korea and Taiwan.

The policies and institutions needed for maintaining competitiveness are different during a crisis (such as the Asian financial crisis) and recession from those in boom times. This requires an understanding of both the volatility of the external economic environment as well as the different types of arrangements needed.

The Asian financial crisis in 1997–1998 provided a test environment for the policies and institutions of Singapore in sustaining competitiveness. Although that crisis was labeled Asian in scope, it varied quite a bit in its symptoms and causes across the countries most affected. In Thailand, Malaysia, and Indonesia, banks, other financial institutions, and property development companies collapsed as a result of their overexposure to speculative lending and investments in stocks and properties. In Korea, the crisis was brought on primarily by industrial conglomerates (*chaebol*) overborrowing from foreign and domestic banks to finance their expansion and competition. Singapore, however, experienced a reduced impact from the crisis because its effective developmental state imposed restrictions on capital flows, restrictive trading rules for the stock exchange, and strong planning controls and active housing provisions in the property sector (see Henderson 1998).

In examining the institutions that support economic development through good and bad economic times, it is important to note Seddon and

Belton-Jones's (1995) observation that the agencies that are charged with maintaining competitiveness in a period of growth are quite different from those that need to be activated in a period of economic downturn.

Economic planners determined that the key to the adjustment and recovery process was a cost-cutting exercise. The cost-cutting strategy arose out of several considerations. Given Singapore's export-oriented production and small domestic economy, the bulk of demand is externally derived. Since this cannot be controlled, the next best measure is to tinker with domestic factors such as wages and other costs. The need to put in place a recovery package was also justified by the drastic falls in regional currencies, which made potential competitors even more attractive. Cost cutting was thus seen to compensate for Singapore's loss in competitiveness as a result of a more stable dollar.

In the cost-cutting exercise, the key organizations were the unions, which needed to convince their workers that such a measure was necessary. With the record high retrenchment figures in 1998 at the height of the Asian financial crisis, the cost cutting was all the more painful for families with reduced household incomes as a result of lower wages or retrenchments. Although cost cutting may benefit the export sector by lowering production costs, it is actually deflationary on the domestic side because of reduced spending. Thus, the retail sector needed to be convinced of such a course of action.

In spite of such complications, the wage cut was successfully carried out for a number of reasons. There was already in existence an institutional structure called the National Wages Council (NWC), which moderated annual wage changes in tandem with the performance of the economy. The NWC suggestions are followed by the government, which provides a demonstrative effect on industry. Precedence was already set fifteen years earlier. In the 1985–1986 recession there was a 15-percentage point cut in the employer's portion of the pension payment (CPF).

The management of this process is another key element in understanding the success. In the process leading up to the announcement, employer associations and the various business chambers kept a low profile. Their position in the institutional structure relegated them to providers of information on the effects of the crisis on business performance. They, of course, worked in their interest and did their lobbying. But decisions were made behind closed doors and primarily within the Committee on Singapore's Competitiveness (CSC), a government-initiated committee to examine the effects of the crisis on the local economy and to recommend solutions.

The key element was therefore the CSC, and in the CSC, all important elements of successful ideological work were present, namely, the appointment of a panel of experts from government, industry, and academia; a due process of consultation involving information collection and deliberation; and the presentation of statistical data as "facts" to the public.

The politicians in Singapore have forged a close relationship with the unions. Singaporean labor history involved a transformation of militant unions into a system where unions became partners in the development process (Chiu, Ho, and Lui 1997, 147–52). This process was spearheaded by the National Trades Union Congress (NTUC). The NTUC in turn had its key officials in the government, thereby forming an interlocking system. It is this close relationship on which the government relied to explain its case to lower-level unionists and workers.

Ideologically, the wage cut was pitched as a call to save jobs. Because it was the government working with the support of the unions to push for the cut, this pitch was ideologically appropriate because it represented union thinking: the larger collective goal of saving jobs by involving individual sacrifice of a pay cut, with government ministers and the civil service leading the way.

Economists examining this initiative have quite naturally asked whether such measures are effective in restoring economic competitiveness. From a political economy perspective, the more important question is whether governments of neighboring countries can ever contemplate such a policy option. The fact that it was considered and carried out demonstrates in a very important way how institutional relations influence policy options. It also became an important demonstration by the government to companies that the government has the ability to make flexible adjustments when the economic climate changes.

Shanghai has experienced a long period of economic prosperity for more than fifteen years, surging during the late 1990s when Singapore and Hong Kong were recovering from the Asian financial crisis. Although strong central controls on foreign bank lending and foreign exchange largely shielded China from the Asian financial crisis, Shanghai might have come close to the bubble of the hot property market bursting around 2005. This triggered a number of central government interventionist measures, including raising down payments on loans for luxury homes from 20 to 30 percent, taxing proceeds from reselling homes within five years, and ending bank loans to developers unless they funded at least 35 percent of project costs from their own capital. And these measures helped cool down the property market in 2006 (Chen, introduction). The more pertinent lesson from Singapore for Shanghai, however, pertains to the social cost if the latter's overall dynamic growth slows down. The wage cuts sustained in Singapore in the wake of the Asian financial crisis, in a different form and context, were manifested in the laying off of large numbers of workers in state-owned enterprises in Shanghai and their subsequently lowered standard of living—done in the name of improving competitiveness in a more open global economy. There are therefore financial difficulties for some segments of the urban population even during overall good economic times.

The process of reinventing new policies and strategies creates internal tensions in state–society relations. We need to understand that the implied flexibility and reinventions needed by cities in the global economy place severe strains on domestic arrangements. This requires not only solutions that work as competitive economic policies but also solutions that manage domestic tensions brought about by inter-city competition.

At the heart of this particular issue are the forces unleashed by economic globalization and their effects on the local political terrain, with capital and global cities the most directly affected.

This externally driven tension is manifested at three levels. Sassen (2001) demonstrated how the expansion of the global economy in the form of the activities of multinational companies led to the growing concentration of service professionals in global cities. As transnational corporate networks expand, management, coordination, servicing, and financing activities proliferate, increasing specialized skill sets and outsourcing and raising demand for service professionals (Sassen 2001, xx–xxi, 11). These trends create dramatic increases in the pay of these professionals, leading to increased urban income inequalities and polarization between this privileged internationally mobile group and the working class that has seen its economic fortunes decline as jobs migrate to distant shores. The driving force for polarization, Sassen (2001, 244–45, 361–62) argues, is the shrinking of the middle class, which could also be a manifested outcome of this process.

The polarization then becomes the driver for the mobilization of a collective response for those at the bottom end of the income ladder, what Margit Mayer (1999, 215) terms antigrowth movements, which organize against specific developments and in defense of threatened communities, and poor people's movements, which are organized around welfare rights.

The government's response to this new economic climate also contributed to the polarization by devoting more attention and resources to economic policies at the expense of social policies (Mayer 1999, 211–12). Body-Gendrot (2000) shows with examples in the United States and France how cities became the locus of social control of the disorders arising from the growing disparities. Writing in a similar vein, Holston and Appadurai (1999) argued that the issue does not lie just in terms of selective attention to policies but also in terms of the treatment of the two classes: the exemption of duty for the professional class and the denial of rights to a migrant working class. The internationally mobile, courted by competing urban governments for the skills and capital they bring, end up with an absence of moral commitment to place, whereas the migrant working class become resentful of their marginal status in society. Margit Mayer suggested that "social policies have been abandoned in favor of punitive and repressive treatments of a growing segment of marginalized population" (Mayer 1999, 213).

Attempts to rework state–society relations are done in recognition of such tensions. This effort involved rallying Singaporeans around values of home, family, and country and touted opening avenues of participation as a means of building ownership. Such efforts at strengthening identity and commitment were a painfully difficult project at a time when the city-state had taken in increasing numbers of expatriate workers and at the same time had record numbers of Singaporeans being sent overseas as a result of regionalization policies as well as their work with transnational companies.

CONCLUSION AND IMPLICATIONS
FOR SHANGHAI

To what extent is Singapore a relevant and useful comparative case with Shanghai? I suggest in closing the following considerations.

THE TIMING AND PACE OF URBAN AND
INDUSTRIAL DEVELOPMENT

The August 9, 2002, issue of the *South China Morning Post* carried an article with the headline "Hong Kong told not to imitate Shanghai" containing the opinion of Wang Zhan, the director of the Shanghai Municipal Government Development Research Center. The headline points to the amazing change of economic fortunes between the two main players in Greater China. Shanghai's rapid development was paralleled by Singapore some thirty-five years ago. Such patterns reflect the geographic switches in foreign direct investments. Singapore grew because of investments into Southeast Asia in the 1970s, and in the 1990s, such investments flowed into China as costs increased in Southeast Asia and as new markets and production possibilities opened up in China. Shanghai caught a favorable wave of development powered by China-bound foreign direct investment (FDI). This good timing was reinforced by Shanghai's rise at a favorable stage of its own development trajectory characterized by the simultaneous coexistence of low-cost manufacturing and opportunities for developing services. The favorable coupling of timing and stage of development has been enhanced and sustained by a strong state. Both the Singapore and Shanghai cases involve sharp breaks with prior economic development, with Singapore moving away from an overdependence on port activities to incorporate industrial development, and Shanghai shifting from socialist industrialization to an export-oriented development strategy (see Wu, this book). These economic reforms were in part influenced by political developments: Singapore gaining independence and Shanghai being part of a larger political change led by a new generation of leaders who saw economic development as playing a key role in the overall development of China and instituted the reforms that increased the power of local authorities. The implications of Singapore's contemporary economic history for Shanghai are that the combination of all three key factors— timing, favorable stage, and strong state—does not last forever.

THE ROLE OF GOVERNMENTS AND AGENCIES

In terms of institutional structures, what is interesting from the Singaporean case has been the creation of specialist institutions and agencies tasked with the performance of specific key roles. In the 1960s, these were agencies such as the Economic Development Board and the Urban Redevelopment Authority, whereas in the 1990s, it was the National Science and Technology Board, with a restructured role for the Jurong Industrial Corporation. What seems also relevant has been Singapore's flexibility in restructuring its economy as particular industrial comparative advantages are eroded by new competitors. Two aspects are crucial in examining this issue. The first has to do with the economic "intelligence" capable of detecting changes and evaluating whether these changes have an economic potential for Singapore. One dimension of this intelligence is the overseas network built up by the Economic Development Board in the 1970s and 1980s, which allowed the republic to be closer to the developments in key industries in North America, Europe, and East Asia. In this regard, the republic's economic history has proven that the government picked the right industry in electronics, which formed the economic backbone of the

Singaporean economy from the 1970s to the 1990s, and perhaps the chemical industry after 2000 when the electronics industry dominance in the city state was weakened.

In the case of China and Shanghai, Segal and Thun (2001) argued that the central government has enlarged the power of local governments, notably through the retention of revenue, thereby providing the freedom and the incentives for subnational actors to move decisively on regional economic fronts. The Shanghai development authorities exploited these new opportunities well because they had both the authority and the experience to guide local economic development, thereby mimicking what Segal and Thun (2001, 566, 580) term as a developmental state operating at the municipal level. In the process, new agencies such as the Shanghai Investment Commission drive foreign investments as well as engineer changes in the urban land market to create the new economic landscape needed. Wu (2000, 1365) observed that by the late 1980s, the pace of economic reform allowed city governments to become the major landowner. This development not only provided the power and authority to effect change but also strengthened the incentives for urban redevelopment through land leasing (Zhang 2002, also this book).

THE EXPERIENCE AND THE SOCIOPOLITICAL CONSEQUENCES OF ECONOMIC RESTRUCTURING

A crucial difference between Shanghai and Singapore's economic trajectories is that Shanghai is still on the path of economic ascendancy, whereas Singapore has seen several bouts of restructuring and economic downturns in the last fifteen to twenty years. Three aspects of this restructuring process are important. The first has to do with the restructuring of the investment promotion agencies themselves and the shifts in relative importance detailed in this chapter. The second has to do with the costs involved in any experimentation with alternatives to the dominant forms of economic activity; several of Singapore's overseas ventures have not fared very well. The third has to do with sociopolitical outcomes of restructuring as the economic capacity to plan and execute them depends largely on state–society relations, specifically an ability to convince the majority of the population at large to agree to such changes even if there is a cost to them.

Sociopolitical outcomes are perhaps of greater significance as Shanghai continues to develop at a rapid pace. The social changes brought about by economic development require a continued attempt at ideological work—convincing the population that such changes are necessary. Thus, governments must pay attention to "softer" infrastructures, in particular to the building of trust and goodwill with the urban population at large. In the final analysis, this proves to be a more difficult and long-term project than that of developing specialist agencies. Despite the different setting, Shanghai, like many other industrial centers in China, is facing a similar challenge in coping with the "pains" of restructuring and downsizing state-owned enterprises, such as providing for the huge number of laid-off workers. With the disappearing socialist ideology and policy of keeping workers permanently employed, residents in the rapidly globalizing city of Shanghai are put in a more precarious position to fend for themselves. This is one major problem that building specialized institutions for a city to compete globally will not solve.

NOTES

I thank Xiangming Chen and two anonymous reviewers for their comments and suggestions.

1. See *The Business Times* (25 February 2003) "EDB to close HK offices as it focuses on China" for the opening of the Beijing and Shanghai office, and *The Straits Times* (28 September 2006) "Singapore Centres to offer one-stop services abroad" for mention of the Guangzhou office.

2. See Perry and Yeoh (2000) for a more detailed assessment of the performance of Singapore's overseas ventures in China and Indonesia.

3. In 2000, this agency was changed to A*Star, Agency for Science, Technology, and Research to better reflect its emerging focus.

REFERENCES

Body-Gendrot, S. 2000. *The Social Control of Cities*. Oxford: Blackwell.

Business Times, The. 2003. "EDB to Close HK Offices as It Focuses on China." February 25.

Castells, M., and P. Hall. 1994. *Technopoles of the World*. London: Routledge.

Chen, Xiangming. 2007. "A Tale of Two Regions in China: Rapid Economic Development and Slow Industrial Upgrading in the Pearl River and the Yangtze River Deltas." *International Journal of Comparative Sociology* 48, no. 2: 79–113.

Chiu, S., K.C. Ho, and T.L. Lui. 1997. *City States in the Global Economy*. Boulder: Westview.

Clarke, S.E., and Gaile, G.L. 1998. *The Work of Cities*. Minneapolis: University of Minnesota Press.

Department of Statistics. 1994. *Yearbook of Statistics Singapore 1994*. Singapore: Department of Statistics.

Economic Development Board. 1970. *Annual Report*. Singapore: Economic Development Board.

Friedmann, J. 1986. "The World City Hypothesis." *Development and Change* 17: 69–83.

Fry, E.H., 1990. "State and Local Government in the International Arena." *Annals, AAPSS* 509: 118–27.

Hang, C.C. 1999. "What It Takes to Sustain Research and Development in a Small Developed Nation in the 21st Century." In *Singapore Towards a Developed Status,* edited by Linda Low, 1–36. Singapore: CAS/Oxford.

Harvey, D. 2000 [1989]. "From Managerialism to Entrepreneurialism: The Transformation in Urban Governance in Late Capitalism." In *City Cultures Reader,* edited by M. Miles, T. Hall, and I. Borden, 50–59. London: Routledge.

Henderson, Jeffrey. 1998. "Uneven Crises: Institutional Foundations of East Asian Economic Turmoil." Unpublished paper WPTC-98-13. Manchester, UK: Manchester Business School, University of Manchester.

Ho, K.C. 1994. "Industrial Restructuring, the Singapore City-State, and the Regional Division of Labour." *Environment and Planning A* 26: 33–51.

Holston, J., and A. Appadurai. 1999. "Cities and Citizenship." In *Cities and Citizenship,* edited by J. Holston, 1–20. Durham, N.C.: Duke University Press.

Hubbard, P., and T. Hall. 1998. "The Entrepreneurial City and the 'New Urban Politics.'" In *The Entrepreneurial City,* edited by T. Hubbard and T. Hall, 1–23. New York: Wiley.

Liu, T.K. 1985. "Overview." In *Housing a Nation,* edited by A.K. Wong and S.H.K. Yeh, 1–29. Singapore: Housing Development Board.

Mayer, M. 1999. "Urban Movements and Urban Theory in the Late 20th Century." In *The Urban Moment: Cosmopolitan Essays on the Late 20th Century City,* edited by S. Body-Gendrot and R.A. Beauregard, 209–40. Thousand Oaks, Calif.: Sage (Urban Affairs Annual Reviews).

Mirza, H. 1986. *Multinationals and the Growth of the Singapore Economy.* London: Croom Helm.

National Science and Technology Board. 1991. *Windows of Opportunity: National Technology Plan 1991,* Singapore: NSTB.

———. 1996. *National Science and Technology Plan.* Singapore: NSTB.

Ng, C.Y., and P.K. Wong. 1991. *The Growth Triangle: A Market Driven Response?* Asia Club Papers (Tokyo Club Foundation for Global Studies), no. 2: 123–52.

Olds, Kris. 1995. "Globalization and the Production of New Urban Spaces: Pacific Rim Mega Projects in the Late 20th Century." *Environment and Planning A* 11: 1713–43.

Pang, E.F., and H.P. Khoo. 1975. "Patterns of Industrial Employment within Public Housing Estates." In *Public Housing in Singapore,* edited by H.K. Yeh Stephen, 240–61. Singapore: Housing and Development Board.

Perry, M., and C. Yeoh. 2000. "Singapore's Overseas Industrial Parks." *Regional Studies* 34, no. 2: 199–206.

Sassen, Saskia. 2001. *The Global City: New York, London, Tokyo.* 2nd ed. Princeton, N.J.: Princeton University Press.

Schein, E.H. 1996. *Strategic Pragmatism: The Culture of Singapore's Economic Development Board*. Cambridge, MA: MIT Press.

Seddon, D., and Tim Belton-Jones. 1995. "The Political Determinants of Economic Flexibility with Special Reference to the East Asian NICs." In *The Flexible Economy*, edited by T. Killick, 325–63. London: Routledge.

Segal, A., and E. Thun. 2001. "Thinking Globally, Acting Locally: Local Governments, Industrial Sectors, and Development in China." *Politics and Society* 29, no. 4: 557–88.

Soldatos P. 1990. "An Explanatory Framework for the Study of Federated States as Foreign-Policy Actors." In *Federalism and International Relations: The Role of Subnational Units*, edited by H.J. Michelmann and P. Soldatos, 34–50. Oxford: Clarendon Press.

South China Morning Post. 2002. "Hong Kong Told Not to Imitate Shanghai." August 9.

The Straits Times. 2006. "Singapore Centres to Offer One-stop Services Abroad." September 28.

The Straits Times. 2004. "EDB to Open Its First Office in Singapore Soon." September 10.

Wu, Fulong. 2000. "The Global and Local Dimensions of Place-Making: Remaking Shanghai as a World City." *Urban Studies* l37, no. 8: 1359–77.

———. 2003. "The (Post-) Socialist Entrepreneurial City as a State Project: Shanghai's Reglobalisation in Question." *Urban Studies* 40, no. 9: 1673–98.

Zhang, Tingwei. 2002. "Urban Development and a Socialist Pro-Growth Coalition in Shanghai." *Urban Affairs Review* 37, no. 4: 475–99.

5. BECOMING A CHINESE GLOBAL CITY

HONG KONG (AND SHANGHAI) BEYOND THE GLOBAL–LOCAL DUALITY

Tai-lok Lui and Stephen W. K. Chiu

Globalization is relatively new to Shanghai, which was cut off from the rest of the world in 1949 and not fully reintegrated with the global economy until the early 1990s. Globalization is nothing new to Hong Kong, which is an open economy with no restrictions on foreign trade and investment. From its early days as a British colony in the nineteenth century, Hong Kong has been an important trading port as well as a commercial city-not only for the advancement of the economic and political interests of the British Empire, but also for the facilitation of regional trade and finance between China and Southeast Asia (Hamasita 1997; Hui 1995; Meyer 2000). Indeed, one of the important factors contributing to both Hong Kong's ascendency to a key position atop the regional trading and commercial networks in East Asia and to its economic success in the postwar decades is this very global connection.

Largely a reflection of its strategic economic position in East Asia, Hong Kong has often been cited in the literature as one of the significant examples of world cities (for a survey of various citations, see Beaverstock, Taylor, and Smith 1999, 448–49).[1] Despite Hong Kong's status among world cities in the global economy, few attempts, perhaps with the notable exception of Meyer (2000), have been made to use the study of Hong Kong enrich the context within which theoretical and analytical concepts have been articulated in recent literature on global cities and/or world cities. This chapter will engage in such a discussion. Particularly, we shall argue that the dual economic and political restructuring of Hong Kong during the past two decades is best understood in light of its integration into its neighboring region and, more important, its repositioning within the national ambit of China.[2]

Instead of becoming more global (in the sense of further integration into the global economy by loosening its attachment to the nation-state), Hong Kong's economic development is increasingly embedded in China's grander national marketization and globalization project. Hong Kong is becoming a *Chinese* global city. By underlining the Chinese dimension and its pertinence, we contend that the national project is increasingly impacting Hong Kong. From Hong Kong's perspective, its own struggle for survival and recovery from the recession triggered by the Asian financial crisis has brought it closer to China. By showing how the "nationalizing" of Hong Kong has undermined its global orientation and local autonomy, our discussion also serves to expose Shanghai's somewhat delicate position across the interstices of the global, national, and local.

Our analysis of Hong Kong as a Chinese global city highlights the place-ness of the global city (Sassen 2001), which is shaped by interactions among the global, the local, as well as the national. Such interactions play a significant role in shaping the restructuring of a global city, and are by no means confined to specific (and given its return to China in 1997, one may say special) cases such as Hong Kong. Empirically, the understanding of Hong Kong's development as a Chinese global city provides broader relevance to our understanding of other Asian cities' (e.g. Singapore) and their respective struggles for economic recovery in the context of the post–Asian crisis (see Ho, this book). Analytically, it also adds a new, national dimension to the dialectics between the global and the local (cf. Wu, this book). Indeed, one must transcend the global–local duality in order to see how both globalization and the role of the state play their part in restructuring global cities.

GLOBALIZATION, GLOBAL CITY, AND THE NATIONAL

Into the 1980s, a new phase of globalization triggered a fundamental restructuring in the global urban hierarchy and the economic and employment structures in specific locales. Scholars such as Friedmann (1986, 1995; also Friedmann and Wolff 1982) and Sassen (2001, this book) have forcefully articulated the theses of the world city and global city, seeking to capture the structural transformation of the world economy toward accelerated globalization and increasing integration. As Friedmann (1995, 26) puts it, the radical break in the world economy began in the 1980s with four major characteristics: "the functioning of industries of a world scale through the medium of global corporate networks; an increase in oligopolistic, progressively centralized power; an ongoing process of corporate decentralization through new forms of subcontracting, joint ventures, and other forms of networked organization and strategic alliances; and finally, a new, more volatile balance of power between nation-states and corporations."

Against this background, a network of global cities has risen from the spatial manifestation of capital accumulation in the new global economy. As Sassen points out, today's global cities are "(1) command points in the organization of the world economy; (2) key locations and marketplaces for the leading industries of the current period—finance and specialized services for firms; and (3) major sites of production for these industries, including the production of innovations in these industries" (2001, 4). A dual process of dispersal of production and centralization of production is typically cited to be the engine behind the emergence of global cities. As the global mobility of capital and commodities accelerated, production—and manufacturing production in particular— became dispersed geographically.

The growing body of literature on world cities and global cities (useful surveys include Beaverstock, Taylor, and Smith 1999; Friedmann 1995; Short and Kim 1999) serves to illustrate the structuring of the global urban hierarchy and the importance and centrality of major cities in shaping the globalization process. However, questions and criticisms have been raised against this argument. It is criticized for using inadequate methodology, whereby "[i]deas are asserted more than demonstrated" (Short and Kim 1999, 8). It is also criticized for being ahistorical, neglecting diversity in different cities' responses to global forces, and rarely taking space seriously (Abu-Lughod 1999; King 1991; Smith 2001). Brenner (1998) and Yeung (2000) argue that world cities research is vulnerable to hyperglobalist hijacking (Held et al. 1999) and as a result it has "generally presupposed a 'zero-sum' conception of spatial scale" and "neglected the role of state-scale transformation in the current round of globalization" (Brenner 1998, 2–3).

The preceding criticisms of world cities research caution against analyzing world cities or global cities too broadly in terms of their functions in the global economy. Equally dangerous is the temptation of seeing a city as a globalizing and autonomous economic unit, and thus oversimplifying our understanding of the global economy as merely consisting of networks and flows linking cities through nodes in the global urban hierarchy. Although the value of these criticisms is noted, it should be pointed out that world cities researchers have long recognized the importance of the place-ness of a global city. As Sassen (2001, 350) states:

> The place-ness of the global city is a crucial theoretical and methodological issue in my work. Theoretically it captures Harvey's notion of capital fixity as necessary for hypermobility. A key issue for me has been to introduce into our notions of globalization the fact that capital even if dematerialized is not simply hypermobile or that trade and investment and information flows are not only about flows. Further, place-ness also signals an embeddedness in what has been constructed as the 'national,' as in national economy and national territory. This brings with it a consideration of political issues and theorizations about the role of the state in the global economy which are excluded in more conventional accounts about the global economy.

This emphasis on place-ness makes it easy to connect global cities research with the new concept of the global city–region (Scott 2001).

The preceding discussion on place-ness draws our attention to a need to unpack the embeddedness of global cities. Instead of seeing global cities as globalizing economic units that are disembedded from their immediate environments, we need to tease out how they are contextualized in different layers of the broader socioeconomic and political structures. There are different kinds of embeddedness of the global cities (cf. Zukin and DiMaggio 1990). At the local level, what Amin and Thrift (1994) describe as "institutional thickness" is crucial to building institutional and organizational synergy for sustaining the competitiveness and innovation of the global cities. Equally significant is the regional factor in reinforcing the centrality of global cities (Scott 2001).

Given our focus on the political in this chapter, it is also important to note that there are different layers of political embeddedness. What is immediately relevant to our present discussion is that the national is more than just the backdrop of the rise and fall of global cities. Despite the fact that globalization has brought about challenges to the capacity of the nation-state in dealing with new issues arising from the management of the national economy, the power and effects of the national remain real enough in shaping parameters that structure the development of global cities, which refutes the argument that the state loses power as globalism gain momentum (as articulated by Weiss, 1998).

State policy at the national level defines and redefines how global cities are connected with their neighboring regions and thus creates boundaries demarcating their hinterlands. It can also develop new rules and regulations that can either enable or restrict the interconnectivity among the global city, the regional economy, and the world economy. This is not to deny or to underestimate the significance of the subnational and the impacts of new regionalism (i.e., local regions taking the initiatives in carrying out economic, political, and social mobilization to deal with economic restructuring in the face of globalization) in the shaping of economic development. Our point is to highlight the fact that whether the national is relevant or otherwise is an empirical question. In different forms, the state continues to exert its influence on regional social formation and thus on the configuration of the global city hinterland.[3] The rescaling of a global city is always closely connected to the state's rescaling project (see Wu, this book, for the reinvented role of the state in Shanghai).

For Hong Kong the scope of economic influence has long transcended its administrative and political boundaries, as evidenced by its almost seamless connections and linkages with Shenzhen, which was used (Ohmae 1995) to illustrate the end of the nation-state and the rise of a borderless world. Hong Kong's rediscovery and redrawing of the boundary of its hinterland (not confining it to the Pearl River Delta [PRD]) was greatly facilitated by its return to China in 1997, when it became a focus of the CCCP's quest to deepen its economic reform and strengthen its integration with the world economy.

China's reentry into the global economy, together with economic and political changes in Eastern Europe, is most critical to making the world economy unequivocally global (cf. Byrne 2001, 87). It opened a new space, both geographic and institutional, for Hong Kong to renegotiate its functions and centrality in the flows of economic transactions in both its region and between China and the world. As a result of such economic reintegration with the national economy, the Hong Kong SAR government has in recent years, increasingly identified Shanghai, rather than Singapore, as its future arch-rival. At the same time, the imposition of Chinese rule over Hong Kong, bringing this global city under mainland control, has reshaped local perspectives. The idea of "one country, two systems" has not, however, stopped Hong Kong from exploring future development in the rapidly changing national parameters. In fact, as we shall show later, in an effort to seek leverage to recover from economic recession, Hong Kong began to look to the mainland for new resources and opportunities. In short, the national is actively shaping Hong Kong's restructuring into a Chinese global city. The same can be said of Shanghai being shaped into a different global city that can complement Hong Kong (see a limited comparison later).

HONG KONG: ECONOMIC RESTRUCTURING AND THE REFIGURATION OF A GLOBAL CITY

As noted earlier, Hong Kong began its integration with the global economy when it was colonized in the nineteenth century, triggering an evolutionary process that transformed Hong Kong from its position as a regional trading port, which grew into an an expanded role as a regional commercial hub, and finally by the early twentieth century, to a key position in Chinese Economic capital markets overseas (Hamilton 1999; Hui 1995; Meyer 2000). However, because of the establishment of the Communist regime in mainland China in 1949 and the Korean War (and the resulting trade embargo on China) in the early 1950s, Hong Kong's entrepôt trade suffered tremendously. However, the 1950s marked a new phase in the development of Hong Kong's manufacturing industries. With modest beginnings, Hong Kong, based upon export-oriented, labor-intensive production, rapidly reinvented itself as a successful industrial city in the 1960s and 1970s. By 1969, (Jao 1997) Hong Kong had emerged as a regional financial center. The rest is a well-rehearsed story, chronicling Hong Kong's successful ascension through the hierarchy of global cities (see Table 5.1; on Hong Kong's economic development, see Chiu, Ho, and Lui 1997).

But the lesson of Hong Kong as a global city does not stop there. Recent years have added to Hong Kong's story, with the most important development being its economic and political restructuring in the context of intensified economic globalization and, not least, the end of what remained of the colonial presence, which opened the door for mainland China to seize sovereignty over the city in 1997. On the economic front, Hong Kong entered a new phase of globalization with the dispersal of local production via massive relocation of its manufacturing industries. Squeezed between high production (labor and land) costs and stiff competition from other newly industrialized economies, local manufacturers began to search for greener pastures abroad (Lui and Chiu 2001). Starting from the mid-1980s relocation became a leading production strategy for Hong Kong's manufacturers.[4] Although many Hong Kong manufacturers extended their production arms to places such as Southeast Asia, Sri Lanka, Mauritius, and as far away as Poland, it is mainland China (particularly the PRD) that constitutes the main destination for their offshore production (see Figure 5.1). Mainland China, with the abundant supplies of low-cost land and cheap labor, is a palatable option for local manufacturers seeking

TABLE 5.1

Ranking of Hong Kong as an International Financial Center, circa 1995

Categories	Asia–Pacific Ranking	World Ranking
Banking		
Number of foreign banks	1	2
Banks' foreign assets	2	4
Banks' foreign liabilities	2	5
Cross-border interbank claims	2	6
Cross-border interbank liabilities	2	4
Cross-border credit to nonbanks	1	2
Syndicated loans and note-issuing facilities (NIFs) (1994)	1	4
Forex market		
Net daily turnover	3	5
Derivatives market		
Net daily forex contract turnover	3	5
Net interest rate contract turnover	4	8
Overall	3	7
Stock market		
Market capitalization	2	9
Value traded	4	11
Number of listed domestic companies	7	16
Gold market	1	4
Insurance		
Number of authorized insurance companies	1	n/a
Premium income	5	27
Qualified actuaries	1	n/a
Fund management	2	n/a

Source: Y.C. Jao, *Hong Kong as an International Finance Center,* Hong Kong: City University of Hong Kong Press, 1997.

ways to expand production without needing to invest in rigorous technological upgrading (Lui and Chiu 1993).

At the end of 1995 the value of realized Hong Kong direct investments in China was US$20.4 billion. Some 55 percent of all foreign direct investment in China came from Hong Kong (State Statistical Bureau 1996, 598). In Guangdong province alone, Hong Kong manufacturers operated 25,000 processing factories and employed three million workers

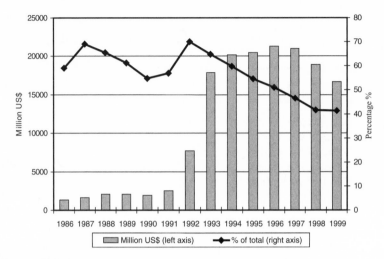

FIGURE 5.1
Growth of Hong Kong investment in China, 1986–1999 (million US$).
Source: State Statistical Bureau, *China Statistical Yearbooks.*

in 1993 (Federation of Hong Kong Industries 1993, 3). Another estimate suggests that Hong Kong firms employed eight times as many workers in Guangdong as in Hong Kong proper in 1996, and their investments in Guangdong were 22 percent as high as domestic investment (Berger and Lester 1997, 24). An MIT team studying the local industry thus coined the term "made by Hong Kong" as opposed to "made in Hong Kong" to capture the shifting in the patterns of production (Berger and Lester 1997).

The change in Hong Kong's role from a production site to an operating center controlling a widely dispersed network of extraterritorial production locales has led to other changes. First, there has been exponential expansion of the reexport trade from China. As Hong Kong manufacturers relocated their production base to China by setting up factories there or by subcontracting parts of the production processes to Chinese factories, the volume of outward processing arrangements surged dramatically. Such outward processing arrangements involve the export of raw materials or semimanufactures from or through Hong Kong to the mainland for processing; subsequently, the processed goods are reimported into Hong Kong. Reexports of products of Chinese origin involving outward processing almost doubled from HK$221 billion to HK$422 billion in four years before 1995. Labor-intensive products such as clothing, electrical appliances, and toys are among the major items. Commodities involving outward processing in China accounted for some 82 percent of all reexports from Hong Kong in 1994 (Census and Statistics Department 1995, F13). One government study made the following observation:

> In a great number of other cases, essentially all manufacturing processes are moved to China, leaving only such functions as marketing, orders processing, materials sourcing, design, product development, prototype making and quality control with the local firms. . . . Besides, many traditional import/export firms have also become engaged in SPAC [subcontract processing arrangements in China] to take advantage of cheap, abundant resources in China. . . . Furthermore, quite a large number of new . . . [trading] firms are also set up in recent years to serve as a local base for new manufacturing firms in China, operating in a way different from traditional importers/exporters. (Census and Statistics Department 1996, FA3)

Indeed, as early as 1991, when the Hong Kong Trade Development Council (1991, 13) surveyed local manufacturers and traders and asked them to describe their respective plans for future operations in Hong Kong, 83 percent of the respondents mentioned controlling headquarters, 81 percent documentation, 73 percent business negotiation, and 72 percent trade financing. In other words, Hong Kong's manufacturers are no longer the primary production contractors for overseas buyers, but instead have positioned themselves as the agents of "triangular manufacturing" (Gereffi 1994, 114).

In the course of this industrial restructuring process, the number of manufacturing establishments fell from the peak at 51,671 in 1988 to 20,380 in 1999, however, the number of import/export firms with manufacturing-related activities rose from 12,580 in 1992 to 22,330 in 1999 (Census and Statistics Department 2001b, FB4). The compilation of statistics on manufacturing-related activities since 1992 actually reflects changes in the business strategy of local traders and manufacturers. In 1992 among those 12,580 import/export firms engaged in SPAC and providing technical support services, 42.3 percent of them were former manufacturers. In other words, many manufacturers changed from directly engaging in production to assuming a role in trading, marketing, and coordination and control between overseas buyers on the one side and the production plants in mainland China on the other.

In 1999 the picture was very different. Only 26.8 percent of the 22,330 import/export firms with manufacturing-related activities previously undertook production in Hong Kong. Among these, about three-quarters (73.2 percent) were originally set up as importers and exporters. This evidence reflects both the flexibility of Hong Kong business (manufacturers taking up more commercial and trading functions and traders integrating into production and related activities) and the strength of local business in the commercial side of global production. The new prototype of successful business is characterized by a competitive advantage in handling dispersed manufacturing, skillful supply chain management, customer-sensitive marketing, and the capability of providing so-called one-stop-shop services (Trade and Industry Department 2001, 2–15).

The growth in cross-border trade and other transactions stimulated the growth of other producer services, such as the financing of production expansions in China, trade-related services, insurance, communication, ports, transportation, and logistics. What is more relevant to our discussion here is the further development of Hong Kong as a locale for coordinating and managing such transnational flows of economic activities. Table 5.2 summarizes the information on the regional representation of overseas companies in Hong Kong.[5] The number of regional headquarters rose from 602 in 1991 to 944 in 2001 and then to 1,167 in 2005, whereas the number of regional offices increased from 278 in 1991 to 2,631 in 2005 (see Table 5.2 for more details). This growth, however, occurred in the more recent shift of a number of regional headquarters of multinational companies to Shanghai (see Chen, introduction, this book).

Available information on overseas companies with Hong Kong–based regional representation does not really reveal too much about the changing pattern of their activities and the complexities of regional coordination and control. However, it should be noted that there are significant diversities among multinational corporations (MNCs) of different country origins in the use of Hong Kong as a center of regional representation, coordination, and control. For example, for Japanese MNCs, "Hong Kong is most important as a location for marketing, sales and customer service functions. . . . for U.S. MNCs, Hong Kong would seem very important for coordinating, supporting, and reporting on regional operations" (Thompson 2000, 182).

In 1991 43.4 percent of the regional headquarters (RHQs) had parent companies engaged in manufacturing. However, upon their arrival in Hong Kong, only 11.5 percent of all surveyed firms were in that business; the majority (51.7 percent) were in wholesale/retail and import/export. In the period 1991–2005, more and more RHQs (either in terms of the business of their parent companies or their Hong Kong–based activity) were found in wholesale, retail, and trade-related services. By 2005 an important line of business conducted by these RHQs in Hong Kong was related to business services, finance, and banking. This picture is largely consistent with our earlier discussion of the restructuring of Hong Kong's manufacturing. If Hong Kong is to

TABLE 5.2
Information on Regional Headquarters and Regional Offices Established by Overseas
Companies in Hong Kong, 1991–2005

	Regional Headquarters	Regional Offices
1991	• 602 total • 258 having U.S. parent companies • 43.4% having parent companies in manufacturing • 51.7% engaged in wholesale/retail or import/export • 78 and 166 responsible for Hong Kong/China and Southeast Asia (including China), respectively	• 278 total • 62 and 61 having U.S. or Japanese parent companies, respectively • 46.4% having parent companies in manufacturing • 40.5% engaged in wholesale/retail or import/export • 126 and 52 responsible for Hong Kong/China and Southeast Asia (including China), respectively
1996	• 816 total • 188 having U.S. parent companies (85 from China) • 40.4% having parent companies in manufacturing • 50.0% engaged in wholesale/ retail or import/export • 314 and 172 responsible for Hong Kong/China and Southeast Asia (including China), respectively	• 1,491 total • 338 and 226 having Japanese or U.S. parent companies, respectively (128 from China) • 39.6% having parent companies in manufacturing • 50.8% engaged in wholesale/retail or import/export
2001	• 944 total • 221 having U.S. parent companies (70 from China) • 27.0% having parent companies in wholesale/retail or trade-related services • 39.7% engaged in wholesale/retail or import/export • 82.8% responsible for mainland China[a]	• 2,293 total • 533 and 420 having Japanese or U.S. parent companies, respectively (172 from China) • 32.7% having parent companies in wholesale/retail or trade-related services • 46.3% engaged in wholesale/retail or import/export • 78.3% responsible for mainland China[a]
2005	• 1,167 total • 262 having U.S. parent companies (107 from China) • 32.6% having parent companies in wholesale/retail or trade-related services	• 2,631 total • 606 and 537 having U.S. or Japanese parent companies, respectively (160 from China) • 35.7% having parent companies in wholesale/retail or trade-related services

(Continues)

TABLE 5.2
(Continued)

Regional Headquarters	Regional Offices
• 52.7% engaged in wholesale/retail or import/export • 89.6% responsible for mainland China[a]	• 52.0% engaged in wholesale/retail or import/export • 84.1% responsible for mainland China[a]

Source: Census and Statistics Department, *Annual Survey of Regional Offices Representing Overseas Companies in Hong Kong.*

Note: [a]The reporting of information regarding these regional headquarters' and regional offices' countries and territories of responsibility was different in 2001 and 2005 from what it was before; the surveyed firms gave multiple answers because their scope of activity covered more than one country.

play a part in global production, either as a gateway of global outsourcing or as a hub of MNC global coordination and control of production, its significance falls primarily in the areas of commerce, trading, and management.

Equally significant is the rise of China as a potential market for consumer products as well as a location of production. In 2005 among the 1,167 RHQs, 1,046 were responsible for the business in mainland China, 479 indicated Taiwan, and 430 Singapore. China figures prominently in the business plans of these RHQs (cf. Thompson 2000). At the same time, there has been an increase in the number of regional offices (ROs) with the parent companies originating from mainland China. It is evident that given its strategic location together with the established business networks, Hong Kong constitutes an important interface between China and global business.[6]

Allied to this is the global increase in the mobility of capital and the rise of Hong Kong as a regional financial center (also see Meyer 2000, 197–218). For example, foreign-incorporated banks increased from 138 in 1990 to 154 in 1995 (Jao 1997, 54). By 1995 Hong Kong emerged as an indisputable center of regional and international finance. As Table 5.1 shows, Hong Kong ranked among the top five centers of financial development in the Asia–Pacific and in the top ten in the world. The net result that the rising share of business services in GDP comes at the expense of manufacturing, and it has had a deleterious effect on the prominence of financial services, trade, and commerce (see Figure 5.2).

Table 5.3 reports on the development of Hong Kong's service sector in 1991–2004. It is evident that Hong Kong has experienced growth not

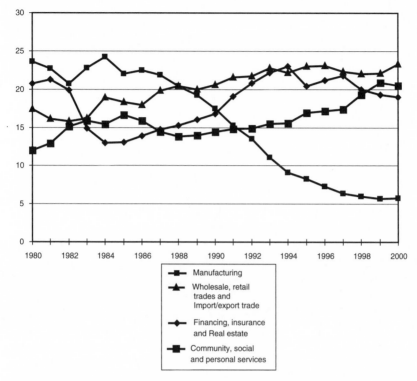

FIGURE 5.2
Sectoral share in GDP of manufacturing and major service sectors (percentage).
Source: Census and Statistics Department, *Annual Digest of Statistics.*

only in banking and finance but also in the areas of professional services, trading, and reexports. Without going into the details of the statistics in Table 5.3, it is worth mentioning that the number of Chinese state-owned companies listed in Hong Kong's stock market increased from six in 1993 to seventy-two in 2004. Echoing the point made earlier, Hong Kong's strategic importance lies in its two-way traffic of investments interflows between the global economy and China.

THE CHANGING NATIONAL CONTEXT UNDER ONE COUNTRY, TWO SYSTEMS

In the past the strategic role of Hong Kong in facilitating economic reform and marketization in mainland China was paramount. However, as China has undergone rapid economic growth, and as Hong Kong's economy recovers from being badly hit by the bursting of its bubble economy in late

TABLE 5.3

Major Statistics on Hong Kong's Service Sector, 1991–2004

	1991	1996	1997	1998	1999	2000	2001	2002	2003	2004
Banking										
Establishments	1,972	1,954	1,936	1,962	1,922	1,837	1,798	1,688	1,588	1,529
Business receipts index (96=100)	n/a	100.0	103.9	97.6	104.0	104.8	107.6	106.7	106.7	111.2
Presence of world's largest five hundred banks in Hong Kong	206	213	215	213	186	186	176	168	170	157
Financial Markets and Fund Management Services										
Establishments	1,802	2,402	2,321	2,200	2,361	2,464	2,523	2,545	2,368	2,354
Business receipts index (96=100)	n/a	100.0	165.2	93.3	98.4	132.9	106.4	91.3	114.0	154.4
Listed companies (Main Board)	357	583	658	680	701	736	756	812	852	892

Chinese state-owned companies listed in Hong Kong	—	23	39	41	44	47	50	54	64	72
Professional Services										
Establishments	5,713	9,199	10,003	9,058	9,686	9,893	10,350	10,723	11,190	11,656
Import/Export										
Establishments	69,066	104,076	101,324	92,604	98,714	104,455	100,438	102,902	97,977	95,451
Import/export firms with manufacturing-related functions	n/a	25,530	25,980	21,640	22,330	19,000	15,647	16,378	15,231	n/a
Reexports of goods produced in mainland China to other places (HK$ million)	221,450	552,822	595,511	559,726	570,126	647,338	578,329	594,708	603,592	684,888

Source: Census and Statistics Department, *Statistical Digest of the Services Sector.*

1997, the Hong Kong SAR government began to turn its gaze to the accu-mulated economic resources in the mainland. It has targeted mainland tourists, particularly those belonging to the so-called white-collar stratum (i.e., the middle class) as potential spenders to boost the economy, espe-cially by the launching of its new Disney theme park. Hong Kong also began negotiating with the central government about securing an advan-tageous position through preferential treatment, that is, by defining Hong Kong's corporations or Hong Kong–related joint ventures as local corpo-rations, before China fully adheres to the WTO rules. Also significant is the intense lobbying to allow mainlanders with foreign currency to trans-fer their funds into Hong Kong banks and/or to invest in the stock mar-ket (*South China Morning Post*, March 12, 2002).

This new orientation was best summarized by the chief executive in his 2002 policy address: that "[f]ollowing China's accession to the WTO, cooperation between Hong Kong and Guangdong will rise to new heights. The government is determined to actively promote economic cooperation between Hong Kong and the Pearl River Delta region with a view to achieving a 'win–win' situation. This is a key element in our efforts to consolidate and enhance Hong Kong's position as an interna-tional center for finance, trade, transport and logistics, as well as a premier tourist destination" (Tung 2001, 8).

The SAR government has its belief that Hong Kong's development as a global city is increasingly linked to China's national development. The Financial Secretary once compared the China–Hong Kong boundary as a "Goretex boundary:" "Hong Kong people and money can flow into the mainland quite freely, but it's not the case the other way around." (Leung 2002) Thus the government was expected to work on the "five flows" across the boundary: people, cargo, capital, information, and services. The intri-cate ties between the national and Hong Kong's drive to become a global city can also be seen as the key strategic aim, as articulated by the city's self-appointed honorific as "Asia's world city." The embeddedness of the global in the national is clear enough: "Hong Kong's position as Asia's world city is built on its role as the gateway to the mainland of China and a hub for busi-ness in the Asia-Pacific region" (Information Services Department 2001). How to manage the flow of people across the border is, however, a tricky task for the SAR government. On the one hand, Hong Kong will maintain a sep-arate customs system, while maintaining a restrictive border control policy consistent with the "one country, two systems" model. Accordingly, freedom of movement across the border, especially from China to Hong Kong, remains out of the question. This has provoked the long constitutional and legal battles between the SAR government and mainland residents seeking right of abode in Hong Kong. Nevertheless, as Hong Kong is fast becoming the hub of and for China in Asia, it will be necessary to relax restrictions on cross-border movements. In particular, the large number of increasingly affluent mainland residents constitutes an important source of visitors yet to be fully tapped by Hong Kong's tourism industry; mainland travelers now account for more than 50 percent of the total number of inbound visitors. The government reached an agreement with the National Tourism Administration for the abolition of the quota system for the Hong Kong Group Tour Scheme from January 2002. Further relaxation was introduced in 2003 with the launching of the Individual Visit Scheme for mainland tourists—first for the residents in the major cities and then, gradually these are to be extended to other regions. Such new initiatives helped to bring more than 13 million Chinese tourists to Hong Kong in 2006.

As the mainland and Hong Kong develop closer economic ties, more businesspeople are travelling between the two places. Previously, however, business travelling was placed under strict regulations even during the first few years of the reunification. To further facilitate visits to Hong Kong, the mainland's public security authorities agreed to extend the validity period for multientry business visas from the present six months to a maximum of three years, with each duration of stay extended to fourteen days. There were schemes letting mainland investors and businesspeople come and settle in Hong Kong. The SAR government also was promoting the exchange of professionals and managers. Over the past few years, the government has, on a progressive basis, reduced the time it takes to process the admission of professionals from abroad to work in Hong Kong and has launched new immigration schemes to admit mainlanders positioning desirable skills and talents.

Even more important is the flow of capital between the national and local economy. As in the case of people, the "Goretex boundary" is heavily skewed toward northbound movements in capital. This situation was found unsatisfactory because Hong Kong could not benefit as much as possible from the prosperous Chinese economy. Hong Kong's well-developed capital market has served as an important conduit for Chinese enterprises to raise much-needed investment funds. At the beginning only state enterprises were allowed to be listed in Hong Kong, but lately an increasing number of private enterprises are also lining up for the opportunity to be listed after the government enacted another round of relaxation of these restrictions. Bond issues have also become more important. As the recession came, the Hong Kong and Chinese governments took steps to reverse this one-way traffic. In 2002 the People's Bank of China began a study on setting up a special financial institution to help mainland residents invest their foreign exchange holdings in the Hong Kong stock market. It was suggested in the same year that a so-called qualified domestic institutional investor (QDII) scheme would create the impetus for investment in Hong Kong consisting, at least part, of the estimated US$80 billion foreign exchange savings held by mainland individuals and US$50 billion waiting in the coffers of mainland companies (*South China Morning Post*, March 17, 2002). Even though much of this money, if the scheme is realized, is expected to be invested only in stocks of Chinese companies listed in Hong Kong (the so-called H shares and red chips), the scheme would still create a much-needed new momentum to the stagnant Hong Kong market. It would also stimulate more mainland companies to be listed in Hong Kong because the current undervaluation of H shares would also be alleviated. In general, Hong Kong is expected to play an even more important role in the gradual opening of the financial system of China.

The year 2003 marked a major turning point in the materialization of various proposals concerning the facilitation of an interflow of resources between the mainland and Hong Kong. The outbreak of SARS and the resultant economic recession significantly contributed to the speeding up of the implementation of various new initiatives (as briefly noted in our previous discussion of tourism and new immigration initiatives), allowing Hong Kong to benefit from the increasingly affluence of the mainland population. They also brought about the signing of the first free trade agreement between China and Hong Kong, the mainland and Hong Kong Closer Economic Partnership Agreement (CEPA), in late June 2003. This agreement was a symbolic step toward developing closer economic cooperation and more intensive economic integration between Hong Kong and the mainland and promised to open opportunities for greater exchange between the former's goods and services and the latter's growing market. But equally significant to bringing about a reinstatement of the importance of maintaining economic prosperity in Hong Kong, and thus social and political stability, is evident in Beijing's recognition that political repression and violence against dissidents must be more discrete. Accordingly, when on July 1, 2003 an estimated crowd of 500,000 gathered in public spaces to express their anger with mainland rule and repression—a rally marking the sixth anniversary of China's political takeover of Hong Kong—the authorities did not openly crack down, and the result was a powerful, but peaceful popular protest (Lui 2005). Though it is important to note that China has its own agenda and concerns about how to manage the domestic economy and its interface with the global economy, a need to ensure Hong Kong's economic prosperity somehow also constitutes a part of its strategic considerations.

After extended deliberations, the mainland authorities finally agreed to give the green light for launching the QDII in April 2006. And more drastic measures allowing Chinese money, both institutional and private, to be invested outside the domestic economy via Hong Kong were floated and are under consideration. Particularly, the details of a so-called through-train scheme, which would allow individual investors in the mainland to buy Hong Kong stocks through selected mainland pilot cities, were under examination and are expected to be put into practice once the concerned authorities have worked out technicalities regarding the implementation and regulation of such a large capital outflow to Hong Kong. It has been suggested that the main impetus behind these new measures includes the mounting pressure on the yuan, the nation's soaring reserve, and the need to give the increasingly affluent urban population more investment choices (*South China Morning Post*, September 10, 2007). China needs to find a means to manage its cash and Hong Kong, given its status of being the most developed financial institution within the country, is expected to take on a new role in national financial matters. All these moves were greeted by positive responses in Hong Kong's stock exchange. A call was made by the chairperson of Hong Kong Exchanges and Clearing for the development of a single China market for shares (*South China Morning Post*, September 15, 2007). It was suggested that further steps toward narrowing the regulatory differences between Hong Kong and the mainland should be made in order to facilitate more cross-border trading and listings. In short, the national is making its impacts on the Hong Kong economy with closer cooperation, more intensive integration, the opening of new opportunities, and through increasing interflows of capital.

This recognition of the significance of the national is best summed up by the organization of the Economic Summit on "China's 11th Five Year Plan and the Development of Hong Kong" by the Hong Kong SAR government in September 2006, which deliberated the merits of future strategies in the areas of "trade and business," "financial services," "maritime, logistics, and infrastructure," and "professional services, information and technology, and tourism." An action agenda was subsequently published in January 2007. It suggested that "Looking ahead, it is worth considering whether and how Hong Kong should be involved in the preparation of the 12th Five-Year Plan (covering the period of 2011–2015) under the 'One Country, Two Systems' principle" (Hong Kong SAR government 2007:29). A self-acclaimed free economy is going to be integrated into national economic planning.

A COMPARISON WITH, AND IMPLICATIONS FOR, SHANGHAI

This chapter has taken steps to contextualize Hong Kong's transformation from an industrial colony to a global city developing in the context of China's new national development strategy since the 1980s. Hong Kong was in a bottleneck at that time, being squeezed by competitors from both the region and from the slowdown in the U.S. economy. In the late 1970s, however, China abandoned self-reliance for an open-door economic policy, aiming for active introduction of foreign capital, technology, and expertise in the hope of achieving the so-called four modernizations. Typically, China used special economic zones and joint-ventured oil field explorations to lure foreign investment. These new developments enhanced the possibility of China establishing a new service center that was close to its territory. Consequently, borderland integration between the colonial Hong Kong and mainland China is deepening. Having been involved in international trade for over a century, Hong Kong is well known for its strength in entrepôt trade, financial connections, and other services. Thus, Hong Kong can develop as a facilitator or intermediary for mainland trade and investment, providing valuable channels of information to China, serving as a contact point for China's trade, financing China's modernization, acting as a conduit for China's technology transfer, and providing a training ground for China to learn and practice capitalist skills in a market environment.

The rise of Shanghai since the early 1990s, however, has cast a long shadow over the bright role of Hong Kong in China's modernization mentioned above, triggering a continuing debate about whether Shanghai might overshadow Hong Kong; the prospect of this rivalry-real or perceived-has unleashed ever more intense competition between the two cities. Aided by a set of comparable indicators and reported survey evidence, we hope to shed some light on this debate using a comparative approach to reveal the relative advantages one might have over the other. As Table 5.4 shows, although Hong Kong still leads Shanghai in total and per capita GDP, it trails Shanghai in GDP and investment growth. The striking difference between the economic compositions of Hong Kong and Shanghai reflects their very different functions. Hong Kong is almost exclusively a service center, whereas Shanghai is more balanced between manufacturing and services. This difference is partly reflected in Hong Kong's much stronger role as a trading and transit trade hub. Hong Kong's growing ties with the PRD were responsible for the drastic decline of Hong Kong's manufacturing sector from 46 percent of total employment in 1980 to 5 percent in 2002, with the overwhelming spatial concentration (almost 70 percent) of Hong Kong–owned factories in the PRD (Chen 2005). In addition, Hong Kong's role in servicing the PRD has shifted. Hong Kong companies have relocated some operations of a service nature such as R&D, design, prototype manufacturing, and logistics to the PRD. However, they have kept high-level services such as advanced R&D, manufacturing management, and offshore trade in their Hong Kong headquarters.

Behind the strong push of the Shanghai government to promote the service sector and downsize the declining state-owned manufacturing industries, the industries' share of the GDP dropped from 63.8 percent in 1990 to 57.3 percent in 1995 and then to 50.1 percent in 2003 (Table 5.4). In terms of employment, the industries' share of the GDP declined from 54.6 percent in 1995 to 39 percent in 2003, whereas the services' share rose from

TABLE 5.4
Economic Indicators for Hong Kong and Shanghai, 2003

Economic Indicators	Hong Kong	Shanghai
Population	6.8 million	17 million
Working population	3.2 million	8.1 million
Area (sq. km)	1,098	6,341
Agriculture's share of GDP	0%	1.5%
Industry's share of GDP	5%	50.1%
Services' share of GDP	95%	48.4%
GDP (2003 price)	$152 billion	$76 billion
GDP per capita (2003 price)	$22,417	$5,644
GDP (based on purchase power parity [PPP])	$22,991	$8,941
GDP 10-year growth rate (2000 market price)	0.4%	15.4%
GDP per capita growth rate (2000 market price)	0.1%	14.8%
Fixed assets investment growth	–3.5%	12.0%
Imports	$226 billion	$64 billion
Exports	$218 billion	$48 billion
Reexports	$203 billion	—
Services' ratio to GDP	44.9%	21.3%
Trade's ratio to GDP	290.4%	18.0%

Source: Adapted from Table 2 of Chen, 2007, "A Tale of Two Regions in China: Rapid Economic Development and Slow Industrial Upgrading in the Pearl River and the Yangtze River Deltas," *International Journal of Comparative Sociology* 48, no. 2:79–113.

33.5 percent to 51.9 percent (see Chen, introduction, Table I.1). Shanghai's shift from a dominant manufacturing to a more service-oriented center with increasing strength in business services and R&D moves it a little closer to the functional profile of a global city such as Hong Kong. This generally favorable transition, however, has thrust Shanghai into a sort of dilemma of balancing the continued growth of its advanced service sector, which is expected of a global city, vs. maintaining its dominance as a traditional regional manufacturing hub for the Yangtze River Delta (YRD). Regardless of whether Shanghai can be successful readjusting and rebalancing its dual role as a globalizing city and a regional manufacturing hub, it is a crucial part of Shanghai's image and functionality which are perceived quite differently from those of Hong Kong. Having spent many years in Hong Kong, China watcher and analyst William Overholt (2004) saw its advantages in many business services such as accounting, law, and investment banking, and some of these have spilled over into the PRD over time and facilitated the latter's edge in logistics and supply-chain management, especially in rapidly changing product areas such as toys, gifts, and fashion. Shanghai, according to Overholt, has advantages in engineering, R&D, and design because of its concentrated human talent and presence of top-notch universities, with another advantage in the economies of scale from the critical mass of heavy industries (e.g. petrochemicals, steel, automobiles, machine tools, and machine technology). Overholt's conclusion was that most Fortune 500 companies focused on China's domestic market belong in Shanghai, whereas most exporters and many sophisticated service industries belong in Hong Kong. Drawing on annual surveys of both multinational and local business executives in both Hong Kong and Shanghai from 2001 to 2004, Tuan and Ng (2006) found that although Hong Kong led Shanghai in economic development conditions, investment environment (by the largest margin), and international image, Shanghai was closing the gaps with Hong Kong on all three indexes.

Although Shanghai may become a competitor against Hong Kong in some functional areas, it is up against the latter's entrenched strengths from a distinct development trajectory. From its reemergence as an entrepôt and transshipment center to its development as a financial hub, Hong Kong benefited tremendously from China's new development strategy. The development of Hong Kong as a financial center, however, has implications on the local path of restructuring because it created path-dependent pressures. Cross-border investment and its high initial returns fuelled a local asset boom and indirectly crowded out local manufacturing production and accelerated the outward relocation of industries. The colonial government pursued a "positive nonintervention" policy, and most Hong Kong firms were small- and medium-sized; therefore, Hong Kong small firms found it highly attractive to relocate their labor-intensive industries to the nearby PRD in Guangdong, which has led to a "hollowing out" of the manufacturing sector in Hong Kong. And Hong Kong has gradually transformed itself as an interface of production in China and the global market through its role in "triangular manufacturing."

So, since the early 1980s there has been a deepening of borderland integration, as Hong Kong firms spread their network of operations into the South China hinterland and therefore turned Hong Kong into the service and financial center of mainland China. Even as the local economy is going through a slow downward trend, the only visible way out for Hong Kong appears to be an through deeper integration with the national economy, capitalizing on its enormous growth potential to further propel Hong Kong into a regional hub for high value–added financial and producer services. Furthermore, reflecting the impacts of a change in sovereignty on Hong Kong's perspective, Hong Kong has been increasingly looking upon China not only as a hinterland for expanding production but also as a neighboring region for the expansion of its service industry, a new source of capital inflow, a potential market for consumer products and services, and a targeted population for the local tourist industry.

This development is to some extent paradoxical. It is almost the opposite of the scenario that was projected in the early 1980s, when Hong Kong was undergoing the political uncertainties created by Sino–British negotiations over its future. Instead of Hong Kong being the exemplar of high capitalism for steering China toward further integration with the global economy, now it is Hong Kong that turns to China to look for new economic energy and resources. In other words, the economic flows between China and Hong Kong are no longer one-way, from the latter to the former. Increasingly, they are two-way flows, tightening the interconnection and interdependence of the two places. Contextualizing such development in the broader historical perspectives of Hong Kong's integration with China (instead of seeing this as a sudden change in their fortunes after 1997), as we have done here, this is hardly surprising. In the wake of China's entry into the global market, Hong Kong's own rescaling process has increasingly been integrated into the ambit of the larger national project. Instead of being disembedded from the larger national and regional contexts, Hong Kong is becoming a Chinese global city. With an influx of Chinese enterprises for raising funds in the stock market, Hong Kong quickly surpassed New York in the value of initial public offerings

(IPO) and has become the second most popular venue, after London, for companies to float new stock listings (Foreman 2006). Equally important, as discussed in an earlier section, is China's need to manage its soaring reserve and the growing demands for investment channels by the mainlanders. In this regard, Hong Kong has all the potential of becoming the leading platform for institutional and private investment outside China proper. Although its prospect as a global city continues to hinge upon its global connections, the China factor is becoming a crucial force in structuring the flows between Hong Kong and the world economy.

It is against this background that we can understand why there has been increased debate regarding competition between Hong Kong and Shanghai, and between Hong Kong and other emerging cities in the PRD (*South China Morning Post*, March 16, 2002; *Ming Pao*, March 27, 2002). Whether Shanghai has already assumed the profile of a global city and challenges Hong Kong's status as the leading global city in China is not the crux of the matter. The important point is that Shanghai is now perceived as a potential challenger to Hong Kong. And competition from Shanghai is an impetus for Hong Kong to enhance its connectivity with the PRD. Suggestions for new projects in infrastructural development for the purpose of turning Hong Kong–Guangzhou into a one-hour commuting zone, speeding up the flows of people and goods within the region, developing collaborative projects among various airports in the region, and the recent statement made by the chief secretary about the role of Hong Kong in making the Greater PRD the main gateway of China's economy (*Ta Kung Pao*, September 19, 2002) are all recent initiatives in coping with the mere prospect of competition that could be posed by a prospering Shanghai.

The paradox is that the more the Hong Kong SAR government and the business community worry about challenges from Shanghai, the more they turn to the mainland as a source of untapped resources and for new economic drives. In comparison, Shanghai has never stepped out of China's national economic and political ambit. But it has become increasingly regionalized with the broader YRD hinterland (Chen 2007) just as it becomes more globally integrated and remains China's own premier economic center. In an ironic way, Shanghai may begin to follow Hong Kong in turning simultaneously more global and regional, without escaping the powerful hold of the national context. The global–local duality perspective prevalent in global city research is simply not sufficient for understanding the multiple opportunities and constraints faced by either Hong Kong or Shanghai. It remains an intriguing scenario as to how Shanghai will balance and exploit these opportunities and constraints at the local, regional, national, and global scales. Hong Kong's "inward turn" to the national after an extended local autonomy as a global city marks one trajectory that helps Shanghai ponder its long-term prospects. If Shanghai continues down the road as "a case of fostering place-based entrepreneurialism through a state project of city remaking" (Wu, this book), Hong Kong is likely to be a beneficiary of "the unfailing support from the mother country" a new, if unexpected, source of strength. Though this may not reduce the global connectivity of Hong Kong, it does imply that this global city is increasingly embedded in the larger economic and political orbit of the nation, from which Shanghai has never left.

NOTES

We thank Xiangming Chen, Dennis Judd, and two anonymous reviewers for comments on earlier drafts.

1. In this chapter, we use the terms "world city" and "global city" interchangeably. We are not unaware of the conceptual implications of different terminologies (see Sassen 2001, xix). Simply it is beyond the scope of this paper to engage in a discussion about how the globally connected cities should best be understood.

2. The Sino–British Agreement was signed in 1984 and it started the work of drafting a miniconstitution for the future Special Administration Region of Hong Kong. It also marked the beginning of the process of political restructuring, with the subsequent return of Hong Kong to China in 1997. Economic restructuring is a longer, extended, and continuous process. But a significant indicator of major sectoral shift in the economy was the dwindling of the manufacturing sector with absolute fall in the numbers of establishments and persons engaged in manufacturing starting from 1987–88.

3. See Yeung (2000) on how Singapore's entrepreneurial state takes the lead in going global. The character of the state in Hong Kong is very different. But instead of being irrelevant, the effects of the state manifest in a different form.

4. At this moment, there are no complete statistics on capital outflow from Hong Kong. A useful set of information is available from the Industry Department's annual survey of manufacturing industries. In 1990, slightly more than a quarter (27.2 percent) of local manufacturers had set up plants outside Hong Kong. In 1995, some 34 percent had done so. Among the larger industries, electronics, electrical appliance, toy, and watch and clocks all had more than or close to half of all firms having factories elsewhere in 1995. These figures, however, are likely to underestimate the magnitude of industrial relocation. The survey was conducted on firms *still* operating in Hong Kong, whereas many firms had actually closed down their local plants and offices and moved entirely overseas. Looking at another question asked in the survey gives a similarly dim view of Hong Kong's industrial view. When asked about their plan for production in Hong

Kong, 13 percent of the respondents said they would phase out part or all of their local production in 1990. In 1995, this had risen to 19 percent (Industry Department 1990, 1995).

5. A regional headquarters is defined as "an office that has control over the operation of other offices or branches in the region, and manages the business in the region without frequent referrals to its parent company outside Hong Kong." A regional office is "an office that coordinates offices/operations elsewhere in the region, in addition to the city in which it is located, and manages the business but with frequent referrals to its parent company outside Hong Kong or a regional headquarters." See Census and Statistics Department (2001a, 5).

6. In addition to geographic proximity, the "soft" side of Hong Kong's connection with China is also very important. On Hong Kong's advantage of being Chinese and at the same time not too Chinese, see Crawford (2001). Also see Chan (2002) for the relevance of Hong Kong businessmen's tacit knowledge in doing business and developing personal networks in China for attracting Japanese companies to come to Hong Kong and see it as a springboard for going into China.

REFERENCES

Abu-Lughod, Janet L. 1999. *New York, Chicago, Los Angeles: America's Global Cities.* Minneapolis: University of Minnesota Press.

Amin, Ash, and Nigel Thrift. 1994. "Living in the Global." In *Globalization, Institutions, and Regional Development in Europe,* edited by Ash Amin and Nigel Thrift, 1–22. Oxford: Oxford University Press.

Beaverstock, J.V., P.J. Taylor, and R.G. Smith. 1999. "A Roster of World Cities." *Cities* 16, no. 6: 445–58.

Berger, Susanne, and Richard Lester. 1997. *Made By Hong Kong.* Hong Kong: Oxford University Press.

Brenner, Neil. 1998. "Global Cities, Global States." *Review of International Political Economy* 5, no. 1: 1–37.

Byrne, David. 2001. *Understanding the Urban.* Basingstoke: Palgrave.

Census and Statistics Department. 1995. "Trade Involving Outward Processing in China 1989–1994." *Hong Kong Monthly Digest of Statistics: June 1995.* Hong Kong: Government Printer.

———. 1996. "Trading Firms with Manufacturing-related Functions." *Hong Kong Monthly Digest of Statistics: August.* Hong Kong: Government Printer.

———. 2001a. *Report on 2001 Annual Survey of Regional Offices Representing Overseas Companies in Hong Kong.* Hong Kong: Government Printer.

———. 2001b. "Trading Firms with Manufacturing-Related Activities." *Hong Kong Monthly Digest of Statistics: September 2001.* Hong Kong: Government Printer.

Chan, Ka Sik. 2002. "Japanese Small and Medium Electronics Firms in South China." Unpublished M.Phil. thesis, University of Hong Kong.

Chen, Xiangming. 2005. *As Borders Bend: Transnational Spaces on the Pacific Rim.* Lanham, Md.: Rowman & Littlefield

———. 2007. "A Tale of Two Regions in China: Rapid Economic Development and Slow Industrial Upgrading in the Pearl River and the Yangtze River Deltas." *International Journal of Comparative Sociology* 48, no. 2: 79–113.

Chiu, Stephen, K.C. Ho, and Tai-lok Lui. 1997. *City-States in the Global Economy.* Boulder: Westview Press.

Crawford, Darryl. 2001. "Globalisation and *Guanxi.*" *New Political Economy* 6, no. 1: 45–65.

Federation of Hong Kong Industries. 1993. *Hong Kong's Investment in the Pearl River Delta.* Hong Kong: Industry and Research Division, Federation of Hong Kong Industries.

Foreman, William. 2006. "Hong Kong Passes New York in Value of IPOs." *International Herald Tribune,* December 26.

Friedmann, John. 1986. "The World City Hypothesis." *Development and Change* 17, no. 1: 69–84.

———. 1995. "Where We Stand: A Decade of World City Research." In *World Cities in a World-System,* edited by Paul L. Knox and Peter J. Taylor, 21–47. Cambridge, UK: Cambridge University Press.

Friedmann, John, and Goetz Wolff. 1982. "World City Formation." *International Journal of Urban and Regional Research* 6, no. 3: 309–44.

Gereffi, Gary. 1994. "The Organization of Buyer-Driven Global Commodity Chains." In *Commodity Chains and Global Production,* edited by Gary Gereffi and M. Korzeniewicz, 96–122. Westport: Praeger.

Hamasita, Takeshi. 1997. "The Intra-Regional System in East Asia in Modern Times." In *Network Power,* edited by Peter Katzenstein and Takashi Shiraishi, 113–35. Ithaca: Cornell University Press.

Hamilton, Gary G. 1999. "Hong Kong and the Rise of Capitalism in Asia." In *Cosmopolitan Capitalists,* edited by Gary G. Hamilton, 14–34. Seattle: University of Washington Press.

Held, David, Anthony McGrew, David Goldblatt, and Jonathan Perraton. 1999. *Global Transformations.* Stanford: Stanford University Press.

Hong Kong SAR Government. 2007. *Our Way Forward: Report on Economic Summit on "China's 11th Five-Year Plan and the Development of Hong Kong," Action Agenda.* Hong Kong: Government Printer.

Hong Kong Trade Development Council. 1991. *Survey on Hong Kong's Domestic Exports, Re-exports, and Triangular Trade.* Hong Kong: Research Department, Hong Kong Trade Development Council.

Hui, Po-keung. 1995. "Overseas Chinese Business Networks: East Asian Economic Development in Historical Perspective." Unpublished Ph.D. thesis in sociology, the Graduate School of the State University of New York at Binghamton.

Industry Department. Various years. *Hong Kong's Manufacturing Industries.* Hong Kong: Government Printer.

Information Services Department, Hong Kong SAR. "Hong Kong: Asia's World City." www.brandhk.gov.hk/brandhk/indexpg_e.htm.

Jao, Y.C. 1997. *Hong Kong as an International Finance Center.* Hong Kong: City University of Hong Kong Press.

King, Anthony D. 1991. *Global Cities.* London: Routledge.

Leung, Antony. Speech at the Hong Kong Business Community Luncheon, March 14, 2002. www.info.gov.hk/gia/general/200203/14/0314152.htm.

Lui, Tai-lok. 2005. "Under Fire: Hong Kong's Middle Class after 1997." In *The July 1 Protest Rally: Interpreting a Historic Event,* edited by Joseph Y.S. Cheng, 277–301. Hong Kong: City University of Hong Kong Press.

Lui, Tai-lok, and Stephen Chiu. 1993. "Industrial Restructuring and Labour-market Adjustment under Positive Noninterventionism: The Case of Hong Kong." *Environment and Planning A* 25, no. 1: 63–79.

———. 2001. "Flexibility under Unorganized Industrialism?" In *Economic Governance and the Challenge of Flexibility in East Asia,* edited by Frederic C. Deyo, Richard F. Doner, and Eric Hershberg, 55–77. Lanham: Rowman & Littlefield.

Meyer, David R. 2000. *Hong Kong as a Global Metropolis.* Cambridge, UK: Cambridge University Press.

Ming Pao. "Mr Anthony Leung Admits That He Sees Shanghai as Competitor," March 27, 2002. (in Chinese)

Ohmae, Kenichi. 1995. *The End of the Nation State.* New York: Free Press.

Overholt, William H. 2004. "Hong Kong or Shanghai?" *The China Business Review* (May–June): 44–47.

Sassen, Saskia. 2001. *The Global City: New York, London, Tokyo.* 2nd ed. Princeton, N.J.: Princeton University Press.

Scott, Allen J., ed. 2001. *Global City-Regions: Trends, Theory, Policy.* Oxford: Oxford University Press.

Short, John Rennie, and Yeong-Hyun Kim. 1999. *Globalization and the City.* Harlow: Longman.

Smith, Michael Peter. 2001. *Transnational Urbanism: Locating Globalization.* Oxford: Blackwell Publishers.

South China Morning Post. 2002. "Zhu's Upbeat Vision for HK." March 16.

———. 2002. "Red Chips Set for Cash Flood from Mainland." March 17.

———. 2007. "Through Train Finds Rail Hard to Ride." September 10.

———. 2007. "Call for Single China Market Finds Broad Support." September 15.

State Statistical Bureau. 1996. *China Statistical Yearbook 1996.* Beijing: China Statistics Press.

Ta Kung Pao. "Hong Kong Participates in the Building of 'Great Pearl River Delta' Economic Region." September 19, 2002. (in Chinese)

Thompson, Edmund R. 2000. "Hong Kong as a Regional Strategic Hub for Manufacturing Multinationals." In *Gateways to the Global Economy,* edited by Ake E. Andersson and David E. Andersson, 169–189. Cheltenham: Edward Elgar.

Trade and Industry Department. 2001. *Techno-economic and Market Research Study on Hong Kong's Textiles, Clothing, and Footwear Industries, Vol. II*. Hong Kong: Government Printer.

Tuan, Chyau, and Linda Fung Yee Ng. 2006. "Hong Kong-Shanghai Metropolitan Competitiveness: Reflections from Surveys of Multinationals, 2001–2005." *Web Journal of China Management Review* 9, no. 2: 1–14.

Tung, Chee-hwa. 2001. *Chief Executive's Policy Address 2001*. Hong Kong: Government Printer.

Weiss, Linda. 1998. *The Myth of the Powerless State*. Cambridge: Polity Press.

Yeung, Henry Wai-Chung. 2000. "Global Cities and Developmental States: Understanding Singapore's Global Reach." GaWC Annual Lecture 2000. www.lboro.ac.uk/gawc/rb/al2.html.

Zukin, Sharon, and Paul DiMaggio. 1990. "Introduction." In *Structures of Capital*, edited by Sharon Zukin and Paul DiMaggio, 1–36. Cambridge, UK: Cambridge University Press.

PART II

GLOBALIZATION AND THE LOCAL TRANSFORMATION OF SHANGHAI

6. GLOBALIZATION, THE CHANGING STATE, AND LOCAL GOVERNANCE IN SHANGHAI

Fulong Wu

The reemergence of Shanghai as a major world city in the 1990s has drawn extensive attention in both scholarly research and opinion journalism (see Gu and Tang 2002; Haila 1999; Murphey 1988; Olds 1997, 2001; Ramo 1998; Yusuf and Wu 1997, 2002; W. Wu 1999; F. Wu 2000a, 2000b, 2002, 2003; Yeung and Sung 1996; Yatsko 1996a, 1996b, 2001, Yatsko and Forney 1998). Joshua Ramo, a senior editor of *Time* magazine, provided a vivid personal observation of the changing urban landscapes, "if you are lucky enough to fly into Shanghai in the late afternoon, up along the coast from Hong Kong, you will be treated to a remarkable sight. As the sun fades to twilight, the pink and then purple light reflects back up at you, first off the East China Sea, then off the Huangpu River, and finally off the 1,000 dappled mirrors of Shanghai's exploding commercial district. After you land, and as you make your way out to a taxi at Hongqiao airport, you will be greeted by another sight—hundreds of twinkling lights atop the city's skyscrapers and construction cranes" (Ramo 1998, 64).

Pamela Yatsko, a journalist for *Far Eastern Economic Review,* reported that "throughout the city, whole blocks are being flattened, turning parts of the former 'Paris of the East' into huge construction sites—a chorus of cranes, jack-hammers and bulldozers chiselling out the foundations of skyscrapers, elevated expressways and subway tunnels. Architects are having their fling with modernism—designing huge glass-faced office complexes and luxury apartment blocks" (Yatsko 1996a, 69). In her recent book, Yatsko (2001) emphasized that Deng Xiaoping, the architect of economic reforms, saw Shanghai's revival as crucial to Chinas' national development strategy: "for Deng, Shanghai and its Pudong project provided perfect symbols at home and abroad that China was forging ahead with reform" (Yatsko 2001, 22). Deng Xiaoping said in his 1992 southern China tour that, "looking back, my one major mistake was not to include Shanghai when we set up four special economic zones. Otherwise, the situation of reform and opening to the outside in the Yangtze River Delta, the entire Yangtze River Valley, and even the entire nation would be different" (Yatsko 2001, 22).

Shanghai's renaissance in China's new open economy is beyond doubt. Considering Shanghai's gateway position in China's embrace of the world economy, it is understandable that the global city paradigm is easily employed to explain rapid urban growth in the 1990s. Shanghai's rise in an era of globalization is seen as a process of transforming a Third World city into a global city—a converging process toward the "favored few—New York, London and Tokyo—that have acquired large economic, cultural and symbolic roles" (Yusuf and Wu 2002, 1213). What can Shanghai's story teach us about worldwide urban restructuring, especially in the developing regions of the globalizing world?

The application of the global city thesis to Shanghai is obviously a catalyst for analytical tension: on the one hand, Shanghai's renaissance cannot be understood without reference to China's increasing integration into the global system; on the other hand, measured by indicators used to quantify global city status, such as the number of multinational headquarters and the size of the finance market, Shanghai is far from being a global city (see Chen, introduction, Sassen, this book). In fact, it may not even occupy a low-tier position on the list of global city hierarchy. Although China has now gained access to the World Trade Organization (WTO) and its economy will subsequently be subject to further integration with and competition in the global economy, it still has a long way to go before becoming a free market economy. Although the tension can be technically solved by arguing that Shanghai will be eventually *re*globalized, (re)gaining its fame as the "Paris of the Orient" after its world relationships were interrupted with the imposition of communist restrictions in 1949, it is indeed questionable whether the global city thesis can be applicable to a city that is under the influence of globalization.

Embellishing and extending the global city hypothesis, Sassen (this book) continues to emphasize the economic logic of creating the global city. In particular, she stresses that "economic globalization and the ascendance of information technologies and industries such as finance have had the effect of concentrating massive resources in major cities. Firms that operate globally need the cutting-edge telematic infrastructure and human resources markets that typically only large cities or metropolises can offer" and, "economic globalization has raised the complexity of economic transactions enormously: firms need to buy more and more specialized inputs and it is still major cities that are the best production sites for such specialized services." On the other hand, she does reiterate the importance of the local: "Yet the term *global city* may be reductive and misleading if it suggests that cities are mere outcomes of a global economic machine. They are specific places whose spaces, internal dynamics, and social structure matter; indeed, we may be able to understand the global order only by analyzing why key structures of the world economy are *necessarily* situated in cities" (Sassen 2001a, 4, emphasis original).

The recent study of Tokyo and Seoul (Hill and Kim 2001) set off debates over whether the global city hypothesis is applicable to cities in the so-called development state (see Wade 1990 for an extensive treatment of the concept and its analytical reference to East Asia state; rejoinders from Friedmann 2001; Sassen 2001b). Is there a different trajectory of becoming a global city or globalizing the city into the world system? Many studies on non-Western regions show some distinct local structures that are more than just accommodating the global (Hill and Kim 2001; Kamo 2000; Machimura 1998). Sassen (this book) identified an important element in the global city, namely, "privatization and deregulation have brought with them a shift of governance/coordination functions from the government to the private sector; this often means that what the national government loses, local (i.e., city) government gets."

At the core of concern is to what extent this element is a precondition or a consequence of climbing into the ladder of the global city? In a recent comment, John Friedmann (2001) carefully distinguished the world city paradigm from the world city hypothesis: "the former concerns the underlying assumptions of a research program that is focused on the incorporation of major city–regions into the global economy; the latter proposes a series of questions for research posed within the broad framework of the paradigm" (2535). This is important because such a distinction removes the burden of the converging assumption from the world city research. The world city does not need to be modeled in accommodating financial and production services because "in my view, the true meaning of hierarchy has less to do with the number of transnational corporate headquarters, financial institutions, and high-level business services than with the overall economic power of the territorial economy which city–regions articulate" (Friedmann 2001, 2535). In this chapter, these issues are addressed by linking globalization of Shanghai with changing state and local governance; the city provides a timely case and context for addressing this complex relationship.

GLOBALIZING SHANGHAI IN A HISTORICAL PERSPECTIVE

The discourse of remaking Shanghai as a global city is embedded in the strategic reorientation of China's national development strategy from self-reliance to participation in the global economy. Globalizing Shanghai is more than just a restoration of Shanghai's past prominent international status; it is a more proactive project—through the "dragonhead" role of Shanghai, China can actively participate in the new global economy. Shanghai is thus a strategic locus for fostering the domestic economy and an important venue where China can host international affairs such as the APEC meeting, the Fortune Global Forum in 2001, and the World Expo in 2010. The role of gateway in the new phase of globalization is very different from Shanghai's historic international role. After Shanghai became a major treaty port as a result of the Treaty of Nanking in 1842, it developed a stronger international orientation than other cities in the Far East. The penetration of foreign capital sped up industrialization and led to the development of local industrial entrepreneurs in Shanghai and its environs. Shanghai played a metaphorical role of the bridgehead—a channel through which foreign products were distributed to the region and domestic agricultural and mineral products were processed and exported. With the unprecedented trade prosperity, Shanghai was truly a cosmopolitan city and a city of services. By the period of its great prosperity in the 1930s, about 90 percent of the nation's banks and over half its foreign trade were concentrated in Shanghai (Gu and Chen 1999; also see Chen and Orum, conclusion, this book).

After 1949, the bridgehead function was transformed into a production-oriented city under socialist industrialization. The service functions such as trade, finance, and distribution dwindled. No longer an *international* city, Shanghai, for the first time in history, developed a comprehensive industrial system, including heavy industries. This would have been impossible in a free-trade world system in which the comparative advantages of industrialized countries would have prevented Shanghai from developing its own industrial sectors. In the 1970s, Shanghai's industrial output accounted for one-seventh of the national total; its fiscal revenue was about one-fourth to one-sixth of the national total; and the volume of freight handled and the value of export goods were about one-third of the national total. In the heyday of socialist development, Shanghai was the source of innovation and production capacity. For example, China developed the large 178-seat passenger jet with the largest take-off weight of 110 tons in Shanghai. Such a preeminent position prevented Shanghai from being tested with bolder policy experiments under the export-oriented development strategy, initially introduced in southern China in the early 1980s.

By 1990 the need for further opening of Shanghai and the Yangtze River Delta had been recognized by the state. In fact, the announcement of the Pudong New Area in 1990 helped to break the temporary isolation of the Chinese government after the Tiananmen Square incident in 1989. Globalizing Shanghai indicated the continuity of economic reform policies and opening to the world economy. Shanghai's reglobalization is of national significance for at least two reasons. First, the politics of Shanghai have been closely associated with the new generation of leadership of China. President Jiang Zemin, Premier Zhu Rongji, and Vice Premier Wu Bangguo were leaders of Shanghai before they moved to Beijing. Second, the significance of Shanghai is defined by its effect on the entire Yangtze River region and further on the national economy. There is a strategic need to have a finance and trade center in the core of the coastal region to engage in economic globalization. In 1992, the 14th Chinese Communist Party Congress (CCPC) announced that the primary task for the development of Shanghai was to "seize the opportunity of development and opening of Shanghai Pudong, and to build Shanghai as the dragon-head and one of international economic, finance, and trade centers, so as to drive the growth of the Yangtze River Delta and in turn the take-off of the whole economic region." This announcement formalized the policy vision of reglobalizing Shanghai as a strategy-based state project.

If we see the emergence of Shanghai's global city functions through the historical imperative, we can understand more deeply its institutional foundation. Such an imperative lies more prominently in the political vision than in the practical need from the arrival of foreign capital in economic globalization. During the Cold War, the confrontation of ideologies and hence the purity of socialist ideology was predominant. With the easing of East–West tension, China reoriented its national politics. Now that military confrontation is no longer a top concern, the coastal region has regained its favorable status. Deng Xiaoping, the architect of the country's reform and open-door policy, pointed out that the key task for the CCP is to focus on economic development. However, somewhat surprisingly, the survival of the state in the era of globalization is of the same urgency as it was in history. Globalizing Shanghai can be justified through Deng's wisdom—"development is the 'hard' truth." The slogan is now widely displayed along many streets and on top of major buildings in Shanghai. The pervasive state power in economic regulation has been translated into fully fledged place promotion, a practice that uses businesslike marketing tactics to promote local attractiveness to external investors (Hall and Hubbard 1998). Only the state has such a regulatory capacity.

CHANGING URBAN DYNAMICS

Globalization has brought about a profound change in the accumulation strategy of the Chinese state. Under socialism the state adopted a productionist view of urban development, which constrained nonproductive investment in the urban environment. Shanghai obtained low-cost materials allocated through central economic planning, sustained cheap labor costs, and thus benefited from the strategy. On the other hand, Shanghai was required to turn over the revenue to support national industrialization. The problem of such a strategy is that it prevents the city from upgrading its economic structure. The strategy of globalizing Shanghai has brought the city to the frontier of a planned urban development regime to encounter the world market. The export-oriented policy in southern China has weaker entanglements with the socialist accumulation strategy because both the resources (materials) and capital come from outside the region. But foreign investment in Shanghai means more than just utilization of cheap labor in industrial processing and assembly.

Shanghai was a major manufacturing center and had established economic linkages with the Yangtze River region before foreign investment flowed into the city. Foreign investment in Shanghai has demonstrated stronger multinational origins and management functions. In short, Shanghai presents an opportunity to access the massive Chinese market for multinationals, and therefore market penetration is a major incentive for businesses to locate in Shanghai. This has effectively boosted land prices. We can compare this process to gentrification. The rent gap theory argues that the potential rent exceeds the current rent due to the constraint of land uses (Smith 1996). Gentrification allows the developer to capture such a gap by changing the social-demographic profile of residents. Although totally different from the context of gentrification, urban redevelopment in Shanghai represents a similar motivation—undervalued urban assets (including land) sustained a high intensity of production capacity. The cost of production factor was low because it was constrained by the socialist accumulation strategy.

Since the 1990s Shanghai has maintained a high rate of investment in urban development. Cumulative infrastructure investment reached 365 billion yuan (approximately US$46 billion) and housing investment accumulated to 350 billion yuan (US$45 billion), accounting for, respectively, 90 percent and 60 percent of the total amount of investment in the previous 50 years. Intensive investment has greatly eased traffic congestion, housing shortages, and pollution, and subsequently improved the urban environment. In the 35th annual meeting of the Asian Development Bank in 2002, Mr. Chen Liangyu, the former mayor of Shanghai, enumerated major achievements. For example, a three-dimensional transport network consisting of elevated roads, fast surface roads and highways, and mass transportation had been constructed. Although the number of vehicles increased by 3.5 times, the average speed in the city area also rose from 10 km per hour to 25 km per hour. The new light-rail system had been built, and by the end of 2000 the length of operational lines had reached 65 km. Pudong and Puxi (west Shanghai) are now linked with four bridges across the Huangpu River. The first phase of Pudong International Airport generated an annual passenger capacity of 20 million (see Kasarda, this book). Since the 1990s about 31 million square meters of old housing has been demolished and more than 100 million square meters has been built, which raised per capita living space from 6.6 square meters in 1990 to 12.1 square meters in 2001. Large-scale greening raised per capita green space from 1 square meter in 1990 to 5.5 square meters in 2001 (Chen 2002).

How did Shanghai sustain such a high level of investment? According to former Mayor Chen Liangyu,[1] there were three main stages of capital formation. In the first stage, from the mid-1980s to the early 1990s, the scale of government investment was enlarged through expanding bank loans. The lack of capital severely constrained infrastructure investment, which amounted to as little as 1.9 billion yuan (US$232 million). Shanghai succeeded in obtaining US$3.2 billion in loans from the World Bank, the Asian Development Bank, and other financial organizations. For example, the Nanpu Bridge and Yangpu Bridge were built with loans from the Asian Development Bank. Meanwhile about ten government investment corporations were set up.

The second stage began in the mid-1990s. The establishment of the land leasing system allowed the government to extract landed revenue. In total, Shanghai raised 100 billion yuan (US$12 billion) through land leasing. The third stage, which began in the late 1990s, raised capital through asset management and the stock market. Since the Asian Financial Crisis in 1997, land leasing has diminished significantly. In contrast, the domestic stock market has witnessed dramatic growth from scratch. Household savings have been increasing, leading to surplus capital within the society. The government thus raised funds through listing profitable projects as companies in the stock market. About 10 billion yuan (US$1.2 billion) has been raised. Moreover, the municipal government authorized user charges for projects such as the highways and tunnels. Through build–operate–transfer schemes and the issuing of domestic construction bonds, the government raised another 10 billion yuan or about US$1.2 billion (Chen 2002).

The change in the capital formation and investment mechanism clearly reflects the initial role of foreign capital in boosting urban investment. Since the designation of Pudong in 1990 and especially since the deepening of economic reform after Deng Xiaoping's tour of the south in 1992, foreign investment has risen rapidly. Actual utilized foreign investment rose from US$0.78 billion in 1990 to US$5.3 billion in 1995, among which foreign direct investment (FDI) increased from US$0.18 to US$4.72 billion (see Table 6.1 below). Utilized foreign investment

TABLE 6.1

Change in the Scale of Foreign Investment and Export Value Relative to GDP, 1985–2004 (Selected Years)

	Actual Use of Foreign Investment (AUFI) (US$ billions)	Realized Foreign Direct Investment (FDI) (US$ billions)	AUFI: GDP	Export Value (US$ billions)	Export: GDP
1985	0.115	0.062	0.72%	3.361	21.17%
1990	0.780	0.177	4.93%	5.321	33.62%
1995	5.298	3.250	17.96%	11.577	39.25%
1996	7.510	4.716	21.50%	13.238	37.90%
1997	6.345	4.808	15.65%	14.724	36.33%
1998	4.816	3.638	10.81%	15.956	35.82%
1999	5.999	3.048	12.31%	18.785	38.55%
2000	5.391	3.160	9.81%	25.354	46.13%
2004	11.69	6.541	12.99%	73.50	81.69%

Source: Shanghai Statistical Yearbook, various years.
Note: Foreign investment and export values are converted into Chinese yuan by actual exchange rates to make the figures comparable to GDP.

continued to grow and peaked in 1996, whereas FDI grew until 1997. After the Asian Financial Crisis in 1997, FDI fell to about US$3 billion in 2000 but rocketed back up to US$11 billion in 2003, US$11.69 billion in 2004, and US$14.6 billion in 2006 (see Chen, introduction). To measure the scale of foreign investment, the ratio of foreign investment to gross domestic product (GDP) is calculated (using the actual exchange rate between the US$ and yuan). The ratio change increased from 0.72 percent in 1985 to 5 percent in 1990. After a dramatic increase to 21.5 percent in 1996, the ratio decreased to 9.8 percent in 2000. The modest level of foreign investment is due to the sluggish increase in foreign investment and a significant jump in GDP. But the ratio increased to 12.99 in 2004. The value of exports, however, shows a strong growth tendency since the 1980s. The ratio of export value to GDP hit a record high of 46 percent in 2000, suggesting Shanghai's strong outward orientation. This figure jumped to 82 percent in 2004, reflecting the role of exports in Shanghai's economic growth (see Table 6.1).

To evaluate the contribution of foreign investment to capital formation, the source of total investment in fixed assets (IFA) is examined (see Table 6.2, information was not available for the period before 1995). Table 6.2 shows the declining share of the state-owned sector in IFA. The figure decreased from 60 percent in 1995 to 44 percent in 2000, and further to 36 percent in 2004. The collective sector share also dropped over time. In contrast, foreign-funded economies (including investments from Taiwan, Hong Kong, and Macao) rose from 13.4 percent

TABLE 6.2

Contribution of Foreign Investment to Investment in Fixed Assets in Shanghai, 1995, 1999, 2000, and 2004 (Billions of Yuan)

	1995		1999		2000		2004	
State-Owned	93.59	60.26%	98.68	53.15%	83.00	44.39%	95.21	36.45%
Collective	24.71	15.91%	22.72	12.24%	15.63	8.36%	14.66	5.59%
Private and Shareholding	15.77	10.15%	30.08	16.20%	54.60	29.20%	66.75	25.47%
Foreign-Funded	20.83	13.41%	32.56	17.54%	31.91	17.07%	85.14	32.49%
Others	0.42	0.27%	1.63	0.88%	1.83	0.98%	0.00	0.00%
Total	155.32	100.00%	185.67	100.00%	186.97	100.00%	262.06	100.00%

Source: *Shanghai Statistical Yearbook,* various years.

to 17.1 percent in 2000 and jumped to 32.5 percent in 2004. However, the biggest growth occurred in the private and shareholding economies, jumping from 10 percent to 29 percent during that period. The share of foreign investment in IFA was higher than the national figure, which stood at 10.6 percent in 1997. Although state investment still dominates in IFA, foreign investment has become an important source of capital. Moreover, the importance of foreign capital is not only in the contribution to capital formation per se but also in enforcing the transition toward a more diversified, market-based mechanism of raising capital for investment.

Globalizing Shanghai means a change in strategy—for the Chinese state it is "using the (domestic) market to obtain the (foreign) technology" (*yi shichang huan jishu*). In this context, "technology" means more than the narrow definition of technological inventions and includes the methods of production. Shanghai has been used as an experimental site for the transition from a socialist productionist regime based on industrial surplus to a regime of flexible accumulation based on the service sector. The strategy of developing Shanghai into an international economic, trade, and finance center marks the shift toward a service-oriented economy (see Table I.1 in Chen's introduction, this book). The development of the stock market is just one example of forging a different mechanism of capital circulation. Property-led development is another case in point. Real estate is the second largest sector in attracting foreign direct investment. In 1997, over US$1.3 billion of actual foreign investment flowed into real estate, accounting for 27.5 percent of the total, in comparison to US$2.7 billion invested in secondary industries. With the building boom, property prices had risen, especially in the high-end market, until the Asian Financial Crisis in 1997. Since then property-led development has been confronted with enormous difficulties, one of which was the persistent high rate of vacancy (Halia 1999). Foreign investment in real estate fell subsequently to US$0.42 billion in 2000, halting property-led development. In contrast, the manufacturing sector has been absorbing more foreign investment, with its share rising to 63.5 percent of the total actual utilized foreign investment (see Table 6.3). Whereas foreign investment contributes to industrial restructuring and facilitates export, it also squeezes out the share of domestic enterprises and exerts a negative impact on local products. Since 2000, foreign investment in the tertiary sector has demonstrated substantial growth. The tertiary sector absorbed about 45 percent of foreign investment.

TABLE 6.3

Distribution of Realized Foreign Investment by Economic Sector, 1996, 1997, 2000, and 2004

Sectors	1996 US$ Billions	1996 Percentage	1997 US$ Billions	1997 Percentage	2000 US$ Billions	2000 Percentage	2004 US$ Billions	2004 Percentage
Primary	0.003	0.064	0.001	0.020	0.006	0.195	0.036	0.550
Secondary	2.520	53.435	2.707	56.309	2.006	63.469	3.587	54.838
Tertiary	2.193	46.501	2.100	43.671	1.148	36.336	2.918	44.614
Real Estate	1.053	22.328	1.326	27.576	0.422	13.340	n/a	
Wholesale and Retail	0.571	12.108	0.223	4.634	0.047	1.484	n/a	
Total	4.716	100.000	4.808	100.000	3.160	100.000	6.541	100.000

Source: *Shanghai Statistical Yearbook,* various years.

REINVENTING THE STATE IN ECONOMIC COMPETITION

Economic globalization brings new opportunities for cities in late industrialization. Inflow of foreign investment helps to transform industrial structures and globalize real estate. More significantly, it creates a new mentality for growth and justifies the reengineering of local governance. Through the hegemonic project of global cities, which invokes a sense of urgency under the challenge of globalization, the state mobilizes and sustains social support and in turn has found a survival strategy in the era of globalization. It is hegemonic because it prioritizes the economic goal and subjects other concerns such as social policy and benefits under this mentality of economic growth (see Ho, this book for Singapore).

PROGRESSIVE FISCAL REGIME SUPPORTED BY THE CENTRAL STATE

Shanghai has always been important to revenue collection for the central state. Between 1949 and 1983, as much as 87 percent of Shanghai's revenue of 350 billion yuan (US$43 billion) was remitted to Beijing (Yeung and Sung 1996, 9). In the late 1980s, recognizing Shanghai's strategic importance and the shift of foreign investment to the Yangtze River Delta region, the central state granted progressive fiscal policies to Shanghai. In 1985, the State Council granted a fixed baseline expenditure to Shanghai, allowing the city to spend more than it had in its local revenue. In accordance, Shanghai government aggressively expanded the fiscal expenditure, increasing from 2.1 billion yuan (US$256 million) in 1984 to 3.6 billion yuan (US$439 million) in 1985, equivalent to a rate of increase of 72.6 percent. In 1988, the central state fixed Shanghai's revenue submission to 10.5 billion yuan (US$1.3 billion). Consequently Shanghai raised its fiscal expenditure to 6.6 billion yuan (US$829 million), a 22.3 percent annual increase. Interestingly, the central state sent a working team composed of ministerial officials to help the Shanghai government get a better deal and prepare the report (Yang and Han 1999, 12). Again, in 1993, in order to get a better position in the 1994 fiscal negotiation, Shanghai's government increased incentives for revenue generation and expenditure. In that year local revenue rose to a record high of 24.2 billion yuan (US$3 billion), a 30.6 percent increase, and local expenditure reached 12.9 billion yuan (US$1.6 billion), an increase of 36.1 percent. In fact, Shanghai began to operate an expansionist expenditure regime. During 1993–1997, local expenditure exceeded local revenue by 19.3 billion yuan (US$2.4 billion). The fiscal balance was maintained by generous central state tax rebates, amounting to 72.5 billion yuan (US$8.8 billion) (Cheng 1999). Deducting a total of 48 billion yuan (US$5.9 billion) revenue submission, Shanghai received a net 24.5 billion yuan (US$3 billion). The substantial support from the central state made it possible for Shanghai to sustain its massive investment in urban development in the 1990s.

STATE-LED MARKETIZATION OF URBAN DEVELOPMENT

Market-oriented reform not only generates entrepreneurial activities *within* the city but also creates the entrepreneurial agency *of* the city. The transformation toward an entrepreneurial city is a major feature of global competition and place promotion (Hall and Hubbard 1998). But in the post-reform context, this also means the use of market instruments to manage state assets so as to generate a return on investment. The term of *jingying chenshi,* literally "the city of business management," emphasizes the operational side of urban entrepreneurialism. The pressure to generate revenue and to capture mobile resources that are unleashed by market-oriented reform has driven decentralized urban asset management. For example, new entrepreneurial space in terms of physical and regulatory preferential treatment has been created. A total of 40 special zones have been set up, among which are three national-level Economic and Technological Development Zones, nine municipal industrial parks, and four development zones in Pudong. Land development corporations have been formed to use the state land as collateral for bank loans. By using land leasing as an instrument, the state no longer invests in urban development through direct capital injection.

STRATEGIC INVESTMENT IN INFRASTRUCTURE

To strengthen structural competitiveness, the state has committed massive investment to infrastructure development since the 1980s. In the eighth five-year plan (1990–1995), 10 major infrastructure projects were completed, amounting to a total of 25 billion yuan (US$3 billion). These projects included the Nanpu Bridge and Yangpu Bridge, Inner Ring Road, and Waigaoqiao Deep Water Berths. In the ninth five-year plan (1995–2000), the second round of infrastructure development included 10 large projects, such as the Pudong International Airport, Metro Line II, Outer Ring Road, and Pudong International Information Port. The total investment from 1996 to 2000 is estimated to be around 100 billion yuan (US$12 billion). Intensive investment significantly improved the urban environment. For example, the opening of Pudong International Airport with the first phase investment of 13 billion yuan (US$1.6 billion) in 1999 enabled the city to host corporate jets for the Fortune Global Forum.

According to former Mayor Chen Liangyu, Shanghai is strategically investing in the development of a Yangshan deep water container port in the tenth five-year period (2000–2005). The start of the second phase of Pudong International Airport and the teleport project will enhance the city's competitiveness for a major aviation and information hub in Asia (see Kasarda, this book). The city also initiated the "city beautiful" movement to construct the "ecological city," which will increase green space to 28–30 percent of the built up area. About 20 million square meters of old housing will be redeveloped. Dilapidated and substandard housing will be demolished, whereas areas with historical values will be preserved and renovated into special areas to attract tourists. The new phase of urban redevelopment will sustain the momentum of urban development started after Deng's southern tour in 1992. During the past decade, about 2.6 million square meters of old housing was demolished, 660,000 households in the inner urban area were relocated, and 115.9 million square meters of new housing was built.

REENGINEERING ENTREPRENEURIAL LOCAL GOVERNANCE

Globalization accelerated the dismantling of the planned regime. The devolution toward the local level is seen as a way to manage and capture mobile resources. For example, an actual occupant of state land is allowed to negotiate with developers to convert its use through state land leasing. In most cases, the negotiation between occupant and developer precedes the approval of the land management authority. In 1995 Shanghai adopted a new administrative structure of "two tiers of government and three levels of management" (also see Lu, Ren, and Chen, this book). Urban districts have thus gained substantial autonomy in organizing urban development (Zhang, this book). The Street Office, which used to be the agent of district government, has been incorporated into the base level of the management structure. In turn, these lower levels of government are not only encouraged to take over the management responsibilities but are also driven to be more entrepreneurial (i.e., increasing local revenue by forging local business partnerships). Local officials are evaluated for their performance in attracting business into their jurisdictions.

The downscaling of the state is effective in that a contract is signed between different levels of the government, thus "hardening" the budget constraint that was "soft" in the past. This in turn mobilizes firmlike government departments (Walder 1995), which become active agents in economic development. The lower levels of government have a strong incentive to promote local development. The downscaling of governance is also a response to the management vacuum left by the dismantling of economic planning in the face of increasing economic and social mobility (e.g., increasing migrant workers and foreign and domestic capital) so as to maintain the state's control over urban development. The aim is to create a governable society during rapid economic growth and social change.

DESIGNING COMPETITIVE STRATEGIES

Since the 1990s a series of policy initiatives have aimed to create competitive strategies. For example, the strategy of "dragon-head" designates Shanghai to be one of the international economic, trade, and finance centers. Subsequently the city government designated six pillar industries (automobile; telecommunication and electronic equipment; iron and steel industry; petrochemical, fine chemical, biological and pharmaceutical industry; power generation and electric equipment; household electronic appliance industry). The city promotes the merger of enterprises to large industrial conglomerations and encourages outward development. Since the Lujiazui finance and trade zone became the new business center, a comprehensive plan has been introduced to integrate it with the Bund, the traditional financial area, into Shanghai's new central business district (CBD). Along the Huangpu River, a new waterfront redevelopment project started in 2002. The 100-billion-yuan project aims to convert warehouses and docks along the bank of the Huangpu River into residential, leisure, and business complexes in anti-cipation of the demand from the World Expo in 2010. The proportion of greenery will be increased to 26 percent of total land from the current 2.53 percent, reinventing an image of world-class waterfront like the River Seine in Paris (Muzi 2002).

CONCLUSION: REGLOBALIZATION AS A STATE PROJECT

The imperative of rebuilding Shanghai into a global city should be understood in light of the state's survival strategy given China's vulnerable position within a new global order. Market-oriented reform and the open-door policy have unleashed the resources that were constrained by the planned system and introduced new forces of globalization, thus leading to enormous complexity and mobility. As such, we witness a dialectic tension between the waning of state capacity and the state reinventing itself in a new regulatory space, following the mentality of the Asian development state. Although the launch of economic reform was initially more a response to its internal logic, remaking Shanghai as a global city is instrumental for the state to justify its legitimacy in the face of globalization. What we have seen in the case of Shanghai is the fostering of place-based entrepreneurialism through a *state* project of city remaking.

Recent change in Shanghai leadership further demonstrates this nature of state project. In 2006, the removal of Mr. Chen Liangyu, the Party Secretary of Shanghai, reflected the continuing role of the central state. Under Mr. Chen, Shanghai did not follow the direction of the central government to implement forceful measures to cool down the property market. Mr. Chen even publicly argued that Shanghai should be treated exceptionally because of its global links. Although the central government acknowledged that major international projects already agreed to, such as the World Expo, should be honored and not be affected by the suspension of land leasing quota, Shanghai's city politics should not be disassociated from larger national politics. In a media interview during the celebration marking the remainder of only 1,000 days until the start of World Expo 2010, the newly appointed party secretary, Mr. Xi Jinping, emphasized that "organizing World Expo is a national behaviour and an important opportunity to implement the scientific development approach [promoted by the central leadership]" (news from sina.com, August 6, 2007). Thus the fate of Shanghai is again positioned within the overall national development strategy.

Shanghai is not a global city and perhaps will never be *re*globalized in the sense of its glorious history as "Paris of the Orient"—if we regard the term as meaning more than just a cosmopolitan metropolis but rather the dominance of international capital. The term in fact referred to its French Concession's resemblance to its Western counterpart. What we have seen in Shanghai is that reglobalization is a strong state-led campaign to rescale and reinvent the state in the era of globalization. The (local) state can use various market instruments to promote property-led redevelopment (He and Wu 2005) as a means to remodel the urban economy. We should remember that China is a developing country now subordinated to the global standards required of WTO members. Therefore, it is irrelevant to ask whether Shanghai is a global city. It may be true that global forces penetrate into the local place according to their economic and technological logics. It is also important to ask what the state can remake so as to conform to global standards. Literally, the image of the gateway city mirrors an intersection where "the track is being connected" (*jie gui*). The case of Shanghai conveys an important message regarding the importance of the local dimension to the formation of the global city.

In the global city literature, no one seriously denies the importance of local conditions in overall urban development in the era of globalization. Sassen (2001b, 2538) stresses that "the development of global city functions is filtered partly through thick local institutional environments and legal/administrative frameworks, so it is not simply a standardized implant that looks the same everywhere." However, the role of local dimension is often seen as secondary if not passive in facilitating the concentration of foreign capital and high-level production services that are major driving forces behind global city status. In this sense, the institutional environment is regarded as essentially the same as resource endowments and more than just a key *condition* for place competition. The literature of place promotion mainly focuses on the linear causal mechanism from increasing mobility of capital to intercity competition and finally to place promotion as a local response (Hall and Hubbard 1996). To a lesser extent, the local dimension is seen as working independently and having its own agenda, whereas the buzzword of globalization is *symbolically* used to justify the local agenda (Machimura 1998).

In fact, the opening of Pudong itself was used to indicate continuing economic reform, which helped to break the state from international isolation after the Tiananmen incident in 1989. What we have seen in Shanghai is a sociopolitical project of building a global city via the state's promotion of local economic development. As such, the development of

Shanghai as a globalizing city does not rely on the quantity of foreign capital per se but rather the subsequent institutional transformations, which generate the momentum of market transition and strengthen the traditional functions of Shanghai and add new ones to it.

What we have seen in Shanghai does not disprove the validity of the global city model—exactly because Shanghai is not a global city defined in global financial terms. But it does suggest a critical implication of globalization. This is related to "how the modes through which a leading international business and financial center . . . articulates with the global economic system are shaped in significant ways by the presence of a development state" (Sassen 2001b, 2537). In the core of the world system, the global (read Western) is indigenous, and therefore a neoliberal discourse adopted by the nation-state in fact facilitates the expansion of the multinational capital to a global scale. In the global periphery, privatization and marketization have created enormous mobility and economic uncertainty. Whereas urban entrepreneurial activities have emerged at an unprecedented rate, it is the responsibility of the state to translate them into structural competitiveness. More often than not global forces and local interests do not overlap. The state thus has to promote place-based competitiveness, transcending its direct involvement in economic production to a broader positioning in strategic management, thus retaining part of its functionality (see Ho; Lui and Chiu, this book, for varied roles of the state in influencing Singapore and Hong Kong).

Two implications for future urban development of Shanghai can be derived from this understanding. First, global cities are not autonomous agents themselves in the triangular relationship between the global economy, national states, and global cities. For example, the dominance of New York in international finance is linked to the U.S. economy and its ability to define the rules of the game in international financial markets. Shanghai's growth cannot divorce itself from overall national growth. Indeed, the headquarters of People's Bank of China (China's central bank) remains in Beijing, which indicates that Shanghai cannot afford to overlook the importance of attracting domestic conglomeration in order to be globally competitive.

Second, instead of emphasizing the quantity of foreign capital, Shanghai needs to devise a strategy to better serve its hinterland and to connect its economy to the world market. This requires different thinking from the import-substitution strategy, which underlies the rationality of the six-pillar industries. Rather, Shanghai needs a new strategy to foster globally competitive high-tech industries (see Markusen and Yu, this book for how this can be achieved via an unconventional strategy) and to nurture

Chinese entrepreneurs in global economic competition. This requires enhancing innovation and production capacity through strategic investment. Meanwhile, there is a need to constrain the property boom and prevent production costs from escalating out of control, which may trigger a decline of these industries. The cooling down of the hot real estate market in 2006 happened only as a result of strong central and local government interventions. Moreover, Shanghai needs to adjust its relationship with the neighboring provinces—Jiangsu and Zhejiang—to seek a greater level of regional cooperation and integration rather than just competition. In fact, the two provinces are often hostile to Shanghai's aggressive policies and unwilling to cooperate in regional integration. Shanghai has to convince them of the benefits that will result from voluntary participation in a globally oriented regional network (see Chen 2007; Chen and Orum, conclusion, this book for ways of bringing region back into global city research).

Finally, China's accession to the WTO has created an enormous opportunity for foreign investors to enter and expand in China, especially in the financial and production services. There is also an enormous opportunity for China to have a broader access to the world market. Shanghai needs to serve its economic hinterland more effectively. In Friedmann's (2001, 2535) words, "world cities articulate territorial economies with the global system, and like cities everywhere, they reflect the power of their 'colonized' space." To further increase its global competitiveness, Shanghai must do much more to "colonize" its space by developing closer and more cooperative ties with the Yangtze River Delta. This strategy calls for a weakened central state and stronger and more aggressive local governments to work across rigid administrative boundaries in creating a new regionally based and yet globally competitive economic system.

NOTES

This research was supported by the Leverhulme Trust project (RF&G/7/2001/0090). Thanks to Xiangming Chen and two anonymous reviewers for comments on earlier drafts.

1. Chen Liangyu, the party secretary of Shanghai, or its de facto mayor, was removed from power at the end of 2006 for his reported lead involvement in embezzling a huge amount of money from the municipal pension fund into the lucrative real estate sector.

REFERENCES

Chen, L.Y. 2002. "Shanghai's Modern Urban Construction and the Reform of Investment and Capital Formation." Shanghai mayor's speech delivered at the thirty-fifth annual meeting of the Asian Development Bank, Shanghai.

Chen, X.M. 2007. "A Tale of Two Regions in China: Rapid Economic Development and Slow Industrial Upgrading in the Pearl River and the Yangtze River Deltas." *International Journal of Comparative Sociology* 48, no. 2: 79–113.

Cheng, J.J. 1999. *Local Revenue Growth.* Shanghai: Shanghai Social Science Academy Press.

Friedmann, J. 2001. "World Cities Revisited: A Comment." *Urban Studies* 38, no. 13: 2535–36.

Gu, F.R., and Z. Tang. 2002. "Shanghai: Reconnecting to the Global Economy." In *Global Networks, Linked Cities,* edited by Saskia Sassen, 273–303. New York and London: Routledge.

Gu, J., and H. Chen. 1999. *Opportunities and Challenges: On the Construction of Shanghai as a Central City in the World Economy.* Shanghai: Shanghai Jiaotong University Press.

Haila, A. 1999. "Why Is Shanghai Building a Giant Speculative Property Bubble?" *International Journal of Urban and Regional Research* 23, no. 3: 583–88.

He, S.J., and F. Wu. 2005. "Property-led Redevelopment in Post-reform China: A Case of Xintiandi Redevelopment Project in Shanghai." *Journal of Urban Affairs* 27, no. 1: 1–23.

Hall, T., and P. Hubbard, eds. 1998. *The Entrepreneurial City: Geographies of Politics, Regime, and Representation.* Chichester, UK: John Wiley.

Hill, G.C., and J.W. Kim. 2000. "Global Cities and Development States: New York, Tokyo, and Seoul." *Urban Studies* 37, no. 12: 2167–95.

Kamo, T. 2000. "An Aftermath of Globalisation? East Asian Economic Turmoil and Japanese Cities Adrift." *Urban Studies* 37, no. 12: 2145–66.

Machimura, T. 1998. "Symbolic Use of Globalization in Urban Politics in Tokyo." *International Journal of Urban and Regional Research* 22: 183–94.

Murphey, R. 1988. "Shanghai." In *The Metropolis Era: Mega-Cities, Volume 2,* edited by M. Doggan and J.D. Kasarda, 157–83. Newbury Park, Calif.: Sage.

Muzi, N. 2002. "Shanghai Reinvents Itself in Its Old Image." Lateline News. http://latelinenews.com/ll/english/1204848.shtml.

Olds, K. 1997. "Globalizing Shanghai: The 'Global Intelligence Corps' and the Building of Pudong." *Cities* 14, no. 2: 109–23.

———. 2001. *Globalization and Urban Change: Capital, Culture, and Pacific Rim Mega-Projects.* Oxford: Oxford University Press.

Ramo, J.C. 1998. "The Shanghai Bubble." *Foreign Policy* 111: 64–75.

Sassen, S. 2001a. *The Global City: New York, London, Tokyo.* 2nd edition. Princeton, N.J.: Princeton University Press.

———. 2001b. "Global Cities and Development States: How to Derail What Could Be an Interesting Debate: A Response to Hill and Kim." *Urban Studies* 38, no. 13: 2537–40.

Shanghai Statistical Bureau, various years, *Shanghai Statistical Yearbook 1996–2000.* Beijing: China Statistics Press.

Smith, N. 1996. *The New Urban Frontier: Gentrification and the Revanchist City.* London: Routledge.

Wade, R. 1990. *Governing the Market: Economic Theory and the Role of Government in East Asian Industrialization.* Princeton, N.J.: Princeton University Press.

Walder, A. 1995. "Local Governments as Industrial Firms: An Organizational Analysis of China's Transitional Economy." *American Journal of Sociology* 101, no. 2: 263–301.

Wu, F. 2000a. "The Global and Local Dimensions of Place-Making: Remaking Shanghai as a World City." *Urban Studies* 37, no. 8: 1359–77.

———. 2000b. "Place Promotion in Shanghai, PRC." *Cities* 17: 349–61.

———. 2002. "China's Changing Urban Governance in the Transition towards a More Market-Oriented Economy." *Urban Studies* 39, no. 7: 1071–93.

———. 2003. "The (Post-) Socialist Entrepreneurial City as a State Project: Shanghai's Reglobalization in Question." *Urban Studies* 37, no. 9: 1673–93.

Wu, W. 1999. "Shanghai." *Cities* 16, no. 3: 207–16.

Yang, Y.Q., and H.J. Han. 1999. *The Open-Door Strategy.* Shanghai: Shanghai Social Science Academy.

Yatsko, P. 1996a. "Field of Dreams: Can Shanghai Re-emerge as a Key Financial Center?" *Far Eastern Economic Review* (July 18): 69–70.

———. 1996b. "Future Shock: Shanghai Remakes Itself as Workers Search for a Role." *Far Eastern Economic Review* 29 (August): 58–60.

———. 2001. *New Shanghai: The Rocky Rebirth of China's Legendary City.* New York: John Wiley & Sons.

Yatsko, P., and M. Forney. 1998. "Demand Crunch." *Far Eastern Economic Review* (January 15): 44–47.

Yeung, Y.M., and Y.W. Sung, eds. 1996. *Shanghai: Transformation and Modernization under China's Open Door Policy.* Hong Kong: The Chinese University Press.

Yusuf, S., and W. Wu. 1997. *The Dynamics of Urban Growth in Three Chinese Cities.* New York: Oxford University Press for the World Bank.

———. 2002. "Pathways to a World City: Shanghai Rising in an Era of Globalisation." *Urban Studies* 39, no. 7: 1213–40.

7. LEAPS AND LAGS IN THE GLOBAL INFORMATION AGE

SHANGHAI'S TELECOM AND INFORMATIONAL DEVELOPMENT IN COMPARATIVE PERSPECTIVE

Zhenhua Zhou and Xiangming Chen

If the globalization of Shanghai is a state project, as argued by Fulong Wu in the previous chapter, it raises the question of whether and how the state's role may vary across sectors and spaces of the local economy in driving Shanghai's globalization. Although the state has served as the initial trigger for and sustained a strong influence on market reforms and the opening up of Shanghai, it has withdrawn or retreated from some economic and social spheres while remaining actively involved in selected others. Therefore, it makes sense to study a specific economic sector of Shanghai that draws continued state involvement to better understand whether and how the state is capable of channeling, and maybe controlling, global forces in building up that sector into a global city function with important local consequences. Following Wu's chapter on the overall role of the state in Shanghai's general drive to become a global city, this chapter is the first of four chapters that will examine local transformations in Shanghai at the sectoral, district, community, and individual levels.

For the sectoral focus on local transformation in Shanghai, we have chosen the telecommunications and information sector over others for both theoretical and empirical reasons. It would be simplistic to suggest that telecommunications and information are more important functions to a globalizing city such as Shanghai than financial service or transportation. In fact, there is ample evidence that the real estate sector has been a more powerful driver of Shanghai's economic growth over the last decade or so (Chen and Sun 2007). By focusing on telecommunications and information, however, we stay consistent with the larger comparative thrust of the first part of the book where we looked at other global cities in the West and Asia with an eye for Shanghai. The analytical focus of this chapter also reflects back on a theoretical perspective on the informational city developed by Manuel Castells (1989). By focusing on the telecommunications and information sector in Shanghai, we attempt to illuminate the debate about the relative role of the state and market in fostering a crucial global city function by rapidly developing a critical sector traditionally under strong state control. Empirically, we examine the rapid development of the telecommunications and information technologies and services, measured by the surging growth in mobile phones and Internet access in Shanghai, as a striking aspect of local socioeconomic transformation, and how it is accompanied by individuals' uneven access to information based on demographic and socioeconomic attributes, as well as personal global connections.

GLOBAL CITIES IN THE GLOBAL INFORMATION ERA

Of the various salient features of global cities that set them apart from other cities, the economic and informational dualities stand out, not only as global cities' constitutive attributes and relational functions but also as twin local outcomes of the larger, global environment in which these cities are embedded and over which they dominate. Although the literature has much to say about both the economic and informational aspects of global cities in advanced industrial economies such as New York and London, we seek and draw relevant perspectives and evidence from the literature, especially regarding the information infrastructure of global cities, to place Shanghai in a broader comparative context and then under a focused analysis in this chapter.

It is a bit ironic that although the earlier literature recognized the associated economic and information technological impacts of globalization on cities, it took some time for the development of a more integrated treatment of the intricate connections between the economic and informational dimensions of global cities. One of the leading studies among this earlier body of literature is Manuel Castells, who in *The Informational City* (1989) developed an ambitious framework for analyzing the relationship between new information technologies and the urban and regional processes in the broader context of historical transformation and spatioeconomic restructuring of capitalism. His core argument was that cities and regions were reshaped by "a historically articulated complex of transformations which concerns, simultaneously, capitalism as a social system, informationalism as a node of development, and information technology as a powerful working instrument" (3). Although Castells evaluated this argument against a variety of cities and regions in the United States and beyond instead of relating it to the number of global cities as we know them today, he alerted researchers to the emergence of the informational city in a global information era in which local places, large or small, central or periphery, have become differentially embedded into a network of powerful information flows (also see Hepworth 1990) and thus risk losing control over the information. As researchers became more cognizant of the locations and roles of more cities in the spatial network of information flows, they also became more sensitive to the unevenness of this location and functional distribution. Global cities have stood out as key sites of the control, coordination, processing, and transmission of information and knowledge flows due to the huge demands for voice, image, and computer communications of all types in these cities (Graham 1999). This argument dovetails with Sassen's notion of global cities as command and control points or nodes in the global economy (Sassen, this book). However, the information technology infrastructure in global cities supports their more dominant economic functions because that very infrastructure has become a crucial component of both the local and global economies.

Are global cities as dominant over the global information network as they are over the global economic system? Knowing the positions and influence of established global cities in the global informational circuit relative to their well-documented economic centrality (Sassen 2001) will shed light on how our case study of Shanghai as a new globalizing city will proceed later. Before focusing on global cities as presumed global informational centers, we make a passing reference to Hepworth's (1990) more general concept of the information city (not the informational city as characterized by Castells), which features an urban economy dominated by information-related wealth creation and employment activities. Both Hepworth (1990) and Horrigan and Wilson (2002) regarded the increasing economic weight of the telecommunications and information sector in urban centers as a major component of the shift from the industrial to the postindustrial or service economy in the United States and Western Europe, where the information sector can be classified as part of distributive services. This distributive service function of information coordination and movement, when elevated to the global level, is exercised only by a select group of global cities where advanced and concentrated telecommunications technologies enable economic control and coordination of spatially dispersed or decentralized production and distribution activities and processes. It is in global cities where we expect to find the simultaneous concentration of and mutual reinforcement between economic and information control functions.

Empirical evidence, however, is mixed regarding global cities as dominant global information centers. Global cities are physically located within national boundaries, and thus their informational development is closely related to the overall level of national development and position in the global system. The United States and the global city of New York demonstrate this relationship at and across the global, interregional, and national scales. First, with the most developed traditional infrastructure systems such as electricity and telephones and as the original developer of the technologies and data networks underlying the Internet, the United States became the absolute global center of the Internet, functioning as a massive switchboard for interregional data traffic, as exemplified by data packets going from London to Australia through a link in New York. Although New York had an overwhelming dominance in U.S. international Internet backbone capacity (measured by megabits per second) and all U.S. cities in the number of domain name registrations in the late 1990s, it is dependent on a number of other major metropolitan areas for the international connection of its Internet users. Specifically, New York needed San Francisco and Seattle for links to Asia, used Washington, D.C., to connect to Europe, and relied on Miami and Washington, D.C. (again), to link to Latin America and the Caribbean. In Europe, whereas London was the central Internet hub for network links to the United States, Amsterdam and Frankfurt became increasingly popular alternative locations for intercontinental links to the United States and other European cities. Armed with this comparative evidence, Townsend (2001a, 2001b) concluded that instead of being completely centralized in global cities such as New York, global and national information networks of Internet links and data flows involve a broader group of information-producing centers, including even a few smaller national or regional cities.

COMPARATIVE EVIDENCE MORE
PERTINENT TO SHANGHAI

If global cities such as New York and London are not as predominant in controlling and coordinating global or regional information networks, it tells us something, but not much, about what to expect of Shanghai's informational power as it rapidly becomes a global city. Although Shanghai is aspiring (and the Chinese state is envisioning and building Shanghai) to a New York–type of global financial center (see Chen, introduction), it is a long way from there not only in the agglomeration of financial assets and influence but also in the information infrastructure to support it. To make the comparative cases more useful for seeing where Shanghai is and how it has done in informational development, we turn to another group of useful indicators on Asian cities and their positions in information capacity, accessibility, and connectivity, as well as their information development strategies involving the varied roles of the national governments vs. local governments vs. the private sector.

Japan had a more centralized and top-down approach to developing its telecommunications and information infrastructure in the 1980s. The metropolitan governments of Tokyo, Osaka, and Nagoya were active in working with private sector actors (telecommunications operators, information service providers, and land developers) to build large-scale projects such as teleports. Tokyo used zoning restrictions to deconcentrate information office facilities of financial and insurance companies from the congested central business district (CBD), whereas Osaka's world's largest teleport comprised 700 acres of zoned land for integrated network services and other information infrastructure (Hepworth 1990). Information supply per capita in Tokyo was 8 times higher than the national average, and consumption per capita was 1.6 times higher (Komatsuzaki 1994). Tokyo also remained the leading international Internet backbone hub in Asia, but Seoul became a major rival for international transmission capacity and the U.S. Internet connections to Asia, primarily through San Francisco. Despite being behind Tokyo and Seoul in this regard, both Hong Kong and Singapore competed fiercely with each other for becoming a primary regional Internet hub. Singapore and Hong Kong also emerged prominently as new centers of international Internet providers and the spatial reorganization of corporate information facilities for data transmission and financial transactions (Townsend 2001a).

In light of the evidence on major Western and Asian cities, we see a spatial dispersal of global and regional information flows, network links, and Internet hubs to a larger set of cities that have begun to supplement or even challenge the consensus top three global cities of New York, London, and Tokyo. New York is somewhat dependent on San Francisco and Washington, D.C., for certain international Internet links, whereas London faces Amsterdam and Frankfurt as growing European information hubs. Tokyo's dominant position as Asia's information center may be somewhat eroded by rival cities of Seoul, Hong Kong, and Singapore. This clear intraregional competition crosses regional lines when we switch from relational indicators on global intercity information flows to measures of telecommunications and information infrastructure and accessibility and connectivity to local information networks within cities. In New York, an estimated 38 percent of its metropolitan households subscribe to broadband Internet services, lagging far behind Tokyo, Seoul, and Hong Kong, where well over 50 percent of the households subscribe to broadband services, which also are ten to twenty times faster than in New York and other American cities (New York City Development Corporation 2005). In fact, it's smaller cities such as San Diego, San Jose, Washington, D.C., Portland, and Austin that have consistently ranked higher than New York as the most wired American cities in terms of Internet penetration.[1] Ironically, although Seoul competes with Tokyo for Asia's information hub status and is sometimes touted as the world's most Internet connected city, its Internet penetration rate of 72.8 percent trailed behind the southern port city of Ulsan at 79.1 percent and Gwangju at 76.3 percent in 2004.[2] However, close to 90 percent of individual Internet users in Seoul use high-speed broadband connection, compared with 38 percent for the New York metropolitan area (New York City Development Corporation 2005). Internet penetration rate and other indicators on more traditional telecommunications infrastructure brings us to a focused examination of Shanghai in the broader comparative context.

SHANGHAI'S LEAPS IN THE TELECOMMUNICATIONS AND INFORMATION INFRASTRUCTURE

Not expecting Shanghai to be where New York, London, or even other Asian cities are today, we trace and chart Shanghai's progress from its primitive past in terms of both more traditional and advanced means of telecommunications. With only one phone for 70 people in 1985, Shanghai came a long way by reaching 97 percent household telephone coverage by 2000 (Harwit 2005) and surpassed full saturation (100 percent) by a wide margin by 2006, with 1.5 phones per household (see left axis of Figure 7.1). Although the growth of fixed-line phones was rapid, Shanghai

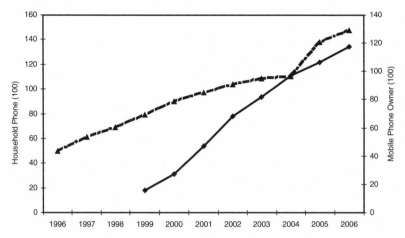

FIGURE 7.1

Growth of household phones and mobile phones in Shanghai, 1996–2006.
Source: Graphed from Shanghai Statistical Bureau (2002, 2004, 2007, Tables 13.13 and 13.14).

leapt forward in the number and rate of mobile phone users, which surged from 15.5 mobile phones per 100 households in 1999 to almost 118 in 2006 (see right axis of Figure 7.1). Mobile phone subscription is poised to rise further as two Shanghai-based companies, working with China Telecom, China's leading fixed-line operator, have already started large-scale 3G (third generation) trial networks of the home-grown wireless technology using the TD-SCDMA (time division synchronous code division multiple access) standard. The trial operation, which has been extended from 16 to 30 base stations in Shanghai, was stable and the technology ready for licensed commercial deployment soon. Given Shanghai's lead position in mobile phone use and technology, the projected growth of mobile phone users from 393 million in 2005 to nearly 500 million in China (already the largest market in the world by far) by the end of 2007 (*People's Daily*, February 11, 2006, 2) bodes well for Shanghai.

Although access to digital information and the Internet in Shanghai has not grown as rapidly as mobile phone usage, it experienced a phenomenal increase through the 1990s. As Figure 7.2 shows, relative to the fast rise in the number of mostly commercial digital data users, which began to decline after 2005, Internet subscribers soared from a few thousand in the mid-1990s to over 9.6 million by 2006, accounting for almost three-quarters of the registered population of 13.7 million. Given the average household size of 2.8 for Shanghai, this translated to almost 50 percent

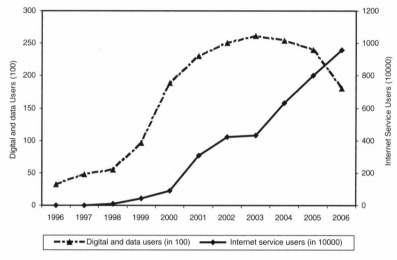

FIGURE 7.2
Digital and data users and Internet service household users in Shanghai, 1996–2006.
Source: Graphed from Shanghai Statistical Bureau (2002, 2004, 2007, Table 13.3).

household penetration (compared to about 20 percent for all Chinese cities), with a little over one-third of those households connected to broadband (Liu 2005). Although this puts Shanghai below cities such as New York, Seoul, Hong Kong, and Singapore, it represents significant progress in light of where Shanghai started and its overall development of information infrastructure.

GROWTH UNDER STRONG STATE PUSH AND REGULATION: SHANGHAI IN COMPARISON

Having surveyed the rapid growth of Shanghai's telecommunications and information sector, especially the acceleration of mobile phone and Internet use, in recent years against the comparative backdrop of what has transpired in a few Western and Asian global cities, it's time to examine whether and how certain forces in the Chinese context may bring about a distinctive trajectory of Shanghai's informational development. The key is to clarify how the relative roles of the national government, local government, and the private sector in developing the telecommunications infrastructure in Shanghai differ from those in other cities. In general, given the security concern and the huge cost of the national telecommunications infrastructure, the central government and policies, especially in developing nations and those with a strong central state, are more instrumental in financing, building, regulating, and managing it, often through a monopoly of organizations and practices. The deregulation of the telecommunications sector in the United States through the breakup of AT&T in 1984 spurred a significant shift to market competition among more companies for better and cheaper equipment and services in industrialized economies. In contrast, China's national government has remained the most powerful player in shaping the telecommunications sector before and since economic reform around 1980. To improve the antiquated telephone system then, the central government provided targeted financial incentives in the late 1980s of allowing 90 percent of central government loans for telecommunications not to be repaid and regional telecom authorities to keep 90 percent of their taxable profits. The central government also limited foreign investment in telecommunications to a few equipment manufacturers and prevented foreign companies from operating domestic companies and offering services (Harwit 2005). This heavy involvement of the central government is similar to the top-down approach taken by the Japanese national government to developing advanced telecommunications and information services across the country but differs considerably from the market-driven and state-level policies for telecommunications in the United States. Given the increasing intercity competition for economic growth and external resources, municipal governments were both expected and under more pressure to play an assertive role in planning telecommunications development and regulating the powerful logic of information flows (see Castells 1989; Hepworth 1990).

Despite strong central direction and because of graduate administrative and fiscal decentralization, the Shanghai city government became more active in the telecommunications sector with a multipronged strategy. It included the following: (1) forming a "telecommunications leading group" headed by then Mayor Jiang Zeming (who later became China's President) in 1985, (2) setting the phone connection fee very high early to collect revenue for financing the infrastructure, (3) working with foreign companies very selectively to purchase equipment, acquire technology, and joint venture with key local companies, and (4) allowing slightly more competition with the original monopoly. The combination of these measures contributed to the rapid growth of both fixed-line and mobile phone subscribers (shown in Figure 7.1), who benefited greatly from the cost of connecting an office or home phone dropping from about US$940 in the late 1980s to US$180 in 1999 and from considerably reduced costs of mobile phones and their initiation charge from 1999 to 2004 (Harwit 2005). Seeing the broadband technology and Internet content as the new wave of information power, the Shanghai government, with central government backing, approved the creation of a monopolistic company to deliver cable television, Internet access, and telephone services through cable lines, making Shanghai the only city in China allowed to do so as of 2003. Unlike other Chinese cities, which left Internet content to private providers, the Shanghai government launched its own municipal Web site (Eastday.com) owned and managed by key municipal corporations in May 2000, and the site became immediately the most popular in Shanghai, with over 10,000 registered users. Although this municipally backed site makes it difficult for other Web sites to compete for content development and delivery, the number of Web sites in Shanghai reached 53,000, accounting for 8.5 percent of China's total in mid-2004 (Harwit 2005).

Shanghai's information infrastructure experienced rapid growth according to additional indicators. During 1996–2000, the main part of Shanghai's "information hub project" consisting of several broadband backbones and key applications was completed. By 2000, the number of Shanghai's fiber optic cables for international communication increased to six, with data transmission speed becoming five times faster than the previous year. Over 1 million cable TV subscribers have access to cable broadband Internet at 860 MHz. The telecom broadband Internet covering 90 percent of the urban area has a 320G key exchange capacity. By the end of 2000, Shanghai also boasted the largest ATM municipal Internet and the largest ATM digital exchange center in the world (Yin 2002). In 2004, penetration of personal computers in Shanghai approached 60 percent, which compared well with New York (66 percent), Tokyo (43 percent), Seoul (60 percent), and Singapore (60 percent) (*Central News Asia*, August 2, 2001, 2). The goal of Shanghai's information infrastructure development is to achieve multimedia content delivery online and further increase information throughput capacity in central parts of the city while building more network links to channel and distribute information to the suburban districts of the city.

WHEN A STRENGTH IS ALSO A WEAKNESS: SHANGHAI'S LAGS IN COMPARATIVE PERSPECTIVE

Shanghai has come a long way in a short period of time to the advanced stage of telecommunications and information development. This would not have been possible without strong and active central and municipal governments working in tandem to drive this development. The strong state push, however, has turned out to be a weakness because it limited opportunities for acquiring more sophisticated informatics that would arise through market competition. The strong state initiative also was not sufficient to overcome the many constraints associated with a late start from a primitive state of telecommunications compared with other global cities. In New York over the last decade, competing firms laid approximately 3 million miles of fiber optic network infrastructure in its five boroughs, and seventeen firms are franchised by the city to operate broadband networks. An estimated 3,700 buildings in New York are "fiber lit" (the so-called "intelligent buildings")—they are wired by fiber optic cables that bring in broadband service. And about 3,000 of these buildings are located in Midtown and Lower Manhattan, which earns the title as the world's most wired CBD. Regarding residential connection to broadband, 85–90 percent of all telephone lines in New York owned by Verizon are eligible for DSL service, whereas all homes in the five boroughs are eligible for cable Internet service (New York City Development Corporation 2005). New York is way ahead of Shanghai in these areas of information infrastructure development.

It may not be fair to compare Shanghai to New York in light of the latter's global dominance in finance, media, and other advanced service industries and their huge demands for informatics, as well as its highly competitive market for information providers. If we turn to Singapore as a reference case, we get a more realistic view on where Shanghai lags in the broader development of information infrastructure and how improvements could be made. In the race to build intelligent or wired cities among top competitors, Singapore has pursued an ambitious goal of "Singapore One" by the year of 2010. It aims at building a high capacity and convertible broadband infrastructure and relevant application and service systems to achieve full interface and interaction between multimedia applications and services for families, enterprises, and schools. The Singapore government adopted some far-sighted, innovative, and liberal policies, which include attracting about 10,000 first-class IT experts and managerial talents from around the world to Singapore, launching a national e-commerce program, and connecting major cities in Asia to form a communications and technology belt and tying it into the backbone digital network in Asia as a foundation for an eventual "digital Asia." Regarding e-commerce more specifically, Singapore drew up "e-Business Industry Development Schemes" (eBIDS) to increase the volume of e-commercial trade. It also established a "National E-Commerce Action Committee" consisting of eight government departments to be responsible for the coordination and promotion of e-commercial activities in main economic sectors. Singapore Information Development Association (IDA) and Singapore Production and Standards Bureau (PSB) invested US$30 million in two programs. One aims at accelerating online service and e-commercial trade mainly for companies with e-commerce capacities to be more creative in e-commerce. The other is the Jumpstart program intended to support local enterprises for e-commerce infrastructure construction and developing online business practices such as consumer relationship management, e-resource plan, and supply chain management (Zhou 2004). The Singapore government recently created a Web portal specifically for small and medium-sized enterprises (SME). The user-friendly portal includes step-by-step guides on how to apply for government financing schemes and market statistics gathered from 25 agencies so that businesses spend less time searching for information.[3] Strategies such as these further illustrate the process of building competitiveness through the involvement of different institutional actors in Singapore (see Ho, this book).

E-commerce in Shanghai is still relatively young. In 2000, enterprise domain names in Shanghai only numbered 11,141, less than three percent of the total number of enterprises in the city. In contrast, 54 percent of the companies in New York had their own Web sites, 79 percent used e-mail, and 30 percent had video conferencing systems. In London, 60 percent of companies had their own Web sites, 70 percent used the Internet, and 25 percent had video conferencing systems. In Tokyo, Internet penetration rate for companies was almost 90 percent. In addition, a low level of internal information development in Shanghai's enterprises hindered their capacity to carry out e-commerce. Cumulative investment in information technology and equipment by Shanghai's enterprises accounted for less than 0.5 percent of their total assets, far less than the typical range of 8–10 percent in developed countries (Zhou 2004). Other external constraints such as a problematic credit system, an inefficient distribution system, a lack of legitimacy for online signature, and poor information security have also limited the development of e-commerce. More recent government statistics, however, show an improvement of e-commerce, whose revenue climbed to 9.1 percent of total sales revenue in 2004. The processing times for import and export declaration were considerably reduced from twenty hours and six hours per sheet in 2001 to thirty minutes and fifty minutes in 2003, respectively, thanks to the introduction of a unified information platform for e-commerce and e-logistics built by the municipal government (Liu 2005). This bodes really well for Shanghai's future e-commerce development in light of China's rapidly growing online sales, which soared 58 percent from 2004 to a record

553.1 billion yuan (US$68.7 billion) in 2005. As well, the turnover of the consumer-to-consumer (C2C) market, worth 13.5 billion yuan (US$1.7 billion), tripled in just one year. More than 71.3 percent of Chinese netizens shopped online by the end of 2005, which was a huge jump from 3.2 percent in 1999 (Yang 2003), whereas the average stood at 70 percent for the Asia–Pacific region.[4] With 162 million neitzens in China by June 2008, about 115 million of them are likely to have shopped online. Because about 83 percent of China's online shoppers aare between 18 and 35 years old—and 70 percent are under 30—the online shopping market will have huge potential for growth.[5]

As the Shanghai municipal government expanded its role to providing information infrastructure (in addition to its dominant role in building physical infrastructure) to sustain high economic growth, it began to redress severe lags in providing more efficient public services through e-government, which has been widely used by major cities in industrialized countries of the West and Asia. In New York in 2000, 50 percent of government services were done online, and this increased to 80 percent by 2002, with the aim of making government work paperless and creating virtual interactions between residents and government service agencies. Tokyo formally launched "the e-government project" in March 2000 and planned to put it into full use by 2003 (Zhou 2004). Singapore was the first country (city) in the world to carry out computerized integration and coordination in public service sectors and civil service programs. By June 2000, more than 130 items of Internet-based public services became available, and over 100 items were on Singapore's government's Web site, which earned a reputation of "providing the most advanced integrated services in the world" (Symonds 2000). In 2000, the Seoul government staged a special campaign of "Information Education for One Million People" for the purpose of informing residents of the wide array of online government services. In 2001, the municipal government shifted the focus to educating the middle-aged and elderly persons about accessing government services electronically. To finance these programs, the government at different levels has raised more than four billion Korean won (US$4.2 million) from private sources, especially IT companies (Tang 2001).

Shanghai's e-government initiative came about as an integral part of the overall reform of the government to make the latter operate according to the principle of "Considerate, Trustworthy, and Reliable." The flagship project of e-government was the launch of the government portal (www.shanghai.gov.cn) in 2002. The site, maintained by the Shanghai

Information Commission, provides links to forty-seven municipal-level commissions and bureaus, nineteen district or county governments, and other affiliated municipal organizations. It posts 2,397 different forms that can be downloaded and offers 640 online services. In May 2004, the municipal government promulgated a new regulation that required all government information, except that concerning national security, commercial secrets, and personal privacy to be viewed and accessed on the government Web site. In 2004, the government portal also unveiled a new feature, "Residents' Mailbox," which allows local residents to send emails directly to concerned municipal agencies to inquire about and access a range of social services (e.g., getting a commercial permit or a marriage license) and to register personal complaints (Liu 2005). Our virtual tour of the Shanghai government portal during the completion of this chapter largely confirmed the existence and availability of these Web features. Nevertheless, e-government in Shanghai remains limited in conducting administrative affairs online and achieving a broader scope and depth of e-administration. In addition, different government agencies and district governments tend to build their Web sites in independent and separate systems without a shared information exchange platform and having cross-listing links. These isolated vertical information sources are a major barrier for Shanghai's e-government development.

BEYOND THE FIREWALL: GLOBAL CONNECTIVITY, INDIVIDUAL ACCESS, AND STATE ACTION

The lagging development of e-commerce and e-government in Shanghai pales in comparison to the striking picture of the city's increasing connectivity to the outside world and telemediated intralocal connections. Although not yet a global or even regional information hub like New York or Singapore, Shanghai's other forms of global telecommunications and information connectivity at both macro and micro levels have brought about local transformations in how unprecedented access to information may change people's daily lives, their relationship with the government, and the latter's response. Given Shanghai's growing global economic links and thanks to the rapid expansion of the telephone system and gradual decline in call rates, the volume of international, Hong Kong, and Macao's calls to and from Shanghai surged through the 1990s, regardless of some fluctuations (see Figure 7.3).

Not revealed by the aggregate number of international phone calls are other forms of information connections of Shanghai residents, especially local residents' personal global ties and the latter's association with

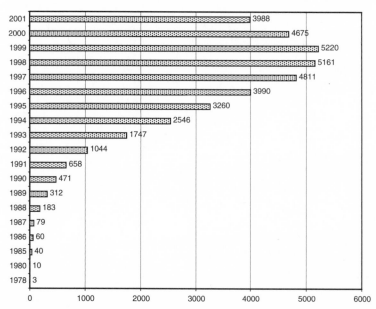

FIGURE 7.3
International, Hong Kong, and Macao long distance calls to and from Shanghai, 1978–2001.
Source: Graphed from Shanghai Statistical Bureau (2002, Table 13.12).

more differentiated individual socioeconomic characteristics. A survey in 2001 involving the second author provides some evidence.

As Table 7.1 shows, age, education, income, residential area, and personal global connections are highly correlated with being knowledgeable about the computer and using the Internet (all Chi-squares are statistically significant). A much higher proportion of younger people (those under 34) answered "Yes" to the question. The proportions of people with the highest education, income, and residential status responding "Yes" were above 80 percent, whereas the corresponding proportions of people on the other ends of the respective distributions were less than 30 percent. In addition, people with more global connections registered a progressively larger proportion of "Yes," with the disparity between the two ends (full vs. zero global connectivity) being even larger than along the other indicators. This information suggests a glaring "digital divide" between people of different ages, in stratified socioeconomic positions, and with varied global connections. Despite the tremendous advances in Shanghai's telecommunications and information infrastructure and its rapidly expanded global connections, local residents have very unequal access to

TABLE 7.1

Level of Knowledge about Computers and Internet Use, by Age, Education, Income, Residential Area, and Personal Global Connections, Shanghai, 2001

	Knowledgeable	Not Knowledgeable
Age (Chi-square = 148.61, PR = 0.00)		
12–18	76.09%	23.91%
19–34	78.95%	21.05%
35–50	37.05%	62.95%
51+	20.35%	79.65%
Education[a] (Chi-square = 182.34, PR = 0.00)		
Low	16.57%	83.43%
Middle	58.53%	41.47%
High	85.28%	14.72%
Income per Capita, in Yuan per Month (Chi-square = 115.14, PR = 0.00)		
60–300	15.79%	84.21%
301–999	31.83%	68.17%
1,000–3,300	68.97	31.03
3,201–25,000	96.67	3.33
Residential Area[b] (Chi-square = 41.31, PR = 0.00)		
Village or Town	28.74	71.26
Traditional Urban Neighborhood	48.16	51.84
New Commercial Housing	64.52	35.48
Luxury Flats and Villas	89.19	10.81
Personal Global Connections[c] (Chi-square = 168.52, PR = 0.00)		
None	21.48	78.52
One	62.03	37.97
Two	79.49	20.51
Three	91.67	8.33
Four	100	0

Notes: [a]Low includes below primary school, primary school, and junior high school; middle includes senior high school and vocational school; high includes two-year college, university, and postgraduate study. [b]Village and town residence includes agricultural villages and town centers, whereas traditional urban neighborhood includes urban residential villages and old urban settlements. The original Chinese term for urban residential villages is *gongren xincun* (workers' new villages), which refers to the main housing settlements in urbanized Shanghai, mostly for factory workers and their families from the 1950s through the early 1980s. From the early 1990s, these residential villages became a main destination for people in old urban settlements who had been displaced by rapid redevelopment in Shanghai. [c]The four global connections are (1) having worked for a foreign company locally, (2) having been abroad, (3) having relatives and friends overseas, and (4) often surfing foreign Web sites.

information in association with their demographic and socioeconomic characteristics and global connections.

The differentiated access to the computer and Internet also reflects the China- and Shanghai-specific information environment or space shaped by a conjuncture of youth's craze for cyberspace, the rapid growth of Internet cafés, and state regulation of information access and Internet cafés. Of the 111 million Internet users in China in 2005, ranking the nation first in the world, an estimated 16 million are Internet café users (Qiu and Zhou 2005), and the overwhelming majority of them are teenagers who mostly play interactive online computer games and chat with their friends, many becoming addicted to the Internet.[6] By some estimates, there are 4 million bloggers in China, and most of them are again young people (Grossman and Beech 2006), who normally do their blogging in Internet cafés. The government at the national and local level tries to place Internet cafés under strict regulation through different means. In Shanghai, the municipally owned Eastday.com had opened 238 Internet cafés by 2002 under a franchise arrangement where private businesspeople could open and operate an Eastday-brand café and pay 5 percent of the revenue and in turn would receive help from Eastday for securing a necessary city permit, with some owners running five or six cafés (Harwit 2005). More recently, Eastday Internet outlets have attracted increasingly less traffic of users than privately owned Internet cafés. As a stringent control and monitoring mechanism, the national government requires all Internet cafés to use software that stores data on each user, and all bloggers must register with local authorities (Einhorn and Elgin 2006).

The Chinese state's monitoring and control of the Internet has been effective to the extent that it blocks access to many sites that express critical opinions on politically controversial and sensitive issues, even making the Chinese-language version of Google.com (running in China) agree to concede in altering certain Web sites (Grossman and Beech 2006). Although the state is able to regulate Internet cafés by using a chain store policy, Qiu and Zhou (2005) argued that the national regulatory regime is a compromised outcome of negotiation involving multiple players at the central level and then imposed onto local authorities, Internet café operators, and millions of users, without guaranteed success. In fact, even when the highly efficient city-state of Singapore imposed the high-tech information technology of Electronic Road Pricing to extract tolls from car drivers coming to and through the CBD during peak rush hours, it ended up creating a sort of local disconnection by filtering out "cash poor/time rich" commuters and improving the mobility for wealthy or "cash rich/time poor" commuters (Graham 2001, 407). In the Shanghai context, even though the municipal government has devised institutional mechanisms such as the Eastday.com Internet café chain to regulate access to the form and content of information, it is severely circumscribed to ameliorate the growing "digital gap" that developed from the increasingly differentiated socioeconomic resources and personal global connections as shown previously. With extensive global connections to different forms and sources of information inflow, Shanghai's residents are rapidly becoming netizens like those in other global cities and beyond. This strong and direct global–local nexus not only is a product of the state's helping hand in building up the information infrastructure but also thwarts the state's outreached hand in regulating access to certain information content.

SHANGHAI'S INFORMATION FUTURE: A GLOBALIZING CITY'S TOUGH CHALLENGES

What will Shanghai's information future look like as it is becoming a global city? It appears "fairly bright" based on the intensity and extensiveness of the state's drive behind Shanghai's rapid economic growth and leaps from a primitive telecommunications past to some of the advanced edges of informatics, at least in electronic information products manufacturing and Internet access. In 2003, the electronic information products industry ranked first in total assets, employment, gross output, sales value, and sales revenue among Shanghai's six "pillar" industries (also including auto, petrochemicals, steel, complex equipment, and biomedicals), which collectively accounted for 63.4 percent of the city's gross industrial output (Shanghai Statistical Bureau 2004). The official national press touted the information sector as Shanghai's "primary backbone industry" as early as 2000 (Harwit 2005). On the other hand, the future of Shanghai's information sector is faced with a set of constraints that need to be overcome by more effective development strategies.

First of all, if the local government is called upon to and can become more active and effective in contending with powerful global information flows and market-driven intercity competition when the national state is already eroded (Castells 1989), the Shanghai government faces a double bind of limited autonomy from the central government in telecommunications and information development and of limited competition among local private companies for information services. Whereas highly competitive private companies account almost entirely for New York's sophisticated telecommunications infrastructure, the city government's hands are tied when it comes to public policy and regulatory decisions regarding telecommunications, most of which are made at the federal and state levels (New York City Development Corporation 2005). The Shanghai government could better synthesize its local autonomy with the power of the central state and local market by integrating telecommunications and information planning with its effort to promote the financial sector and its success in building the physical (transport) infrastructure. As the cases of New York, Tokyo, and Hong Kong indicate, the huge push for becoming global financial centers through reliable telecommunications and information processing is key to these cities also being information hubs. Since countries and cities with well-developed traditional network infrastructures such as roads and telephone systems also have done well with the deployment of the Internet infrastructure by retrofitting the latter to existing telephone networks (Townsend 2001a), Shanghai could do better in expanding its Internet infrastructure from its extensive transport and telephone systems already in place.

Second, Shanghai faces the challenge of achieving a more balanced and unified development of its information infrastructure. The lack of e-commerce and e-government development has kept Shanghai behind the global cities of the industrialized West and East Asia. Institutional hurdles include the People's Bank of China's lid on the maximum electronic payment amount in a single deal. Although this restriction might help guard against the risk of online fraud, it hinders fast growth of the e-commerce market. The uneven access to the Internet of different socioeconomic groups threatens to leave a large proportion of the population, particularly the older, the less educated, the poorer, and the less globally connected, behind in the global information age. Given its strong government and planning legacy, Shanghai is capable of achieving balanced and unified information development by avoiding duplicative and incompatible network platforms for different municipal government agencies and promoting a broader awareness of and community-based training in Internet usage. In addition, the mutual reinforcement between the growth of Internet usage and civil society in China (Yang 2003) poses a continuing dilemma to the central and local state regarding the promotion of information development at the expense of losing more power over nonstate groups and actors.

Finally, as a late globalizing city, Shanghai has duly emphasized building the hardware infrastructure of the "information superhighway" with financial capital and has neglected the software human capital for developing applications and maximizing usage, exemplified by a shortage of well-trained and skilled professionals. Given the projected shortage of professionals in several fields for Shanghai (see Chen, introduction), Shanghai's eventual catch-up with established global cities in information access, usage, and distribution will depend less on building more Internet backbone hubs and fiber optic networks by the government than on training a new generation of skilled information workers (see Markusen and Yu, this book). It is ironic that some of them may emerge from the existing generation of young computer gamers who spend long hours in the hundreds of the city Internet cafés.

NOTES

We thank Dennis Judd and two anonymous reviewers for comments and suggestions on an earlier draft, and Jiaming Sun for helping update the data in Figures 7.1 and 7.2.

1. Chris Charron, "The Top 10 Most Wired American Cities," July 5, 2005, Forrester Research, www.forrester.com/Research/Document/Excerpt/0,7211, 37114,00.html.

2. Kim Tong-hyung, "Seoul Is Not the World's Most Wired City, " August 12, 2004, http://urban.blogs.com/seoul/2004/08/seoul_is_not_th.html.

3. Christie Loh, "One-stop Business Info Hub for SMEs," *Central News Asia,* www.channelnewsasia.com/stories/singaporebusinessnews/view/194616/1/.html.

4. Reported by a study released by the China Internet Development Research Center under the auspices of the Chinese Academy of Social Sciences, , "More than 70 percent of Chinese neitzens shop online." China Daily, online, www.chinadaily.com.cn/english/doc/2006-02/25/content_523974.htm, accessed on February 22, 2006.

5. "Thrifty is nifty," China Daily, December 2, 2008, 18, www.chinadaily.com.cn/cndy/2008-12/02/content_7259015.htm, accessed on Friday 6, 2009.

6. A recent survey conducted by the Shanghai Youth Federation at the end of 2005 found that at least 14 percent of the city's teenagers (youth aged 11–17) were addicted to the Internet. Whereas 11.6 percent were slightly addicted to the Internet, logging on for long periods every day, 2.5 percent of the survey respondents were seriously addicted, unable to restrain themselves from the Internet and frequently skipping classes, as reported in "Youth workers try to pull the plug on Internet addicts," metro section, *Shanghai Daily,* December 12, 2005, A4.

REFERENCES

Castells, Manuel. 1989. *The Informational City: Information Technology, Economic Restructuring, and the Urban–Regional Process.* Cambridge, Mass.: Basil Blackwell.

Chen, Xiangming, and Jiaming Sun. 2007. "Untangling a Global–Local Nexus: Sorting Out Residential Sorting in Shanghai." *Environment and Planning A* 39, no. 10: 2324–45.

Einhorn, Bruce, and Ben Elgin. 2006. "The Great Firewall of China." *Business-Week* (January 23): 32–34.

Graham, Stephen. 1999. "Global Grids of Glass: On Global Cities, Telecommunications, and Plenary Urban Networks." *Urban Studies* 36, nos. 5–6: 924–49.

———. 2001. "Information Technologies and Reconfigurations of Urban Space." *International Journal of Urban and Regional Research* 25, no. 2: 405–10.

Grossman, Lev, and Hannah Beech. 2006. "Google under the Gun." *Time* (February 13): 53–54.

Harwit, Eric. 2005. "Telecommunications and the Internet in Shanghai: Political and Economic Factors Shaping the Network in a Chinese City." *Urban Studies* 42, no. 10: 1837–58.

Hepworth, Mark E. 1990. "Planning for the Information City: The Challenge and Response." *Urban Studies* 27, no. 4: 537–58.

Horrigan, John B., and Robert H. Wilson. 2002. "Telecommunications Technologies and Urban Development: Strategies in U.S. Cities." *International Journal of Technology, Policy and Management* 2, no. 3: 338–54.

Komatsuzaki, Seisuke. 1994. "A History of the Concept of and Research on Information Development in Japan." In *Informational and Economic Development,* edited by Jingwen Li, 10–14. Beijing: Social Sciences Literature Publishing House (Shehui Kexue Wenxian Chubanshe).

Liu, Yadong. 2005. "Upgrade City Administration and Municipal Public Service Based on IT." PowerPoint presentation. http://unpan1.un.org/intradoc/groups/public/documents/APCITY/UNPAN020015.pdf.

New York City Development Corporation. 2005. "Telecommunications and Economic Development in New York City: A Plan for Action." Report to Mayor Michael R. Bloomberg. http://newyorkbiz.com/about_us/Telecom Plan-March2005.pdf.

Qiu, Jack Linchuan, and Liuning Zhou. 2005. "Through the Prism of the Internet Café: Managing Access in an Ecology of Games." *China Information* 19, no. 2: 261–97.

Sassen, Sassen. 2001. *The Global City: New York, London, Tokyo.* 2nd edition. Princeton, N.J.: Princeton University Press.

Shanghai Statistical Bureau. 2002. *Shanghai Statistical Yearbook 2002.* Shanghai: Shanghai Statistics Press.

———. 2004. *Shanghai Statistical Yearbook 2004.* Shanghai: Shanghai Statistics Press.

Symonds, Matthew. 2000. "The Next Revolution: A Survey of Government and the Internet." *The Economist* (June 24): 11–12.

Tang, Hua. 2001. "Korea Accelerating Its Informational Development." *Overview of the Global Technological Economy* 11: 10–13.

Townsend, Anthony M. 2001a. "Network Cities and the Global Structure of the Internet." *American Behavioral Scientist* 44, no. 10: 1697–1716.

———. 2001b. "The Internet and the Rise of the New Network Cities: 1969–1999." *Environment and Planning B* 28, no. 1: 39–58.

Yang, Guobin. 2003. "The Co-Evolution of the Internet and Civil Society in China." *Asian Survey* 43, no. 3: 405–22.

Yin, Jizuo, ed. 2002. *Blue Book on Shanghai's Economic Development in 2001.* Shanghai: Shanghai Academy of Social Sciences Press.

Zhou, Zhenhua. 2004. "Xinxihua yu Shijie Chengshi Xin Fazhan" (New Developments in Informatics and World Cities). In *World City: International Lessons and Shanghai's Development,* edited by Zhou Zhenhua, Chen Xiangming, and Huang Jianfu, 48–68. Shanghai: Shanghai Academy of Social Sciences Press.

8. STRIVING TO BE A GLOBAL CITY FROM BELOW

THE RESTRUCTURING OF SHANGHAI'S URBAN DISTRICTS

Tingwei Zhang

.

FROM ONE SECTOR TO SEVERAL SPACES

Following the sectoral focus on the telecommunications and information sector in the preceding chapter, this chapter turns to the urban district level by examining local transformation within and across three distinctive administratively bounded areas of Shanghai in the larger context of China's reforms since the early 1980s. The transition of the economy from centralized planning to market-oriented and the devolution of decision power from the central government to municipalities on local economic decisions have attracted the attention of many scholars (Yeh and Wu 1996; Logan 2001; Zhang 2002a). China's transition takes place in the era of globalization, which indeed plays a certain role in China's reforms. China's reform is a typical top-down process and was initiated by a small group of top leaders, and thus, things that happened in other countries encouraged, taught, and warned these reformers in formulating policies and scheduling steps of the reform. More important, economic gains from joining the world economy provided an opportunity to reformers when they were convincing other leaders of the necessity for reform and show-ing the Chinese people the legitimacy of the reform. Therefore, it is not surprising to see that most discussions about globalization are positive in China, which is quite different from studies in some Western nations. In the United States, for instance, many scholars view globalization benefiting international corporations at the expense of the working class and old cities (Brecher 1994; Fitzgerald and Leigh 2002; Marcuse and van Kempen 2000; Ranney 2002).

The consequences of China's reforms in the last twenty years have been widely reported. Besides impressive economic growth, rapid urbanization, and China's closer integration into the world economy, scholars focused on the growing gaps between the "new rich" and the poor and between the urban and rural residents in a more stratified social order (see Logan, Bian, and Bian 1999; Wang and Murie 1996). Another dimension of inequality manifests itself across places locally in terms of differentiated land use and uneven development. Although global capital is partially responsible for this spatial outcome, local urban politics, "Chinese style," may matter more, especially in a diverse city such as Shanghai. To help account for interdistrict disparities in Shanghai's global rise, I draw selectively from a "growth coalition" or "growth machine" perspective, which sees both the conflicting and compatible interests of different growth-oriented actors, such as real estate developers and local government officials, as crucial to urban growth in the United States (Logan and Molotch 1987). Experience drawn from Atlanta and other American cities reveals that outside of the formal government responsible to all constituencies, an informal coalition consisting of local politicians and the business community is formed in promoting urban development/redevelopment in certain districts, especially in strategically important areas such as downtown. The downtown prioritized strategy is considered critical to the economic growth of American cities in the postindustrial age; it is also becoming popular in Shanghai and other Chinese cities, although their respective economies are still based on manufacturing.

Uneven local development is a major consequence of broader changes in Chinese cities, including huge investment in infrastructure and building projects as an effort to sell place to the growing social–spatial differentiation among urban communities. The reforms from internal pressure and the economic opportunity brought by globalization from outside have stimulated more Chinese cities to be "international" or even "global." Although the theme of this book is local transformations that might accompany or result from the measures taken by cities aspiring to be "global"—a common phenomenon in the era of globalization—the important question that is the subject of this chapter is as follows:

A city often restructures its economic and spatial activities to respond to global change. In urban China, the unit directly experiencing a city's restructuring is the district right below the municipality. Because urban districts are the administrative as well as economic foundation of the municipal government, economic and spatial restructuring always starts from the bottom, at the district level. What happens in urban districts will be critical to understanding cities' actions to reach their "global" objectives. Unfortunately, not many Chinese case studies at the urban district level have been done. Scholars have correctly pointed out that the main obstacle is the lack of small-area data, together with the fact that microdata at a high resolution often remains confidential in China (Wu 2002). Although many researchers have contributed to the study on Shanghai at the municipal level (see Kong 2001; W. Wu 1999; Yeung and Sung 1996; Zhao 1998 on Shanghai in general; see F. Wu 2001 and 2002 on the real estate industry and housing; and see Zhang 2002b on the progrowth coalition), case studies at the district level are still rare.

This chapter intends to fill the gap by examining Shanghai's restructuring measured by changes of land use pattern and the spatial-functional structure through an analysis of three Shanghai urban districts: Huangpu, Luwan, and Yangpu. Huangpu district is the traditional central business district (CBD), whereas Luwan is the main retail and residential area and now has been planned to be a world-class commercial district. Yangpu is a traditional industrial district with a concentration of manufacturing factories. The respective development patterns and magnitudes of the three districts differ significantly since the reforms. Changes in the development pattern in the three districts reveal the fundamental shift of Shanghai's economy from manufacturing to service industries as a response to the global change (see Chen, introduction, this book). Because land and buildings are essential vehicles for carrying economic activities, the restructuring of the spatial structure reflects the city's restructured economy. This study thus provides a valuable illustration of "acting from the bottom," that is, how Shanghai has spatially restructured itself at the district level to become "the dragon-head of China's economy" and "one of international economic, finance, trade, and port centers," as defined by the central government. Indeed, the national government views globalizing Shanghai a state project (Wu, this book).

Data used in the study were collected in interviews with directors and planners of the three district planning bureaus in 2001 and 2002. Secondary data are from district statistical yearbooks, district history books, and district fact books from 1985 to 2001, and from the municipal statistics bureaus. Except where otherwise noted, most of the data comes from the city's statistical yearbooks up to 2007.

Shanghai's administration system has changed many times in the last two decades, and it is still changing in terms of its land/population classification system (urban–rural), and district boundary adjustment. It is worth emphasizing that boundary adjustment itself was employed as an administrative tool to empower and reinforce some districts to be "global players," such as the CBD of Huangpu district. However, boundary changes make it hard to conduct a consistent comparative study over several decades. For example, today's Huangpu district was the outcome of the merge of (the "old") Huangpu district and the then Nanshi district in 2001, which makes it impossible to extract "old" Huangpu data from the Huangpu data after 2000. Therefore, data from the 2000 census (before the main boundary adjustment) is used as the baseline to provide consistency in this study. The drawback of this methodology is that the study may miss some new developments in recent years.

This chapter starts with background information from the city and profiles of the three districts. It then compares differences in building use and urban development patterns of the districts in the process of economic restructuring, followed by an analysis of spatial restructuring policies and politics, as well as factors that influence the function redistribution decisions. The findings are discussed and conclusions drawn in the last section.

SHANGHAI'S ECONOMIC AND SPATIAL RESTRUCTURING AFTER THE 1990S

Shanghai, China's largest city and its economic center, has a population of 18.4 million (13.7 million "registered residents" and 4.7 million migrants) and a land area of 6,341 square km in 2006. The city government reports directly to the central government, a status similar to a province.

In 2008, the city had 18 districts and one rural county (Chongming County). This administration system was a result of boundary adjustment in 2001. Before the adjustment, there were sixteen urban districts, among them, nine were "central" or "old" urban districts, meaning that they were located within the traditional urbanized core and recognized as urban districts before the 1978 reforms. These central urban districts formed the conventional "city proper" (see Map 8.1).

Shanghai's past has important impacts on the composition of its economy and on the decisions of economic restructuring today. Shanghai became a "treaty port" to foreigners in the 1840s and China's primary economic center by the 1920s. Located at China's richest area, the Yangtze River Delta, Shanghai also attracted domestic investors following foreign entrepreneurs. Financing, trading, and manufacturing industries formed the base of the city's economy. Even in 1952, in the earliest days of "a socialist

MAP 8.1
The location of three districts in Shanghai.

Shanghai," the proportion of the city's agriculture, manufacturing, and service industry output remained 6:52:42. After nationalizing all industries in 1956 the financing industry almost disappeared, and Shanghai became China's manufacturing center, especially for textile and steel industries. The proportion of the city's agriculture, manufacturing, and service industry output became 4:77:19 in 1978 (Kong 2001). From 1950 to 1976, Shanghai contributed one-sixth of the nation's revenue with a population comprising only 1 percent of the nation (also see Wu, this book). The city was China's gateway to the outside world. The Shanghai port handled one-third of the nation's import/export cargoes until the 1980s.

Since carrying out the reform policy in 1978, Shanghai's economy has grown rapidly. Total GDP increased from 27.3 billion yuan (US$3.4 billion) in 1978 to 455.1 billion (US$57 billion) in 2000, an increase of 750 percent in 22 years from a small base. (The city's GDP increased further to 10,366 billion or US$132.9 billion in 2006.) The growth should be attributed to restructuring the economy of the city, which has shifted from a manufacturing center to a service and transportation hub. In 1978, the manufacturing industry contributed 77.4 percent to the city's GDP; the share dropped to 47.6 percent in 2000. The service industry, on the contrary, increased from 18.6 percent in 1978 to 50.6 percent in 2000, an increase of 172 percent. In 2006, the share of the service industry remained 50.6 percent and manufacturing was 48.5 percent (see Table I.1 in Chen, introduction, this book).

The composition of the service industry has also changed. In 1978, almost half (45.6 percent) of the tertiary industry was from retail, wholesale, and catering. The real estate industry composed only 0.5 percent of the service sector, and the financing business's share was 13.8 percent. In 2000, the largest share in the tertiary sector was the financing industry (29.7 percent) followed by "others," meaning consulting, tourism, educational, and cultural businesses (24.6 percent). The real estate industry's share increased to 10.9 percent in 2000 (Table I.1 in Chen, introduction). Today, Shanghai has been closely integrated into the world economy and become a key regional financing and trading center in East Asia.

Economic transition should be supported through and reflected in the city's spatial restructuring. With more emphasis given to the service industry, especially the financial business, the city needs an attractive, world-class CBD with office buildings armed with cutting-edge facilities. The increasing domestic "new rich" and foreigners look for better housing and entertainment amenities close to the CBD. Foreign investors seeking joint venture opportunities in Shanghai prefer new factories served by good infrastructure systems and with sufficient space for potential expansion. These locations are available only in ex-urban areas.

However, in 1990, the city's condition was far from attractive. The central area had dense population and many small-scale manufacturing factories, a legacy of the proindustry era. Surrounding the downtown—areas that could be ideal locations for high-end housing—were residential developments for average residents built decades ago when housing was a main form of state welfare. So when the city was striving for an "international center," its spatial structure reflected more of the prereform era rather than the needs of a "globalizing city." It was obvious that Shanghai's space structure had to be reformulated.

Spatial restructuring is aimed to redistribute functions among districts. Before the reforms, each urban district was a small society—each had its own "CBD," industrial zone, and residential quarters, and the functional division among districts was vague. The Shanghai government saw a global city as needing a clear division of functions among districts—a world class CBD with others functioning as "working zones" or "bedrooms" to support the CBD. In an approach reflecting these new economic goals, Shanghai adopted three strategies to restructure its space. First, the city re-created/reinforced the CBD through relocating and redistributing existing residents and factories from the central district to periphery areas to give way to new commercial developments. Second, inner city residential zones were created for elites and foreigners by reducing population density and constructing high-end housing in districts near the CBD. Third, industry parks were built in ex-urban and periphery areas to locate joint ventures and relocate profitable existing factories moved out from the central area. After 10 years, the result of spatial restructuring is evident in Table 8.1.

Among all building types, office building increased the most. From 1978 to 2000, office space increased by 952.2 percent, and an increase of 303.3 percent took place from 1990 to 2000, the period when Shanghai accelerated its engine to be an "international financing and trading center." The rapid increase in the number of office buildings demonstrates the city's economic restructuring toward the service industry. This trend continued in the 2000s. In 2006, total office space reached 131 million square meters, an increase of 440 percent from 2000.[1]

In both of the periods of 1978 to 2000 and 1990 to 2000, plants (factories) increased only by 126 percent and 19.1 percent, respectively; this

TABLE 8.1

Functional Composition of Buildings in Shanghai, 1978, 1980, 1990, and 2000 (in millions of square meters)

	1978	1980	1990	2000	Change 1990–2000	Change 1978–2000
Housing	41.2	44.0	89.0	208.7	134.5%	406.6%
Plants	25.4	26.5	48.2	57.4	19.1%	126.0%
Offices	2.3	3.4	6.0	24.2	303.3%	952.2%
Shops	2.3	2.4	4.0	11.9	197.5%	417.4%

Source: SSB (2001).

category increased the least. Most new factories were actually built before the 1990s when Shanghai started its race to globalize. Factory buildings increased only 9.2 million square meters from 1990 to 2000, or 19.1 percent in ten years. With the increasing injection of foreign direct investment (FDI) into Shanghai since 1990, new factories are basically built for and by joint ventures in the Pudong New Area. Many "old" urban industrial districts, such as Yangpu, experienced little change in manufacturing space, as is discussed later. However, a new phenomenon is the significant increase of factory buildings in the 2000s. Shanghai statistics reveal that factory buildings increased 413 percent from 2000 to 2006. We have reasons to suggest that some leaders tried to keep a balance between service and manufacturing while facing increasing challenges from other Yangtze River Delta manufacturing bases. Most new factories were built in new suburban towns. Shanghai's six new manufacturing bases led by Pudong New Area took a total of 57.8 percent of all factory buildings, whereas Yangpu, Shanghai's traditional manufacturing base, only housed 5.4 percent of all factories in 2006.

Shops increased by 417.4 percent from 1978 to 2000 and 197.5 percent from 1990 to 2000, the second largest increase in all building types. This trend continued in the 2000s, when the amount of shops increased by 292 percent from 2000 to 2006.

Housing is the third rapidly growing category. Housing stock increased by 406.6 percent and 134.5 percent, respectively, in the period of 1978 to 2000 and 1990 to 2000. The city's 2006 statistics indicate that the housing stock doubled from 2000 to 2006 (with a 96 percent increase.) These changes are products of spatial restructuring strategies.

The distribution of spatial restructuring was uneven. The city decided to give development priority and the comprehensive functions to the CBD and new industrial parks at the cost of reducing the importance of traditional industrial districts, a strategy employed by many American cities in the economic restructuring period of the 1970s to 1980s (Brenner and Theodore 2002; Rast 1999). Also like American cases, the policy reflects the switch of Shanghai's development goal to a more service-oriented economic center. We can find more evidence through a comparison of development patterns of the three urban districts from 1985 to 2000.

RESTRUCTURING SPACE AT THE URBAN DISTRICT LEVEL

The three urban districts analyzed in this study are Huangpu, Luwan, and Yangpu. Table 8.2 summarizes statistics on the three districts. The three districts were selected because Huangpu is the CBD, Yangpu is the largest

TABLE 8.2

Profiles of Three Urban Districts, Shanghai, 1985 vs. 2000

	Land (in sq. km)		Population		Administrative Units[c]	
	1985[a]	2000[b]	1985[a]	2000[b]	1985	2000
Huangpu	18.7 (5.3)	12.4 (4.3)	683,700 (9.8)	661,800 (10.5)	n/a	9
Luwan	7.5 (2.2)	8.05 (2.8)	480,000 (6.9)	355,900 (5.7)	n/a	4
Yangpu	53.0 (15.1)	60.7 (21.0)	975,000 (14.0)	1,070,000 (17.2)	n/a	10
Urban Area Total[b] (100%)	351.1	289.4	6,983,000	6,282,400	134	99

Source: SSB (1986, 2001).

Notes: [a]Parenthesized numbers indicate the share of districts in the total of the city's urban districts in 1985. In addition to a large rural area in the city's jurisdiction, there were twelve urban districts in 1985, and the number increased to sixteen in 2000. Most rural areas have been developed and added to the urban area since 1992, and the total urban area increased to 3924.24 square km, with a population of 1,136,820, in 2000. The "urban area" of 2000 refers to the central urban district, which is the "older" urban area consisting of nine of the sixteen urban districts. [b]The 2000 percentage is a district's share in the city's entire "central urban district." [c]Administrative units are urban subdistrict offices (called "street offices" by the Chinese government), which are government bodies at the lowest level in an urban area in China.

old industrial district, and Luwan is in transition from a "general/average" district to assuming a key role in the city's economy. The CBD, a major industrial area, and several "general" districts comprise the main parts of a city's spatial structure. An analysis of the three representative districts can paint a picture of how the spatial structure changes following alterations of the city's development goal. In the Shanghai case, the analysis can shed light on the bottom-up strategies adopted to help the city to become global.

Huangpu, located in the center of the city, was traditionally the CBD and the home of the municipal government. The area managed by the district was the core of the British concession from 1845 to 1940. Many buildings, especially those in the riverfront area known as "The Bund," were headquarters of banks and international corporations established by foreigners in the 1930s. Nanjing Road, the main retail street in the district, was, and still is, the foremost shopping street in China (see Cochran 1999). The economic base of the district consisted of trading and retailing businesses. This position is reflected in the district's building uses.

In 1985, out of a total of 10.65 million square meters of building areas, 45.4 percent (4.84 million) was for "nonresidential uses," including office, commercial, and retail uses. Offices (1.27 million square meters) and shops (0.56 million square meters) accounted for 37.8 percent of the total nonresidential buildings. Office building in Huangpu alone accounted for 29.9 percent of all office space in the city (all data from Shanghai Statistical Bureau [SSB], see Table 8.3).

Luwan is located next to the CBD at the central-south of the city. The district was once the French concession from the 1890s to the 1930s. Shops of luxury goods, especially fashionable clothes and shoes, together with luxury restaurants were featured on the main shopping street, Huaihai Road, in the district. Also, there was a concentration of villa and high-class apartment buildings in the district. In 1985, the areas of both villas (120,000 square meters) and apartment buildings (190,000 square meters), which provide the best quality housing in Shanghai, in Luwan exceeded the sum of that in the two other districts. Retail business formed the foundation of the district's economy. Today, retail is still the main business of the district; for example, 57.5 percent of the district's tax revenue was from retail and catering in 1998 (LDSYC 1999).

Yangpu was developed as the city's main industrial zone in the 1920s, in part because of its location near the Huangpu River, the main waterway of the city. During China's industrialization period of the 1950s to the 1960s, the district received a considerable amount of public

TABLE 8.3A

Comparison of Urban Development in the Three Districts, 1985 vs. 2000 (I) (in millions of square meters)

	Total Building Area		Residential Use		Nonresidential Uses	
	1985	2000	1985	2000	1985	2000
Huangpu	10.65	16.54	5.81	7.55	4.84	8.99
	(9.5)	(8.1)	(9.0)	(6.2)	(7.7)	(10.9)
Luwan	6.72	10.62	3.84	5.88	2.88	4.74
	(5.3)	(5.2)	(6.0)	(4.9)	(4.6)	(5.7)
Yangpu	19.43	36.12	8.62	21.35	10.80	14.78
	(15.2)	(17.7)	(17.1)	(17.7)	(17.1)	(17.9)
Urban Area Total[a] (100%)	127.47	203.49	64.44	120.83	63.04	82.66

Source: SSB (1986, 2001).

Notes: [a]See notes to Table 8.2.

TABLE 8.3B

Comparison of Urban Development in the Three Districts, 1985 vs. 2000 (II) Residential Building Uses (in tens of thousands of square meters)

	Villa		Apartment		Staff Housing		Slum	
	1985	2000	1985	2000	1985	2000	1985	2000
Huangpu	2	1	3	3	194	367	15	4
	(1.5)	(0.6)	(3.2)	(1.5)	(7.1)	(3.8)	(5.3)	(10.8)
Luwan	12	16	19	30	78	342	5	1
	(8.8)	(9.5)	(20)	(15.3)	(2.9)	(3.5)	(1.8)	(2.7)
Yangpu	4	3	1	1	494	1,921	44	12
	(2.9)	(1.8)	(1.1)	(0.5)	(18.1)	(19.7)	(15.7)	(32.4)
Urban Area Total[a] (100%)	136	168	95	196	2,730	9,743	281	37

Source: SSB (1986, 2001).
Notes: [a]See notes to Table 8.2.

TABLE 8.3C

Comparison of Urban Development in the Three Districts, 1985 vs. 2000 (III) Nonresidential Building Uses (in tens of thousands of square meters)

	Plant		Office		Shop	
	1985	2000	1985	2000	1985	2000
Huangpu	106	110	127	423	56	135
	(3.0)	(3.5)	(29.9)	(25.5)	(18.8)	(18.6)
Luwan	160	116	20	154	18	71
	(4.6)	(3.7)	(4.7)	(9.3)	(6.0)	(9.8)
Yangpu	745	935	25	62	34	62
	(21.4)	(29.8)	(5.9)	(3.7)	(11.4)	(8.5)
Urban Area Total[a] (100%)	3485	3138	425	1657	298	726

Source: SSB (1986, 2001).
Notes: [a]See notes to Table 8.2.

investment into state-owned manufacturing factories. Most of this public investment went to the district's heavy industry, which absorbed 93.9 percent of the total amount from 1949 to 1959. As a result, the district was the city's "backbone" for 30 years, especially in the 1950s and 1960s when the district contributed one-fifth of the city's revenue, peaking in 1964 with a share totalling 29.3 percent of the total revenue (YDSYC 1995).

Even in the 1980s when the reform was just beginning, the district still had 14 percent of the city's factories and contributed 26 percent of the city's total industrial output in 1985 (SSB 1986). However, the district's economic status was challenged after the service industry–oriented restructuring in the 1990s.

In order for Shanghai to shift from China's manufacturing and business center to an "international trading, port, and financing center of the twenty-first century," a series of policies have been formulated and implemented.

1. Investing more in infrastructure improvement and beautification projects for the service sector in CBD rather than in manufacturing industry districts.

2. Promoting the service industry in the city's most attractive areas to replace existing manufacturing factories and housing of the average people.

3. Encouraging FDI enterprises in new industrial zones in Pudong and ex-urban areas rather than renewing old manufacturing factories in Yangpu.

4. Transferring central city industrial land to high-end housing and commercial buildings, and relocating factories to industrial campuses in ex-urban areas, especially in Pudong.

5. Reinforcing the CBD position by increasing its population/activity density through adjusting district boundaries.

6. Revising the master plan by changing the development axis from north–south to west–east. Shanghai's main manufacturing factories are located at the north (the steel industry) and the south (the oil refining and chemical industry) but service centers are at the west (Hongqiao) and east (Pudong/Lujiazui), and the revision reveals the shift of the development strategy.

The economic and spatial restructuring have contributed to rapid economic growth, especially in the tertiary industry, and social stratification among districts. After ten years of spatial restructuring, the three districts have experienced considerable differences in urban development pattern and magnitude. Table 8.4 summarizes differences of urban development in Huangpu, Luwan, and Yangpu districts. The differences are measured by changes in population, land, and the amount and use of buildings from 1985 to 2000. The remainder of the chapter takes a separate and more in-depth look at each of the three districts in turn.

TABLE 8.4

Changes in Urban Development in the Three Districts, 1985 vs. 2000

	Huangpu			Luwan			Yangpu		
	1985	2000	Change	1985	2000	Change	1985	2000	Change
Land (sq. km)	18.7	12.4	−33.7%	7.5	8.1	7.3%	53.0	60.7	14.5%
Population	683,700	661,800	−3.3%	480,000	355,900	−25.9%	975,000	1,070,000	9.7%
Population Density (per sq. km)	36,561	53,370	46.0%	64,000	43,938	−31.3%	18,396	17,627	−4.2%
Total Building Area (millions of sq. m)	10.65	16.54	55.3%	6.72	10.62	58.0%	19.43	36.12	85.9%
Building Area per Capita (millions of sq. m)	15.57	24.99	60.5%	14.0	29.8	112.9%	19.93	33.75	69.3%
Residential Use (millions of sq. m)	5.81	7.55	29.9%	3.84	5.88	53.1%	8.62	21.35	148.0%
Residential Use per Capita (sq. m)	8.5	11.4	134.1%	8.0	16.5	106.3%	8.8	19.95	126.7%
Nonresidential Use (millions of sq. m)	4.84	8.99	85.7%	2.88	4.74	64.6%	10.82	14.78	36.6%
Nonresidential Use per Capita (sq. m)	7.1	13.6	91.5%	6.0	13.3	121.7%	11.1	13.8	24.3%
Villa (millions)	2	1	−50.0%	12	16	33.3%	4	3	−25.0%
Apartment (millions)	3	3	0%	19	30	57.9%	1	1	0%
Slum (millions)	15	4	−73.3%	5	1	−80.0%	44	12	−72.7%
Plant (millions)	106	110	3.8%	160	116	−27.5%	745	935	25.5%
Office (millions)	127	423	233.1%	20	154	670.0%	25	62	148.0%
Shop (millions)	56	135	141.1%	18	71	294.4%	34	62	82.4%

Source: SSB (1986, 2001).

Note: Land is in square km, building areas are in millions of square m, and changes are as percentages.

HUANGPU DISTRICT

Huangpu is the CBD of the whole city, so its functions are comprehensive as the city's administrative, service, business, and retail center. Spatial restructuring in Huangpu aims to strengthen its functions and make it ready to be a CBD of an international center.

After boundary adjustment from the middle of the 1990s to 2001 to reach a "better distribution of functions among districts," the land of the district was reduced and the population dropped, but the total building area increased from 1985 to 2000. A smaller land area and fewer people with more buildings means that both population density and building density have increased. Huangpu's population density in 2000 (53,370 persons per square km) is the highest in the three districts. High density is a typical CBD phenomenon in Chinese cities. Areas removed in the adjustment were basically lower-quality residential quarters and land at the east side of the Huangpu River so that the remaining area could be strengthened through adding more high-quality developments of nonresidential uses. Buildings for nonresidential uses increased by 85.7 percent from 1985 to 2000, almost three times the increase of residential uses (29.9 percent) in the same time period. As a result, per capita nonresidential use building area almost doubled (91.5 percent). The amount of office space increased by 233.1 percent, and shops also increased by 141.1 percent in this period. After completing the city-sponsored downtown renewal project of the Nanjing Road Pedestrian Mall, more projects along the Huangpu River have been implemented. Today the district, with a heavy concentration of office and retail developments, looks more like a typical CBD of a city in a developed nation (data from SSB, as provided in Table 8.4, the same for the other districts).

The overall quality of the district has been improved, evidenced by the significant increase of new buildings and the decrease of slum area (73.3 percent in the 15 years). On the other hand, the average residential area of the district is still less than that of the two other districts, partly due to the high housing price in the CBD. The average housing price in Huangpu was 5,800 yuan (US$707) per square meter in 2000, which is the highest among the three districts.

LUWAN DISTRICT

Luwan's new function for the city is threefold: retail center, entertainment center, and provider of high-end housing for elites and foreigners. The district gained some land in the boundary adjustment, but its population dropped by one-quarter from 1985 to 2000. The mechanism of district boundary and population adjustment was to redistribute district functions based on district merits, which itself was a means to strengthen the city's competitiveness as a whole. In the same period, the total building area increased by 58 percent. With fewer people and more space, the district's overall physical environment has been improved. The increase is especially significant for office buildings: total office space in 2000 was 670 percent of that in 1985. The same is true for retail. Per capita non-residential uses increased by 121.7 percent, the highest growth rate among the three districts. These changes demonstrate that the district is becoming a booming retail center or experiencing a "rebirth" of the district's splendid past when it was the number one commercial center for a "high class" clientele in the French concession. Is this a microscopic comeback of the "Paris of the Orient"?

Luwan is also becoming a better but more expensive place to live: good quality housing (new villa and luxury apartment buildings) has increased considerably, whereas slum area (defined as a statistical category and refers to huts and sheds built before the 1949 revolution with no tap water or toilet) has been reduced by 80 percent in the period. The average housing price was 5,700 yuan (US$695) in the district in 2000, which was much more expensive than housing in other urban districts (average less than 5,000 yuan) except the CBD. The shift of the land use, such as the decrease of plant buildings, also reveals the district's new role. Today, the district has become a main attraction to the "new rich" and foreigners for its glamorous restaurants and night life.

YANGPU DISTRICT

In contrast to the Huangpu and Luwan districts, spatial restructuring in Yangpu is much less geared toward the glamour of urban renewal but has a twofold purpose: retaining some of its traditional industrial zone and developing a housing stock for the average Shanghai resident. From 1985 to 2000, Yangpu gained both land and population. Many residents moved in from Huangpu, Luwan, and other central urban districts where the housing price soared with the improvement of housing quality and the appreciation of property values. As a result, Yangpu has become a "bedroom" for the average person; total residential building area increased by 148 percent, but the share of good quality housing decreased (25.0 percent for villa and no change for apartments). The average housing price in Yangpu was 3,000 yuan (US$366) per square meter in 2000, not only lower that that in both Huangpu and Luwan but also one of the two lowest of the central city (supported by evidence in Wu 2002).

Yangpu's share of staff housing, the ex-public housing for ordinary urban residents, was 19.7 percent in 2000. The amount of staff housing in the district alone doubled the sum of that in the two other districts (see Table 8.3b earlier). The overall living conditions have been improved, evidenced by the decrease of slum area and the increase of average residential space. But the amount of slum remaining in Yangpu is still more than the sum of that in the two other districts. Without detailed income data available, the best measurement for people's economic status is their living conditions, including housing type and housing price. With less good quality housing and lower housing price, Yangpu is home to ordinary Shanghai residents.

The district has made efforts to diversify its economic base: whereas industrial buildings increased slightly, office buildings grew significantly from 1985 to 2000. However, the amount of office space is still much less than in either Huangpu or Luwan. Shops have increased as well. But again, the amount of shops is less than that in the two other districts. On the other hand, factories in Yangpu (9,350,000 square meters) are more than the sum of all plants in the two other districts. This reflects the district's manufacturing-oriented economy shaped by the district's past and the legacy of the proindustry era. The district's effort for diversification is evident in new developments in the 2000s. As discussed previously, the district's share of factory buildings dropped to 5.4 percent in 2006, and real estate became the new direction of economic development.

FROM THE BOTTOM UP: FACTORS IN REDISTRIBUTING FUNCTIONS AMONG DISTRICTS

Guided by the new development goals, Shanghai's spatial restructuring follows the redistribution of functions among districts. In the last ten years, some districts were given comprehensive functions whereas others received less attention. What factors did Shanghai's decision makers take into consideration in redistributing district functions? From the analysis of the three districts, we found that a district's geographical location, history, economic base, and local leadership all were influential. These factors affected the restructuring decisions in various ways. The existing economic base usually played an important role, but other factors worked together with the economy factor. For instance, when more service functions were given to a particular district, its location and history as well as the economy may all have been used as reasons. When a decision was actually made based on political considerations, the economic factors were often used at least as an excuse. Internal politics had certain effects, but played only a minor role.

LOCATION

Location matters in urban development and function distribution. Downtown receives more functions and development attention, especially in the post-Fordist era as reported in many cases, such as in Chicago (Brenner and Theodore 2002; Rast 1999). In Shanghai, the Huangpu district—the CBD and the home of the municipal government—is a favorite place of investors and residents. Its functions range from administration to commercial, retail, and residential developments. On the contrary, with a location on the north side of the city with a distance to downtown, Yangpu has limited function and is less attractive to development activities. In the past, due to Yangpu's convenient access to the waterway (both the Huangpu and Yangtze River) and long waterfront/port exposure, Yangpu stood as a manufacturing district for 80-some years. But manufacturing is no longer the major direction in Shanghai's economic transition, and the district's geography becomes a disadvantage. The competition between the city's CBD and its traditional industrial base is typical when it is compared to other "internationalized cities." The real conflict is between "the new economy" and the traditional manufacturing industry, and between the "domestic" and the "global." In all cases reported, the CBD, with its privileged location, is generally the winner.

HISTORY

A district's past may have a considerable impact on its functions and development pattern. Huangpu has been Shanghai's traditional CBD for over 70 years. Luwan was the French concession and a high-end retail center before the 1949 Revolution. Its history has fostered a local culture rooted in the district's relation with Western culture and business. The rebirth of the district as a world-class commercial center has thus received support not only from the government but also from the marketplace and even the district's ordinary residents.

Yuangpu was a manufacturing district since the 1920s, and manufacturing was Shanghai's most important economic base and the largest employment sector until the 1990s. As the number one contributor to Shanghai's revenue, the district generated 9.3 percent of the city's total revenue in 1964 and remained the second contributor (after Huangpu) in 1989 and 1990. But its position has dropped to a much lower rank than Pudong New Area, Huangpu, Jingshan, and Baoshan in recent years, according to interviewers, although no official ranking report is available (interview with Wang, July 2001[2]). The district's past has a strong influence on its economic role in Shanghai.

ECONOMIC BASE

A district's economic base contributes significantly to its functions. Huangpu's economic base has always been financing and retail businesses since it was founded in the 1850s, although its economy was hurt severely after the 1949 Revolution due to the nationalization of banks and other businesses. In the reform era, Huangpu has regained its position as the heart of Shanghai's economy. Even confronting challenges from other districts, especially the Pudong New Area after 1998, it still holds over a quarter (25.5 percent) of the office space and one-fifth (18.6 percent) of the shops of the city's central urban districts (see Table 8.3c earlier).

With less population and limited land, Luwan was economically a "little brother" among urban districts from 1949 to the 1980s. But the district's retail-based economy remained strong even during the socialist period of the 1950s to the 1970s. The reforms provided the district's redevelopment with a new opportunity. Given a well-developed business foundation and less manufacturing, and thus less pollution in the district, it was relatively easier to convert land to commercial and residential uses here than in other industrial districts. Luwan's share of office buildings increased from 4.7 percent of all urban districts in 1985 to 9.3 percent in 2000. The share for shops increased from 6 percent to 9.8 percent in the same period. There is strong evidence that the district's retail/commercial-oriented economy has not only been self-sustained but also strengthened.

Manufacturing industry was and still is Yangpu's main economic base. The district's textile, steel, ship-making, machinery, and other factories contributed 26.5 percent of Shanghai's industry output in 1965 and dropped to 14.6 percent in 1990 (YDSYC 1995). The importance of the district's manufacturing sector to Shanghai's economy was reflected in Yangpu's building use; its share of plants was 21.4 percent of the city's urban districts in 1985. The share increased to 29.8 percent in 2000 as a result of other districts converting more manufacturing land to service and residential uses. However, with the shift of the city's development strategy toward the service industry, many factories are facing the fate of being relocated to planned industrial zones in periphery and ex-urban areas. The shutting down of most of the city's textile industry in the early 1990s laid off 400,000 workers (also see Chen, introduction, this book); the majority of the workers were in Yangpu district, the base of the city's textile industry. Industrial land was then converted to housing and other "profitable" uses. In the process of economic restructuring, the Yangpu district government has tried to keep a balance of manufacturing and service industry. In the 2000 government report, the district director asked for "promoting the development of both manufacturing and service industry" as the goal of the district's Tenth Development Plan (2000–2005) (GYYDC 2000). But the legacy of the proindustry era may still play a role in defining the district's new functions.

LEADERSHIP

Leadership makes a difference in urban development outcomes, with a mayor being a key actor in local urban growth, as many researchers have pointed out (Fitzgerald and Leigh 2002; Logan and Molotch 1987). In China, the jobs and promotion of local government officials depend largely on their relationship with the superior government. Connection to the municipal government is critical to district officials for their careers. Because Huangpu district hosts the municipal government, district leaders have more chances to contact city leaders and build personal connections with officials of the municipal government. Chen Liangyu, the former Party Secretary of Shanghai removed in 2006 (see Chen, introduction, this book), was the Mayor in the early 2000s and the director of Huangpu district in the 1980s. He received favorable promotion in part because of his connection to several ex-mayors, including the ex-President of China Jiang Zhe-ming, who at that time was Mayor. Many ex-leaders of the district now serve in the municipal government, and they are channels to current district officials in accessing the municipal government. Surely those current district officials are potential municipal leaders, and they themselves will be channels to the city government for the district leaders of the next generation.

Many leaders of Luwan district start their career in local government branches, but their connection to the city government is more related to their performance. Fostered by the district's entrepreneurial culture, officials of the district have a reputation of "official entrepreneurs" because they are sensitive to business opportunities. Once a new policy is announced by the central or the municipal government and a policy window is opened, the officials react quickly in identifying and catching development opportunities resulting from the policy. Hang Zheng, the current Shanghai Mayor, was formerly the district director in charge of urban development. Two former deputy mayors, Zhou Yupeng and Zhou Muyiao, also served in Luwan district.

Most leaders of Yangpu came from the domestic manufacturing industry. They are veterans of the manufacturing industry but new to service businesses and urban development. In China, experience is more valuable than education in the manufacturing industry. Many leaders with manufacturing backgrounds thus have relatively less education, which makes them less competitive in seeking promotion in the new "globalizing" economy, which requires higher education and foreign experience. No main figures in the municipal government came from Yangpu in the last 30 years, although Yangpu has the second largest population among all districts (after Pudong).

This situation in turn makes it difficult for district leaders to bring the district's needs to the municipal agenda, which hurts the district in various ways. Although it is hard to link the city's decisions that have been unfavorable to the district directly to Yangpu's lack of participation in municipal decision making, some critical policies have brought negative impacts to the district in the postreform era. In the past, Shanghai practiced an equalitarian policy in which all districts shared their revenue though the city government's redistribution measures. When Yangpu was the big contributor to the city's revenue, it gave much help to other districts. This revenue redistribution policy was removed in the early 1990s, when Yangpu urgently needed funding to update its very old factories; other districts, however, became richer through economic restructuring. Locating more average residents to the district means consuming its limited land and space resources and thus reducing its development of other economic activities, which hurts the district's revenue base. All those policies work against Yangpu. District officials complained in interviews that the district has become a "little brother" due to weak leadership, but none could pinpoint a particular policy that they believed was aimed at hurting the district. Many negative consequences may be side effects to the city's rapid growth, but it is Yangpu that has to pick up the balance of the bill.

The removal of the revenue sharing policy also intensified competition among districts and their leaders. Only when the municipal government intervenes can meaningful cooperation among districts be established. Large infrastructure projects, such as the elevated highway, are usually used and directly managed by the city to mobilize citywide resources and reduce any possible conflicts among districts.

CONCLUSION: SHANGHAI'S WAY OF GLOBALIZING FROM BELOW

Lured by the economic growth opportunity brought by globalization, cities all over the world to strive to be global. The case of Shanghai reveals that economic restructuring following changes of global systems is the main approach practiced in all "successful" cities. The efforts to make an international city always start from the bottom at the district level, especially key districts such as the CBD, or some other submunicipal levels. Economic restructuring is realized by functional redistribution among districts, which in turn is guaranteed through spatial restructuring in districts.

Global capital and cross-national corporations are moving to Shanghai (Chen, introduction, this book). To satisfy the needs of the global forces, Shanghai has mobilized its resources to strengthen its traditional CBD (Huangpu) and create an "expanded CBD" (the Lujiazui zone of the Pudong New Area). In doing so, a huge stock of existing low-quality buildings in the downtown area have been torn down, the bulk of manufacturing factories in the central area have been moved out, and many local residents have been relocated to give way to world-class commercial and residential developments. Other districts have been given different functions: some are "direct" supporters to the CBD, such as Luwan, a retail and residential district for the elites and foreigners who work in the CBD. Others have to be "secondary citizens," such as Yangpu, a district for the average residents and for the retained "old" industry. New factories have been built in ex-urban or periphery suburban areas. Workers of these factories live in housing developments near the factories in periphery areas or in districts such as Yangpu. The restructuring of the spatial structure thus curries favor with the global forces at the cost of social-spatial segregation among local districts.

What factors determine a district's fate? In addition to public policy, location, history, the economic base, and the leadership of a district all contribute to spatial restructuring and functional differentiation of the districts, as seen in the case of Shanghai. As discussed previously, these factors affect the restructuring decisions in various ways and often in an interactive manner. Many factors are "given" (such as the location and the history of a district), and a district's functions are predetermined to a certain extent. Here new policies are of course most critical. One recent example is that the area that used to be one of the poorest neighborhoods in Luwan has become a top-class entertainment and housing attraction called "*Xingtiandi*" ("New Heaven and Earth"). For both political and financial considerations, the project has received support from governments at all levels, including the central government. The Hong Kong–based developer (*Shui-On*) has built a solid coalition with the government and its efforts were rewarded. It seems that poor historical legacy does not necessary mean a hopeless future. Should a prodevelopment coalition come into place, historical inertia can be modified, although it might not be completely reversed by new policies. A coalition of a "growth machine" appears to be the key to a district's fate, with the municipal government the most influential member in this coalition, resembling the power of local government in driving urban growth and renewal in the United States after the 1960s. In another interpretation from a "growth coalition" angle, the coalition in Shanghai involves the advancement of district leaders' political careers, whereas it focuses more on the growth of the built environment in U.S. cities (Ma 2006).

So "to be global" may cost some districts, while bringing opportunities to others, especially the downtown, thus enlarging gaps between the lucky ones and the disadvantaged ones. The uneven distribution of opportunities and costs spurs competition among districts for resources, both material and political. In this sense, leadership matters and creates winners and losers.

We may find similar situations at the national level. Shanghai has been designated as the locus of China's economy and a potential international center largely due to its location, history, economic base, and leadership. It could also be said that while Shanghai has gained opportunities to serve international corporations, some older industrial cities, such as those in northeast China, are struggling for survival, although the situation has been largely changed since 2003, when the current central government was formed. To what extent the new administration can realize its goal of a "harmony society through balanced development" in the globalization era remains to be seen.

NOTES

I would like to thank Xiangming Chen and two reviewers for their suggestions and comments on an earlier draft.

1. Shanghai's administration system has changed many times in the last two decades, especially because of district boundary adjustments and the merging of districts. These changes make it hard to conduct a consistent comparative study over several decades. Today's Huangpu district was the outcome of the merging of (the "old") Huangpu district and what was then Nanshi district in 2001. Therefore, data from the 2000 census (before the main boundary adjustment) are used as the baseline to provide consistency in this study.

2. Interview with K. Wang, Director of Housing Bureau, Yangpu District, Shanghai, July 2001.

REFERENCES

Brecher, J., and T. Costello. 1994. *Global Village or Global Pillage: Economic Reconstruction from the Bottom Up*. Boston: South End Press.

Brenner, N., and N. Theodore. 2002. *Space of Neoliberalism: Urban Restructuring in North America and West Europe*. Malden, Mass.: Blackwell.

Cochran, Sherman, ed. 1999. *Inventing Nanjing Road: Commercial Culture in Shanghai, 1900–1945*. Ithaca, N.Y.: Cornell University Press.

Fitzgerald, J., and N. Leigh. 2002. *Economic Revitalization: Cases and Strategies for City and Suburb*. Thousand Oaks, Calif.: Sage.

GYYDC (General Yearbook of Yangpu District Committee). 2000. *General Yearbook of Yangpu District*. Shanghai: Shanghai People's Press (in Chinese).

Kong, Y. 2001. *Jiedu Shanghai* (Understanding Shanghai). Shanghai: People's Publishing.

LDSYC (Luwan District Statistical Yearbook Committee), 1999. *Luwan District Statistical Yearbook*. Shanghai: Shanghai Statistical Press (in Chinese).

Logan, J. ed. 2001. *The New Chinese City: Globalization and Market Reform*. Malden, Mass.: Blackwell.

Logan, J., Y. Bian, and F. Bian. 1999. "Housing Inequality in Urban China in the 1990s." *International Journal of Urban and Regional Research* 23: 7–25.

Logan, John, and Harvey Molotch. 1987. *Urban Fortunes: Toward a Political Economy of Place*. Berkeley: University of California Press.

Ma, Laurence J.C. 2006. "The State of the Field of Urban China: A Critical Multi-disciplinary Overview of the Literature." *China Information* 20, no. 3: 363–89.

Marcuse, P., and R. van Kempen, eds. 2000. *Globalizing Cities: A New Spatial Order?* Malden, Mass.: Blackwell.

Ranney, D. 2002, *Global Decisions, Local Collisions*. Philadelphia: Temple University Press.

Rast, J. 1999. *Remaking Chicago: The Political Origins of Urban Industrial Change*. DeKalb: Northern Illinois University Press.

SSB (Shanghai Statistical Bureau). 1986–2007. *Shanghai Statistical Yearbook*. Beijing: China Statistics Press.

Wang, Y.P., and Murie, A. 1996. "The Process of Commercialization of Urban Housing in China." *Urban Studies* 33: 971–89.

Wu, F. 2001. "Housing Provision under Globalization: A Case Study of Shanghai." *Environment and Planning A* 33: 1741–64.

———. 2002. "Sociospatial Differentiation in Urban China: Evidence from Shanghai's Real Estate Markets." *Environment and Planning A* 34: 1591–1615.

Wu, W. 1999. "Shanghai." *Cities* 16, no. 3: 207–16.

YDSYC (Yangpu District Statistical Yearbook Committee). 1995. *Yangpu District Statistical Yearbook*. Shanghai: Shanghai Statistical Press (in Chinese).

Yeh, A., and F. Wu. 1996. "The New Land Development Process and Urban Development in Chinese Cities." *International Journal of Urban and Regional Research* 20: 330–53.

Yeung, Y.M., and Y.W. Sung, eds. 1996. *Shanghai: Transformation and Modernization under China's Open Policy*. Hong Kong: Chinese University Press.

Zhang, T. 2002a. "Decentralization, Localization, and the Emergence of a Quasi-Participatory Decision-making Structure in Urban Development in Shanghai." *International Planning Studies* 7, no. 4: 303–23.

———. 2002b. "Urban Development and a Socialist Pro-growth Coalition in Shanghai." *Urban Affairs Review* 37, no. 4: 475–99.

Zhao, M. 1998. *The Reform of Land Use Regulation and Urban Development*. Shanghai: Tongji University Press (in Chinese).

9. DOWNWARD PRESSURE AND UPWARD BUBBLING

Global Influence and Community (Re)Building in Shanghai

Hanlong Lu, Yuan Ren, and Xiangming Chen

PEELING AWAY LAYERED LOCAL SPACES

Following Tingwei Zhang's examination of local transformation in Shanghai at the urban district level, we move a notch down the spatial scale to the community in this chapter, which aims at probing how the structure and meaning of communal life have been directly and indirectly impacted by both the "touch-down" of global forces and the "bottom-up" collective and individual responses. Recent research links the structure and meaning of local communities to the process and impact of globalization by moving away from the classical (and dated) sociological idea of a society and a community as a well-bounded system and replacing it with an alternative perspective on how social and urban life is (re)ordered across time and space within and beyond local and national boundaries (Chen and Sun 2007; Sun and Chen 2005; Wellman 1999). In this new research direction, Marcuse and van Kempen (2000, 2) posed two related questions: "Is there a clearly visible direct impact of globalization on the internal spatial pattern of cities? How (if at all) can the impact of globalization be separated from other macro-societal changes that are linked to globalization and/or parallel it?"

As the direct impact of globalization on city space is reflected through the new disparities across three of Shanghai's urban districts, this impact also should be observable at the smaller scale of local communities, which make up the urban districts. Moreover, as globalization reaches through the urban district to impinge on communities, it can get tangled up with national and local forces, such as economic, administrative, and housing reforms that have already changed communities in important ways. When global or external and domestic or internal forces interact and intersect in community space, they reshape its boundary, composition, and meaning, thus differentiating it into multiple layers, each of which reflects a different interaction of global and local dynamics. In this sense, although the community may appear as the most disaggregated spatial whole for observing globalization's local footprint, its complexity challenges us to take a more nuanced analytical approach. To do so in this chapter, we first discuss the ways and mechanisms by which globalization has exerted influence on local communities in China's cities, particularly in Shanghai. Then we provide an overview of community development in Shanghai, focusing on the broad changes at the community level since the 1980s, followed by an analysis of how community residents perceive both global influence and local changes in terms of their level of satisfaction. Finally, we explore the practical implications of a more autonomous local community, a growing number of nongovernmental organizations (NGO), and more diverse residents for local urban governance in Shanghai.

GLOBALIZATION AND THE LOCAL COMMUNITY IN CHINA AND SHANGHAI

Globalization has inflicted varied influences on different aspects and layers of the Chinese city. There is ample evidence to support the argument that globalization has left the strongest and most visible mark on the Chinese city at the macroeconomic level, which is especially true if we focus on relational measures of foreign investment and trade for major coastal cities such as Shanghai (Chen, introduction, this book). The impact of globalization has also been strongly felt at the mesoeconomic level of urban district, albeit unevenly, in terms of differential growth and restructuring induced by the varied spatial location of foreign investment (Zhang, this book). Global influence on the telecommunications and information sector of Shanghai has been found to be present in both a macrorelational sense and individual-level connectivity (Zhou and Chen, this book). There is abundant evidence on the penetration of globalization into the microcultural domain in terms of local consumer behavior (Sun and Chen, this book). The global–local influence, however, is by no means one-way or direct. On the contrary, it is often reflected and filtered through the local state's overall policies to globalize the city (Wu, this book).

We see the community in Shanghai as a distinctive sociospatial microcosm of transformations that occurred as a combined result of deeply penetrated global influences; state-initiated community reforms; the growing autonomy of nonstate, grass-roots organizations, such as NGO; and the changing composition and identity of community residents. There are two ways to differentiate how these processes and factors interact to bring about community transformations. We could look at the relative weight and varied mechanism of their influence, on one hand, or separate the external vs. internal sources of the influence, on the other. This is difficult due to the lack of both attribute and relational measures across all spatial scales. To circumscribe this constraint, we take a simplified but integrated approach to first identifying some local connections to globalization as capable of exerting external direct and indirect influence on the community and then examining community reforms and rebuilding as powerful internal forces of change that mediate the impact of globalization.

Globalization affects communities of different national and local political contexts differently through varied channels. In the Chinese urban context, globalization has the strongest impact on the local economy of coastal cities through the latter's reception and absorption of foreign direct investment in spatially clustered export-oriented factories, especially in such cities as Shenzhen and Dongguan in South China (Chen 2005). Although this process remade the economic structure and spatial form of these cities, it left a less visible footprint on their local communities because they were much newer and somewhat smaller cities with a rural background and a weaker administrative control in the past. Shanghai is different because its local communities responded to and changed with the growing local impact of globalization in more differentiated ways.

GLOBAL FOOTPRINTS ON LOCAL COMMUNITY SPACES: VARIED AND MUTATED

Globalization didn't accelerate in postreform Shanghai until the development of Pudong began in the early 1990s. As it gained economic strength through the huge influx of foreign direct investment into local industrial parks, globalization spread out and trickled down to a variety of the sociocultural and residential community spaces. Rather than remaking these spaces by replacing their local sustenance and meaning with totally new and alien counterparts, global forces were moderated and integrated by various strong and resilient trappings of local communities. As a result, we witness the simultaneous presence of globalization's striking marks and their altered or adulterated forms and guises at the local community level.

First, globalization helped bring about more differentiated residential spaces in local communities. At the municipal level, the proportion of overseas funds directly flowing into Shanghai's real estate sector rose from 16.1 percent in 2001 to 25.4 percent in 2003, and further increased to 32.6 percent in the first five months of 2004, exerting a strong pressure on the market. The average sales price for residential property in Shanghai has doubled since 1997, with a surge of 26 percent in 2004 to US$784 per square meter (Chen and Sun 2007). This broad market effect aside, some of this localized global real estate capital went into the construction of gated communities, which contain either luxury villas or upscale townhouses for foreign expatriates and wealthy local residents. Tucked behind security cameras, hired guards, and fences or walls, the gated communities, some of which carry exclusive addresses (like a string of the same lucky number such as 8), are part of a global trend toward an elite urban lifestyle characterized by the physical separation from crime, the poor, and other "undesirable" elements (Smets 2005). But the fact that this occurred in Shanghai is highly significant and consequential for community development because it forever ended the dominance of the traditional, state-regulated, and largely undifferentiated residential space. Mixing more global elements with the varied residential space is the growing trend of Shanghai's long-term foreign residents, who are moving out of or bypassing gated communities to settle in mixed neighborhoods with locals. Ronghua Community under the Hongqiao Street Office of Changning District is home to over 4,000 households of foreign nationalities, many of whom see themselves as becoming "indigenous Shanghaiese" and actively participate in community affairs and community-organized Chinese arts, crafts, and cooking classes. This is also partly reflected in the rapid growth of foreigners marrying local Chinese through the 1990s before the trend fluctuated to around 2,500 couples in 2006 (see Figure 9.1), and most of these couples tend to settle in Shanghai for the long haul. A few communities in Shanghai have even included representatives of long-term foreign residents in local governance as members of residential committees. Some foreigners have made genuine efforts to assimilate themselves as local residents by adopting local customs and ways of life, even though they face difficult barriers,

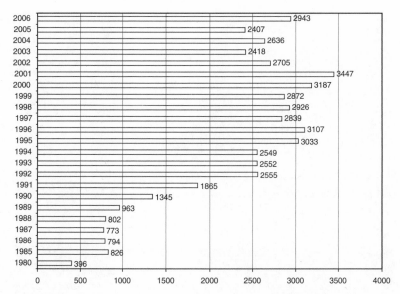

FIGURE 9.1
Chinese-foreign marriages in Shanghai, 1980–2006 (in Number of Couples).
Source: Graphed from *Shanghai Statistical Yearbook* 2007, Table 3.11

such as very different Chinese neighbors and administrative-based community regulations (see next section).

If foreign residents' infiltration of the local residential space represents one kind of global–local interaction in communities, another type involves the creation of new glamorous commercial and entertainment spaces that encroach upon traditional local communities. The most illustrative example is the *Xintiandi* district (meaning "New Heaven and Earth") located near the old French Concession. Designed by an American architect and covering seven acres, *Xintiandi* (see Figure 9.2) takes up a two-block pedestrian street filled with fancy restaurants, cafés, night clubs, and luxury boutiques, including Christian Dior. Although the complex was created as a "festival marketplace" like New York's South Street Seaport and Boston's Quincy Market, its design is a mixture of renovated old buildings and new construction imitating the style of *shikumen* (meaning "stone gate")—the gray brick townhouses built in many of Shanghai's neighborhoods for relatively wealthy families dating back to the early 1900s (Goldberger 2006). This makes *Xintiandi* an architectural fusion of the Western and Chinese and global and local influences. Functionally, *Xintiandi* draws primarily Shanghai yuppies and foreigners (both long-term

FIGURE 9.2
The refurbished Shikumen Lane in Xintiandi, Central Shanghai.
Source: Xiangming Chen

residents and short-term tourists). It's ironic that this "capitalist enclave" was built next door to the state-designated historic house, which hosted the founding and first congress of the Communist Party of China in 1921 with the attendance of Mao Zedong. The irony aside, iconic or signature commercial real estate projects such as *Xintiandi* have brought about drastic transformations to the original communities that they have replaced and also exerted strong spillover effects on existing surrounding communities, pushing up property prices if nothing else (see Wai 2006; Zhang, this book).

As globalization further invaded both the residential and commercial community spaces in Shanghai, it also began to affect community life through other channels as exemplified by the rapid expansion of chain convenience stores in various neighborhoods. Names such as Huanlian, All-Day, and Rowson cropped up around street corners and within alleys. Whereas most of these chains are Chinese companies, they represent the concept of convenience neighborhood shopping embodied by the

American franchising chain of 7-Eleven. In this sense, they reflect an indirect extension of a global or primarily American influence. Collectively, these convenience chains constitute a large share of neighborhood shopping on an everyday basis. On one hand, they replaced the *danwei* (work unit)-run stores associated with the collective housing compounds that had largely disappeared as self-contained residential communities. On the other hand, they offer a greater variety of items and goods of everyday needs than privately (often family)-owned and operated eateries and stands. In the meantime, global fast food chains such as McDonald's and Kentucky Fried Chicken (KFC), which used to locate primarily in and around shopping centers and office buildings, have made some inroads into residential areas, especially near large blocks of newly developed apartment high-rises. Although convenience stores and fast food chains may be global or external in origin, they began to meet some daily needs of busier and more diverse and wealthy local residents, some of whom prefer convenience shopping and eating to buying at more centrally located supermarkets and cooking formal meals at home. They have also helped ameliorate the shortage of shopping facilities in some of the new residential communities (Wu and Li 2002). The local community in Shanghai has indeed become a "micro environment with a global span" (Sassen, this book).

STATE-DIRECTED COMMUNITY REFORM AND REBUILDING: OPEN CHANNELS AND PROTECTIVE SHIELDS

The impact of globalization on the local community in Shanghai would not have been as strong and varied if there were fewer channels for that impact to penetrate down to the grass roots. The community-level influence of global forces would be even more powerful and potentially disrupting if there were fewer or no mechanisms associated with the traditional community system. These serve as protective shields to cushion or moderate external sources and stimuli of change that may be perceived as undesirable or pose actual threats to community stability. This coexistence of change through reform and continuity, through keeping reforms somewhat limited, created both opportunities and constraints for the width and depth of global influences on the local community. State-initiated community reforms, coupled with market-driven community change, are powerful mediators of the global economy-local community nexus. To understand these complex relations across multiple scales, we need to chart the evolving course of community change or transition in response to administrative reforms and market dynamics before and through growing local–global connections.

Prereform Community Administration: All Top-Down and Vertical

During the planned economy era, Chinese urban management was highly centralized and rigid, which meant an almighty government covering all fields of society and economy. City residents were attached to *danwei* (work units) and received necessary living resources and benefits from and through them. This administrative-driven urban management system created huge financial burdens for both the local governments and enterprises. In the wake of, and as part of, market-oriented economic reforms, the state no longer controlled all resources as it did before. The competitive pressure from global economy integration pushed major cities such as Shanghai to take certain measures to adapt to the global market and to increase governmental capacities to compete. As the Shanghai municipal government adopted more rational policies to compete in the global economy, it started to economize on the deployment of resources by gradually shifting from the vertical, top-down administrative structure to a more community- and neighborhood-oriented model of urban governance. This involved reducing the government's welfare outlays and pushing the local community to providing more social service functions, especially taking care of the economic and social needs of a growing number of unemployed workers from financially strapped state-owned enterprises.

As we grapple with the significant implications of these dramatic changes, we must not forget that they stemmed from a very different recent history. It took several years after 1949 for the Chinese Communist government to consolidate an "almighty government" and "command-obedience" pattern of governance characterized by the central government taking full control over all aspects of people's economic and social life. Under this system, governments at various levels owned all enterprises and operated them directly, whereas the latter not only were engaged in economic production but also carried out social functions, including housing provision, health care, and social control. In other words, they were simultaneously economic and social organizations. This system embodied the Communist political ideology and its development strategy of "high employment, low consumption, high enterprise–based welfare." The top-down relationship among the different levels of government, work units, and urban residents in the prereform period is shown in Figure 9.3.

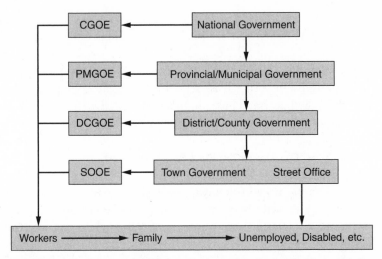

Figure 9.3
The hierarchical government management model before reform.

Under this system, employees in work units owned by higher level governments had higher social status and enjoyed more material resources (Bian 1994; Walder 1986). Even dependent family members and retired employees maintained close relations with their work units, whereas only the unemployed and disabled lived in local communities and were managed by street offices and resident committees. Urban management was based on the *danwei* model under which local communities played hardly any role.

In all urban localities, the vertical "District–Street Office–Resident committee" structure was firmly established and in full operation. The street office was the representative organization of district government, and the resident committee practically became the representative organization of the street office. Street offices and resident committees possessed limited resources and their main function was to help maintain political and social control on behalf of the Party and serve as the agency of local government. There were three kinds of social organizations in local urban areas before the economic reform. First, there were Party and Government Representative Organizations (PGRO), including Street Offices; the Chinese Communist Party Executive Committees (CCPEC); and the Executive Offices of different District Government Departments, such as the Civil Affairs Office, the Citizens' Social Culture Office, the Public Sanitary Office, the Social Security Office, and community hospitals.

Secondly, there were working units in local urban areas that were owned by governments of different levels. Usually, street offices and resident committees had difficulties in managing those enterprises owned by upper level governments in their jurisdictions. Finally, there were some social groups and organizations in local areas, including resident committees, study groups, clubs, and so on. Those units and groups received very limited financial support from street offices and they had hardly any autonomy.

POSTREFORM COMMUNITY RESTRUCTURING:
MORE FROM BELOW THAN ABOVE

Postreform community restructuring followed the reform of state-owned enterprises and turned them into more autonomous market-oriented actors. In the meantime, large numbers of non–state-owed enterprises, including joint ventures and private businesses, were set up and began to absorb the growing number of workers laid off from the state-owned enterprises. As marketization led to more erosion of the "Work Unit Institution" (Cao and Chen 1997; Hua 2000; Liu 2000), enterprises began to reduce some of their social responsibilities, especially the provision of housing and other welfare benefits. This brought about a significant change in the relationships among the state, work units, and urban residents.

Urban residents became less dependent on work units as they developed stronger ties with local communities. Moreover, due to increasing rural–urban migration, greater occupational mobility, growing unemployment, rapid population aging, and rising living standards, citizens' social demands grew stronger, which pressured local communities to take on the social functions that used to be carried out by the state through work units. The local community emerged from a marginal status to become an important arena for social development. No longer an "industrial reserve," as it was during the prereform period, the local community became the primary public space for local citizens.

Recent urban community development emphasizes the strengthening of roles of street offices and resident committees, which could be characterized as "government building up society." Zhu (1998) described it as an "administered community development" process. Since the mid 1990s, in Shanghai and some other Chinese cities a system of "two levels of government and three levels of administration" has been put in place. The cadre administration rank in the street office has been raised, meaning that the municipal and district governments shifted much administrative power to street offices in distributing economic resources and managing public affairs. In 1996, the Shanghai municipal government issued the "Policies for Strengthening Street Offices, Resident Committees, and Community Development." This set of policies was intended to strengthen street offices' power in community service, education, sanitation, social security, social safety, and so forth. For example, the Shanghai government instituted a new approach of returning 1–2 percent of taxes to street offices for community development. Measures such as this began to change the street office from a weak branch of the district government to a sort of grassroots-level governance, fostering the transition from the "Two Levels of Government and Two Levels of Administration" model to the "Two Levels of Government and Three Levels of Administration" model.

Shanghai began to promote the construction of model communities in the late 1980s by launching campaigns, such as constructing spiritual civilization. In 1995, Shanghai launched the campaign of "Development Planning on Community-based Spiritual Civilization Construction," which facilitated the annual award of model communities at both the city and district levels. Civil organizations located within the local community also set community involvement as one of their targets and arranged necessary resources and human capital to advance community development. The use of model community created a grassroots system for dealing with various public affair problems instead of relying on the commands and instructions from various higher-level government agencies.

Nongovernmental organizations (NGO) also emerged as an important force in community building and in meeting residents' social demands. The Luoshan Community Service Center, for example, was allowed by the Social Development Bureau of Pudong New Area to be operated by the YMCA, which returned to Shanghai, after decades of absence since its pre-1949 presence, beginning in 1997. It has since provided high quality and professional service to local citizens. However, social NGO are insufficient in numbers and in capacity-building to become an independently strong force for community development at the present. Some social organizations such as the Labor Union and the Women's Association have very limited public participation and little involvement in community affairs. In addition, most social organizations are highly dependent on governmental support and thus carry the reputation as Government Organized Nongovernment Organizations (GONGO). They not only face the difficulty of obtaining resources outside the government system but also are constant targets for interference from the government about how they should operate.

In sum, the "Shanghai Model" of community reform is characterized by the power transition from higher-level government to the local level as well as the reconstructing of the local administrative system. Restructuring the local administrative system and community development are two closely related but different processes with different orientations. Any blurring of these two processes could burden a local community with governmental tasks and turn it into another local administrative unit, which would lead to an expansion of existing government functions and a deviation from the essence of community building. Whereas the local community gained more autonomy through the variety of reforms mentioned previously, the Communist Party maintains its role in managing local communities. Shanghai's Communist Party Committee took some steps to strengthen its role in local communities in light of local social transition. First, it enhanced its organizational structure in street offices and resident committees in order to keep a leading role in community development. Second, it established party organizations or party branches in the new types of enterprises and social organizations. These efforts reaffirmed the Party's functions in community development and local society and allowed the Party to acquire greater support from local citizens and represent a wider range of social groups' interests (Lu 1994; Ren 2005).

FROM STRUCTURAL DYNAMICS TO ATTITUDINAL REFLECTIONS: AN EXAMINATION OF STATE-MEDIATED AND COMMUNITY-BASED GLOBAL–LOCAL CONNECTIONS

Despite the Party's effort to sustain its influence in local communities, the variety of community reforms and associated growth of nonstate actors such as the NGO converged to reduce the top-down, vertical administrative Party-state control over local communities and thus enhanced the latter's relative autonomy in both governance and resources—a mixed blessing of being less dependent on the municipal government but facing more demand for social services. This process subjects local communities more directly and broadly to global economic and sociocultural influences that pierce through the large open space created by the gradual withdrawal of the central and local states from community governance and affairs. In the meantime, broader economic reforms, especially of the urban housing sector, produced both intended and unintended consequences for local communities. Whereas housing commodification was intended to provide better quality and more varied residential choices, it created the largely unintended outcome of greater residential mobility and diversity that affects all aspects of the local community, such as residents' satisfaction and participation. The housing reform's unintended consequence for the community is complicated by global capital in the real estate sector (see earlier) and local residents' global connections.

Housing Reform and Community Satisfaction

One empirically meaningful way of assessing the impact of both domestic dynamics (e.g., housing reform) and global connections on the community is to examine residents' satisfaction with community. A relative rather than an absolute concept, residential satisfaction varies over time and across contexts (Topçe and Dökmeci 2005). The notion of "community satisfaction" is related to residents' evaluations of physical and social features of their environments such as the objective characteristics of a neighborhood (e.g., its age, appearance, upkeep, and access to resources and services), the demographic and social characteristics of residents (e.g., their age, income, and length of residence), and residents' social ties and subjective definitions of the neighborhood (Fried 1982; Hummon 1990; Kasarda and Janowitz 1974; Tepperman and Wilson 1996). Satisfaction is also strongly influenced by the individual's perception of the condition of the neighborhood housing, of the friendliness of its residents, of its security from criminals, and of the convenience to work and shopping (Baldassare 1982; Lee and Guest 1983).

By diversifying housing types and, especially, allowing private property, housing reforms in the 1980s and the 1990s reshaped the residential environment and thus induced different reactions to, and satisfaction with, its various aspects. As a survey by the Institute of Sociology at Shanghai Academy of Social Sciences in 1998 showed (see Table 9.1), residents in the two types of private housing were more satisfied with their dwelling than residents in the two types of public housing. On the different measures of community life, private housing residents exhibited a higher level of satisfaction than their public housing counterparts. However, because traditionally government-owned housing compounds were more favorably located, their residents were more satisfied with their location. The generally higher level of satisfaction with private housing not only reflects its better community amenities but also indicates that property ownership, as a major private investment, fosters a stronger identification and satisfaction with different aspects of a community.

Even as residents derive satisfaction from private property ownership and the services offered by new community-based organizations, their level of community satisfaction may also depend on how they perceive the continued presence of the traditional resident committee. A survey in Shanghai showed that 38.4 percent of the respondents saw the resident committee's function as "governmental," and 34.9 percent viewed it as "managing

TABLE 9.1

Residents' Evaluation of Housing and Community Life by Property Types, Shanghai, 1998

		Satisfaction with Housing[a]	Community Safety[b]	Community Integration	Environment and Sanitation	Location within the City	Convenience in Daily Life
Private Property through Market Purchase (N = 162)	Mean	2.62	4.52	4.27	3.78	5.10	5.46[c]
	S. D.	0.73	1.22	1.15	1.38	1.15	1.03
Private Property through Preferential Purchase (N = 178)	Mean	2.50	4.78[c]	4.43[c]	4.17[c]	5.06	5.35
	S. D.	0.63	1.25	1.01	1.34	1.04	1.04
Work Unit–Owned Property (N = 35)	Mean	2.74	4.66	4.37	4.09	4.40	5.03
	S. D.	0.66	1.14	1.14	1.38	1.54	1.25
Government-Owned Property (N = 633)	Mean	2.94[c]	4.65	4.26	3.72	5.16[c]	5.42
	S. D.	0.73	1.35	1.18	1.48	1.28	1.21
Overall (N = 1,008)	Mean	2.80	4.65	4.28	3.82	5.11	5.40
	S. D.	0.73	1.30	1.14	1.44	1.23	1.15
Significance of Difference among Types		0.000**	0.35	0.78	0.002*	0.005*	0.203

Notes: $*p < 0.01$. $**p < 0.001$. [a]Satisfaction with housing is measured by a four-point scale, with 1 being "most satisfied" and 4 being "least satisfied." [b]Evaluation of the different aspects of community life is measured by a seven-point scale, with 1 being "least satisfied" and 7 being "most satisfied." [c]Indicates the highest score among different property types.

residents as a government representative," whereas only 13.3 percent regarded the resident committee as an "autonomous local organization."[1] The survey also showed that 50.7 percent of the respondents "did not know the staff members of the resident committee," and 27.5 percent "just knew the names of the resident committee's staff but had no contact with any of them," whereas only 7.7 percent said that they were "very familiar with the resident committee's staff." If the resident committee cannot function as an autonomous organization to serve the interests of local residents but remains an extension of the hierarchical administrative system, it loses its value and credibility as a source of community satisfaction and an important actor in community development.

GLOBAL CONNECTIONS AND COMMUNITY SATISFACTION AND PARTICIPATION

Whereas residents' satisfaction with their communities originates mostly from the immediate and surrounding local environment and their personal characteristics, the expanding global ties of local communities and their residents provide other avenues through which community satisfaction may be obtained. As people reach out and transcend their neighborhood and kinship boxes into the global community, they encounter a variety of interesting and eye-opening experiences through travel and the Internet, which may stimulate more or less satisfaction with their local residential communities. Unfortunately, the literature on community satisfaction has not quite caught up to examining the existence and strength of this relationship.

Data from a survey in Pudong, Shanghai, in 2001 allow us to look into whether there is a relationship between personal global connections[2] (PGC) and local residents' satisfaction with community. As Table 9.2 indicates, community satisfaction varied greatly by the number of PGC, with seven of eleven measures showing stronger between-group differences. For five of the measures, people with the most (or four) PGC had the highest level of satisfaction including neighborhood harmony, convenience in seeing a doctor, and transport convenience. Because PGC are highly correlated with income and residential status in the same data (Chen and Sun 2007; Sun and Chen 2005), one should not be surprised that people with more global connections tend to be wealthy residents in more socioeconomically homogeneous communities with superior health care and private cars. Regarding community safety, air quality, and the ecological environment, people with the most PGC were less satisfied than those without or with few PGC. This suggests that more globally connected

TABLE 9.2

Level of Satisfaction with Community, by Number of Personal Global Connections (PGC),[a] Pudong, Shanghai, 2001

	Zero	One	Two	Three	Four	Average across (1)–(5)	Statistical Significance for Difference among the Groups (Chi-squares)
1 = Extremely Dissatisfied 10 = Extremely Satisfied							
Neighborhood Harmony	7.17	7.00	7.05	6.95	7.55	7.29	52.26*
Convenience in Seeing Doctors	5.78	7.17	6.69	6.92	7.34	7.03	54.97*
Community Safety	7.83	7.36	6.80	6.06	6.52	6.51	66.08**
Public Cultural Facilities	6.39	6.36	5.95	5.71	6.48	6.13	64.67**
Public Stadium and Athletic Facilities	6.44	5.94	5.61	5.63	6.13	5.86	49.30
Community Cultural Activity	6.44	5.44	5.03	5.41	5.97	5.60	56.27**
Residential Participation	6.22	4.81	4.95	5.13	5.82	5.40	68.39**
Community Organizing	7.00	5.22	5.31	5.28	5.70	5.49	63.43**
Housing Management	6.56	6.11	5.61	4.47	5.19	5.08	60.16**
State of the Migrant Population	4.94	4.92	4.28	4.23	4.29	4.27	49.38
Social Service Network	5.59	5.83	5.55	5.26	5.44	5.42	50.71
Air Quality	7.06	6.43	5.94	5.49	5.90	5.84	49.58
Ecological Environment	7.72	6.64	6.21	5.83	6.63	6.34	53.19*
Transport Convenience	7.83	7.39	7.46	7.26	8.06	7.66	53.85*
Volunteer Work	4.72	5.58	5.40	5.54	5.96	5.61	59.16**

Notes: * $p < 0.1$. ** $p < 0.05$. [a]There are four dummy responses (Yes = 1): (1) Have you worked for a foreign company locally? (2) Have you been abroad? (3) Do you have relatives and friends overseas? (4) Do you often surf foreign Web sites? Although responses to these four questions are not mutually exclusive, we choose to use the number, instead of differentiating or weighting the four connections, to emphasize the scope and strength of personal global connectivity.

residents, who are more in tune with the importance of a safe and clean living environment, tended to find the local conditions lacking. Finally, with regard to community-based cultural, organizing, and participatory activities, whereas the level of satisfaction for people with the most PGC was lower than those without PGC, it was higher than people with fewer PGC. We see this as evidence that more globally connected people are more interested in engaging in these activities in their communities and thus are more satisfied with them.

Public participation is critical to any effort in community building. It involves citizens' input in decision-making, volunteer activities of different kinds, and other ways of democratic administration. However, public participation is of a very limited scale in urban China today. According to the "Urbanization, Housing Patterns and Community Development Survey" in Shanghai mentioned previously, only 3.4 percent of the surveyed residents participated in volunteer community activities; 17.2 percent saw community volunteering as very necessary and were willing to participate; 56 percent expressed their willingness to participate in community volunteering if it is well organized; whereas the remaining 23.3 percent had very little interest in community participation. Currently, the local government organizes much of the community-oriented participation. Government uses top-down procedures to recruit volunteers, which blurs the difference between volunteer activity and government organizing. Despite the government's strong hand in pushing community volunteer activities, there is some empirical evidence that community participation may increase as people become more concerned with major domestic and global events, although the overall level of participation is rather low (see Figure 9.4). This could strengthen local residents' interest in linking their community concerns to national and global dynamics and being involved in addressing them in a relational context. It also bodes well for greater bottom-up community participation without government interference or facilitation.

COMMUNITY LOST? REBUILDING THE NEW COMMUNITY

The direct and indirect local impacts of globalization, coupled with the state-driven administrative and housing reforms, has set in motion some powerful forces that began to transform the traditional local community in China's cities. This process has been particularly intense in Shanghai, where global influences penetrated the local urban fabric and reform-generated market dynamics are strong and omnipresent at the grass roots.

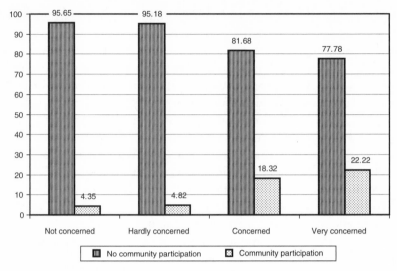

FIGURE 9.4
Percentages of residents who have or have not participated in community affairs, by level of concern for major domestic and global events, Pudong, Shanghai, 2001.
Source: Graphed from the survey (N = 600) conducted by a team of researchers led by Yuan Ren in Pudong, Shanghai in 2001.

The salient features of the traditional community prior to opening and reform, such as strong top-down administrative control, an undifferentiated residential landscape, and homogeneity of residents in discrete neighborhoods, largely disappeared. In their place emerged more local governance initiatives, diverse housing stocks, and more mixed residents within and across neighborhood boundaries (Bray 2006). On balance, the loss of the traditional community appears to be greater than the growth of elements that herald the rough contour of a new community. Nevertheless, the future of this new community looks promising for its own growth and the well-being of its residents, despite and because of the growing range of change-inducing global–local ties and deepening of reforms. Building on earlier analyses, we identify a few bottom-up initiatives and strategies that could foster the development of the new local community in Shanghai.

First of all, to take advantage of the new community spaces created by the entrance of global influences and the departure of a less intrusive state hierarchy, there is the timely opportunity to build the new community by strengthening community-based organizations and groups as important elements of an emerging civil society. Members of these social organizations are likely to share common interests and be willing to work together to promote the public good of the entire community. There also is a need to coordinate and fine-tune the relationship among resident committees, property management companies, and homeowner associations, which have both complementary and conflicting interests vis-à-vis one another (see Chen and Sun 2006). This bottom-up community organizing has the potential to replace the traditional administrative model and reconstitute the local community as a new independent social sphere filled with active public participation and community involvement.

Second, we advocate the community-oriented involvement of social organizations such as the Labor Union, the Youth League, and the Women's Federation. Previously entrenched parts of the work unit system prior to reforms, these organizations now confront the challenge of extending their work, rather than their unduly influence, into local communities. For example, the Labor Union can help stimulate a three-way dialogue among government, new business organizations, and employees. The Youth League could assist community involvement by strengthening the ties between its local branches, young volunteers, and other youth organizations. Shanghai built up a Youth Community Service Network, which promotes long-term and sustainable community involvement through a "Time-Saving Bank" approach. It allows people to save hours in the bank when they perform some social services and to withdraw the saved time when they need other peoples' service. The Women's Federation can explore opportunities to reemploy the large number of laid-off women from closed state-owned enterprises into community-based businesses such as housekeeping and long-term care.

Third, we see the opportunity and need for local resident committees to carve out a more autonomous governing space. Long embedded in the vertical "District–Street Office–Residents Committee" structure, the resident committee has thus far operated with growing but still limited autonomy. In recent years, however, Shanghai took several steps to improve the autonomy of resident committees. One such step involves reconstructing a more equal relationship between the street office and the local resident committee. This helps weaken the vertical pyramid and makes the resident committee a more independent partner in collaborating with the street office. In some local communities in the Pudong New Area, the government employs professional social workers to carry out public affairs. Resident committee members are elected by the residents to provide voluntary services to local residents, whereas street offices employ social workers to carry out tasks for the upper-tier government. This allows resident committees to be free of the heavy burden of governmental tasks and to concentrate on meeting the residents' demands and to better represent local residents' interests. The resident committee therefore tries to be a self-administrative organization.

Another effort is focused on reconstructing the relationship between the resident committee and local residents themselves, from a "manager vs. being managed" relationship toward a "deputy vs. client" relationship. In recent years, democratic elections for local resident committee leaders in Shanghai have been widely held to bring about more openness and accountability in democratic decision-making, democratic administration, and public superintendence. Still another measure adopted in Shanghai is capacity building for the local resident committee. By holding residents' conferences, organizing community councils, setting up subcommittees under the resident committee, and employing professional staff, the resident committee found various ways to augment its operational autonomy.

Finally, we see the benefit from empowering NGO and NPO to become more active players in local community development. Some problems, however, constrain the external environment and internal operation of NGO, including the lack of clear and pertinent legislations, difficulty in registration, strong government intervention, and a serious shortage of human and financial support. It is extremely important to foster a favorable institutional environment for NGO development, which may include promoting more volunteer activities and developing committed and effective community leaders.

All these suggested measures are consistent with the broad trend toward rebuilding local communities from the ground up. Some of them, however, may encounter the established local presence of global influence. The effort to set up resident committees in some gated communities with mostly foreign residents in Shanghai met with resistance, irrespective of the local government's intention and facilitation. On the other hand, the involvement of foreigners in a few resident committees mentioned earlier, rare and symbolic as it may be, is a positive sign of integrating the global into new local communities. The more important and ultimate yardstick for measuring the long-term success of bottom-up community rebuilding is how they can enhance local residents' community satisfaction and participation. The uneven evidence shown earlier points to a long road ahead for building the new local community with satisfied and involved residents in Shanghai.

NOTES

Hanlong Lu would like to thank the Ford Foundation for supporting the Re-Construction of Grassroots Organizations in Urban China: A Research on Chinese Neighborhood Committees project, and the Mumford Center at the State University of New York at Albany for its support of the Urban China Research Network Program that facilitated some of the work reported in this chapter. Xiangming Chen acknowledges the support of a Faculty Scholar Award from the Great Cities Institute of the University of Illinois at Chicago during fall 2005. We thank Jiaming Sun for assisting with data analysis, and two anonymous reviewers for suggestions and comments on earlier drafts.

1. The Urbanization, Housing Patterns, and Community Development Survey was conducted in 2001 and was supported by the Urban China Research Network Program in Mumford Center at the State University of New York at Albany. The survey focused on citizens' community involvement, their attitudes about social participation, their degree of satisfaction with community life, and the factors of urbanization and resident patterns associated with their community activities. The survey was based on a two-level random sampling at the district and residents' committee levels in Shanghai. We sampled twenty communities to conduct household interviews, yielding a final sample of 517.

2. Personal global connections are measured by four dummy variables: (1) having worked for a foreign company locally (1 = yes); (2) having been abroad (1 = yes); (3) having relatives and friends overseas (1 = yes); and (4) often surfing foreign Web sites (1 = yes). These measures were derived from a survey conducted in Pudong, Shanghai, in 2001 by Yuan Ren and Xiangming Chen.

REFERENCES

Baldassare, M. 1982. "The Effects of Neighbourhood Density and Social Control on Resident Satisfaction." *Sociological Quarterly* 23: 95–105.

Bian, Yanjie. 1994. *Work and Inequality in Urban China*. Albany: State University of New York Press.

Bray, David. 2006. "Building 'Community': New Strategies of Governance in Urban China." *Economy and Society* 35, no. 4: 530–49.

Cao, Jinqing, and Zhongya Chen. 1997. *Stepping outside the Ideal Castle: Research on the Work Unit in China* (Zou Chu Lixiang Chengbao: Zhongguo Danwei Xianxiang Yanjiu). Shenzhen, PRC: Haitian Press.

Chen, Xiangming. 2005. *As Borders Bend: Transnational Spaces on the Pacific Rim*. Lanham, Md.: Rowman & Littlefield.

Chen, Xiangming, and Jiaming Sun. 2006. "Sociological Perspectives on Urban China: From Familiar Territories to Complex Terrains." *China Information* 20, no. 3: 519–51.

———. 2007. "Untangling a Global–Local Nexus: Sorting Out Residential Sorting in Shanghai." *Environment and Planning A* 39, no. 10: 2324–45.

Fried, Morton. 1982. "Residential Attachment: Sources of Residential and Community Satisfaction." *Journal of Social Issues* 38: 107–19.

Goldberger, Paul. 2006. "Shanghai Surprise." *The New Yorker* (January 2): 144–45.

Hua, Wei. 1997. "The Shift from Unit Society to Community Society: A 50-Year Transition of Chinese Local Governance" (Danwei Zhi xiang Shequ Zhi de Huigui: Zhongguo Chengshi Jiceng Guanli Tizhi 50 Nian Bianqian). *Strategy and Management* (Zhanlue yu Guanli) 1: 5–10.

Hummon, David Mark. 1990. *Commonplaces: Community Ideology and Identity in American Culture.* Albany: State University of New York Press.

Kasarda, John D., and Morris Janowitz. 1974. "Community Attachment in Mass Society." *American Sociological Review* 39: 328–39.

Lee, Barry A., and Avery M. Guest. 1983. "Determinants of Neighborhood Satisfaction: A Metropolitan-Level Analysis." *Sociological Quarterly* 24: 287–303.

Liu, Jianjun. 2000. *Work Unit China: The Individual, Organization, and Government during Social Reconstruction* (Danwei Zhongguo: Shehui Tiaokong Tixi Chonggou zhong de Geren, Zuzhi he Guojia). Tianjin, PRC: People's Press of Tianjin.

Lu, Hanlong. 1994. "Community Development in Urban China: Problems and Perspectives." In *Social Security in the People's Republic of China,* edited by Renate Krieg and Monika Schädler, 206–16. Hamburg: Institut für Asienkunde.

Marcuse, Peter, and Ronald van Kempen. 2000. "Introduction." In *Globalizing Cities: A New Spatial Order?,* edited by Peter Marcuse and Ronald van Kempen, 1–21. Oxford: Blackwell Publishers.

Ren, Yuan. 2005. "Globalization and Grassroots Practices: Community Development in Contemporary Urban China." In *Globalization and the Chinese City,* edited by Fulong Wu, 292–309. London: Routledge.

Smets, Peer. 2005. "Gated 'Community': Their Lifestyle and Urban Governance." Paper presented at the forty-fifth meeting of the European Regional Science Association, Amesterdam, August 23–27. http://econpapers.repec.org/paper/wiwwiwrsa/ersa05p403.htm.

Sun, Jiaming, and Xiangming Chen. 2005. "Personal Global Connections and New Residential Differentiation in Shanghai." *China: An International Journal* 3, no. 2: 301–19.

Tepperman, Lorne, and Susannah J. Wilson. 1996. *Choices and Chances: Sociology for Everyday Life.* Boulder: Westview Press.

Topçe, Emine Ümran, and Vedia Dökmeci. 2005. "Neighborhood Satisfaction in Modern and Old Neighborhoods in Istanbul." A paper from the European Regional Science Association. http://econpapers.repec.org/paper/wiwwiwrsa/ersa05p512.htm.

Wai, Albert Wing Tai. 2006. "Place Promotion and Iconography in Shanghai's Xintiandi." *Habitat International* 30: 245–60.

Walder, Andrew G. 1986. *Communist Neo-Tranditionalism: Work and Authority in Chinese Industry.* Berkeley: University of California Press.

Wellman, Barry. 1999. *Networks in the Global Village: Life in Contemporary Communities.* Boulder: Westview Press.

Wu, Duo, and Taibin Li. 2002. "The Present Situation and Prospective Development of Shanghai's Urban Communities." In *The New Chinese City: Globalization and Market Reform,* edited by John R. Logan, 22–36. Oxford: Blackwell.

Zhu, Jiangang. 1998. "Power Change in the Local Urban Area: Strong Government and Strong Society" (Chengshi Jiequ de Quanli Bianqian: Qiang Guojia yu Qiang Shehui Moshi), *Strategy and Management* (Zhanlue yu Guanli) 4: 10–12.

10. FAST FOODS AND BRAND CLOTHES IN SHANGHAI

How and Why Do Locals Consume Globally?

Jiaming Sun and Xiangming Chen

SCALING DOWN TO THE INDIVIDUAL

It is only fitting that we undertake an individual-level analysis of Shanghai as closure to the analytical flow of the four preceding chapters. This chapter completes the multiscaled analysis of the transformative impact of globalization on Shanghai in Part II of the book by examining the reactions and adaptations of local residents toward global brand fast foods and clothes. Using individual-level data, this analysis complements the more aggregate approaches of the earlier chapters and thus completes a full range of analytical scales for understanding the multiple dimensions of local transformations in the globalizing city of Shanghai.

If local transformations in Shanghai at the institutional and spatial levels are rather dramatic as shown by the other chapters, behavioral changes in Shanghai consumers may be either more striking or more subtle due to closer global–local interactions in everyday consumption. More than any other domain and scale of analysis in this book, consumer behavior best illustrates the local as the place where global impacts are either received or resisted and where global flows fragment and are transformed into something place-bound and particular (Wilson 1997). By examining local consumer behavior, we intend to demonstrate how global values and trends spread and penetrate locally to invoke varied responses, which contribute to the transformation of local cultural practices and lifestyles.

Globalization generates tendencies toward the widespread standardization of consumer products such as McDonald's (see Ritzer 1996, 2003). However, globally standardized products in local places may not appeal to all consumers. The varied response of local consumers to global brands reflects complex ways in which global forces help bring about adaptations or transformations in local consumer culture and lifestyle. The analysis in this chapter shows that clear intergroup differences in consumer choice of fast foods and brand clothes are accounted for by both demographic and socioeconomic factors, as well as personal global connections. We argue that despite the seemingly universal appeal of global brands, local consumption of global brands varies by individual characteristics, resources, and ties to the outside world.

UNPACKING THE GLOBAL–LOCAL CONSUMPTION NEXUS

Despite the myriad conceptualizations of the global–local relationship such as "glocalization" (Robertson and Khondker 1998), it is not always clear how the global and local are linked and interact in different empirical contexts. According to Robertson and Khondker (1998), globalization refers both to the compression of the world and the intensification of consciousness of the world as a whole. They posit that globalization involves the structuration of a social system at the global level and that there is an intensification of global consciousness in the sense that individuals are increasingly oriented toward the world as a whole. From a cultural perspective, Appadurai (2001) argues that global cultural flows are shaped by the multiplicity of perspectives generated by flows of people, money, ideologies, media technologies, and symbols. Local cultures incorporate global symbols but in ways specific to the local context. There is no pure local culture that is untainted by global culture but rather a variety of local cultures that are increasingly interpenetrated and constantly remade out of elements of global cultural flows (Held 1999).

Focusing on consumption, Ritzer (1996) used *The McDonaldization of Society* (the title of his book) to describe the process by which the principles of the fast food chain become globally influential. Treating McDonald's as the "paradigmatic case" of social regimentation, Ritzer argues that McDonaldization may be an inexorable process as it sweeps through seemingly impervious institutions in different parts of the world. However, firms that produce and market globally, including McDonald's, also develop necessary local connections. That is, their production and selling must be able to stand on local feet, and globally marketable symbols must be "creamed" off local cultures. In this sense, global business not only involves "delocation" but also "relocation" or translocation (Bocock 1993).

In reality, the global–local nexus of consumption is often a two-way street involving both changes in local consumption and local modifications of a global company's standard products and operating procedures. Whereas the key standard elements of the McDonald's system—queuing, self-provisioning, and self-seating—have been accepted by consumers throughout East Asia (Watson 1997), some aspects of this model have been rejected, notably those concerning time and space, particularly in local settings. A mall in one part of the world (London or Hong Kong) may be structured much like that in another location (Chicago or Mexico City, for example), but there will be some differences in their specific contents (Ritzer 2003). In China, consumers have turned their local McDonald's restaurants into leisure centers, after-school clubs, and social and dating places (Yan 2000). The meaning of "fast" has been subverted in these settings, where it refers to the delivery of food, not to its consumption. An interesting case in which the global adapts to the local is that McDonald's introduced rice dishes in Hong Kong to broaden their appeal during the economic downturn, taking business away from some traditional chain rice restaurants (Yu 2002).

In consumption, globalizing and localizing dynamics are not necessarily conflicting but unfold simultaneously, and when they interact, they do so in different ways at different times in different parts of the world. Whereas traditional societies may experience the powerful impact of global consumer culture and thus change quite drastically, they exhibit continuities that may be reflected in mixed values and adaptable behaviors of individual consumers. Our analysis seeks to unpack the global–local consumption nexus through explaining the differential consumption of global brands in Shanghai as a result of both individuals' attributes and global connections.

LOCAL CONSUMPTION OF GLOBAL BRANDS

Consumption mirrors cultural tradition and evolution. McCracken (1990) described consumption as a thoroughly cultural phenomenon and argued that in Western developed societies culture is profoundly connected to and dependent upon consumption. Without consumer activities, modern societies would lose key instruments for the reproduction, representation, and manipulation of their culture. Thus, how we consume and why we consume influences how we construct our everyday lives.

If culture changes with consumption, it does so slowly in a general sense but unevenly across space depending on how consumers react to new and different products. As globalization stretches the boundary of the world market to include more local places, new and different consumer goods of global brands become more available to local consumers. Global brand products became available in many Chinese cities, especially coastal cities such as Shanghai. Take foreign fast foods as an example. The number of Kentucky Fried Chicken (KFC) restaurants in China has already exceeded 1,000 in 230 cities in all provinces and regions except Tibet, whereas McDonald's has been adding about 100 restaurants annually over the last few years with over 960 outlets with over 60,000 employees in approximately 200 Chinese cities today. McDonald's and KFC accounted for 8 percent of the total income of fast food restaurants in China, which stood at US$22 billion in 2003.[1] Shanghai alone hosts over 200 KFC and McDonald's restaurants, which have spread throughout the city and penetrated local residential areas since their early clustering in the downtown and busy commercial areas (Lu, Ren, and Chen, this book). The American fast food chains are betting on the growing purchasing power and open-mindedness of consumers in Shanghai. Since opening its restaurant in Shanghai in 1989, KFC ran its cumulative sales to US$300 million by 1999. Capitalizing on the appeal of its hamburgers, McDonald's in 2004 opened its first McKids retail store in Shanghai (before introducing it in the United States, Western Europe, and Japan) featuring action toys, casual clothing, interactive videos, and books. Hamburgers ranked at the top of preferred fast foods, as shown by a consumer survey in Shanghai, although three traditional Chinese items also had some appeal (see Figure 10.1).

As American fast foods caught on, Shanghai consumers also began to chase global clothing brands, so much so that the city became a shopping haven for such brands as Nike, Pierre Cardin, Puma, Tommy Hilfiger, and Valentino. Although fake clothes with these labels can be bought on the side street in Shanghai for much less than the real thing, the fancy stores on Nanjing Road and Huaihai Road, including the world's busiest H&M women's store carry authentic wear and attract the growing number of affluent local consumers. It appears that the relatively small number of people with high incomes can afford to purchase brand name clothes, whereas more people and families go to McDonald's and

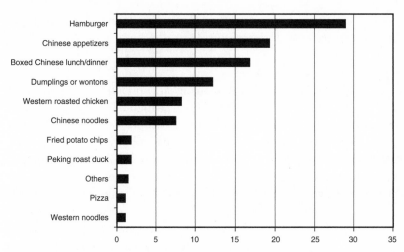

FIGURE 10.1

Type of fast foods preferred by consumers in Shanghai, 1999.
Source: Xue Ling, "Digitized Fast Food," Branded Bulletin (1999, 29).

KFC restaurants as mass consumers. In reality, why people choose to spend money on different global brands such as American fast foods vs. brand name clothes is much more complex. Whereas all global brands have certain general appeal to local consumers, the latter choose the former for a variety of different reasons based on individual characteristics shaped by local contexts. More importantly, when the local context is the rapidly globalizing city of Shanghai, factors reflecting growing global–local connections are likely to come into play in people's decisions on consuming global brands. It behooves us to find out how much personal characteristics and resources vs. global connections matter to the consumption of global brands in Shanghai.

UNDERSTANDING NEW CONSUMPTION IN SHANGHAI

Whereas the previous chapters on Shanghai used more aggregate information consistent with their levels of analysis, this chapter calls for individual-level data with which we can gauge people's behavior toward global brand products as a form of new, global-style consumption. More specifically, we need data and variables to answer two questions: (1) How do local consumers choose global brands and fashions given their basic demographic and socioeconomic characteristics and a shifting cultural context? (2) How are consumers' choices influenced further by other complicating factors, especially personal global connections that reflect local consumers' locations and distance relative to the outside world?

THE SETTING AND DATA

We have collected the needed data in Shanghai's Pudong New Area, whose launch in 1990 marked the beginning of Shanghai's "renaissance" and remarkable rise as a globalizing city. Pudong itself has undergone arguably the most remarkable transformation of any part of any city in the world over the 1990s (see Chen, introduction, this book). In addition to the symbolic aspect of its skyline, Pudong developed different areas for Shanghai's new financial district (dubbed "the Manhattan of China") and high-tech manufacturing. The modern bank and factory buildings aside, a number of McDonald's and KFC restaurants opened up and so did upscale department stores such as Yaohan and other commercial outlets. Residents in Pudong District do not need to cross the Huangpu River to enjoy a McDonald's meal and to find brand-name consumer goods.

The rapid transformation of Pudong from a backwater of Shanghai to the latter's "crown jewel" is reflected in demographic, urbanization, and economic trends and weights, which have translated into a booming consumer market. In 1990, Pudong had 1.3 million people with permanent residence; the number rose to 1.8 million in 2003, accounting for 13.2 percent of Shanghai's total registered population, even though it only occupies 8.4 percent of the city's land area (Shanghai Statistical Bureau 2004). Pudong's GDP as a share of Shanghai's total rose from 8.1 percent in 1990 to 21.9 percent in 2001, when it also accounted for 27.1 percent of the total foreign investment in Shanghai. From 1990 to 2001, agricultural labor in Pudong dropped from 277,000 to 196,000 as the share of agricultural employment in the total labor force declined from 47.7 percent to 21.9 percent (Pudong Social Development Bureau and the Pudong-Fudan Social Development Research Center 2002).

Despite this rapid urbanization in Pudong, in 2001 it administered thirteen towns (*zhen*) that were officially defined rural areas in addition to thirteen wards (*jiedao*) in urban areas. To obtain a representative sample for our study, we employed a three-layered sampling procedure with three steps. First, we selected nine wards and three towns to give more weight to the larger urban population. Second, we selected two neighborhood committees in every ward, one neighborhood committee in two of the three towns bordering or close to the urban wards, and one community in the third and more rural town located farther away from central Pudong. This spatial coverage of our sample gave us a broad spectrum of urban–rural differences, knowing that rural residents in Pudong were exposed to the influence of rapid urbanization and globalization. Third, we randomly selected 25 households in every chosen neighborhood committee for interviews using a questionnaire. We ended up conducting 450 interviews in the urban areas and 150 interviews with officially rural households in the more and less urban towns for a total of 600 cases (see Chen and Sun 2007 for a detailed account of the sampling procedure).

Although the survey yielded fairly rich data, we chose a set of most germane variables to address the topic of this chapter. The two dependent variables are dummy responses to the questions "Have you been to McDonald's or KFC?" (yes = 1) and "Have you bought foreign brand-name clothes?" (yes = 1). The independent variables include the standard demographic and socioeconomic characteristics such as gender, age, residential status, education, and income. To gauge the impact of personal global connections on the consumption of global brand fast foods and clothes, we use responses to these questions: 1) Have you worked for a foreign company locally? (yes = 1), 2) Have you been abroad? (1 = yes); 3) Do you have relatives and friends overseas? (1 = yes); and 4) Do you often surf foreign Web sites? (1 = yes).

IT ALL GOES TOGETHER: WEALTH, YOUTH, FAST FOODS, BRAND-NAME CLOTHES

We begin the analysis by focusing on how two crucial variables— income and age—are related to brand-name consumption in Shanghai. Economics analysis has long established a strong positive relationship between income and consumption (i.e., people with higher income consume more). Whereas this relationship tends to hold for different educational and occupational groups, it varies by demographic factors and life-cycle events. Newly married couples in the United States may save more for a house, whereas young singles tend to spend rather than save (Browning and Lusardi 1996). How does the influence of income and age manifest itself in Shanghai? One may very well expect that in a cosmopolitan city of rising but increasingly differentiated wealth and consumption, people with higher income are likely to spend more. It is also reasonable to expect younger people to be more avid consumers in a more modern and materialistic city. Nevertheless, it is sufficiently intriguing to find out if and how these expectations are borne out by the consumption of global brands, especially in terms of preference against more traditional goods and the various reasons behind brand consumption.

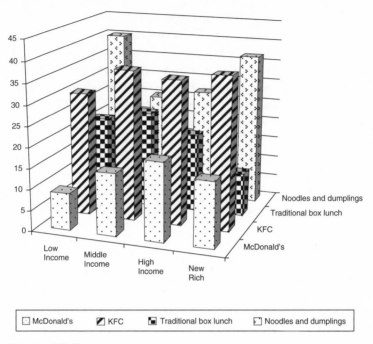

FIGURE 10.2
Percentages of most preferred fast foods for different income categories (in Chinese yuan),
Shanghai, 2001.
Source: Based on analysis of data from a survey conducted by Yuan Ren and Xiangming Chen
in the Pudong New Area, Shanghai in 2001.

Figure 10.2 demonstrates an interesting and somewhat unexpected
association between income and consumption of foreign fast foods vs. traditional Chinese items. First, whereas people with higher income have a
stronger preference for McDonald's, this preference attenuates among the
really wealthy consumers (monthly household income between
US$1,220–6,100). In addition, income is not a strong differentiating factor
among the income groups for preferring KFC. Second, even as American
fast foods are broadly popular, Shanghai consumers maintain some preferences for traditional Chinese foods. In this comparative vein, the differential influence of income becomes clearer. Affordability is clearly a factor in
low-income consumers' strong preference of noodles and dumplings over
McDonald's, as a lunch at the latter for a family of three (two adults and a
child) may cost almost 20 percent of the lower bound of the monthly
income for those in the bottom income group (see Figure 10.2). Although
the so-called new rich also prefer noodles and dumplings to McDonald's, it

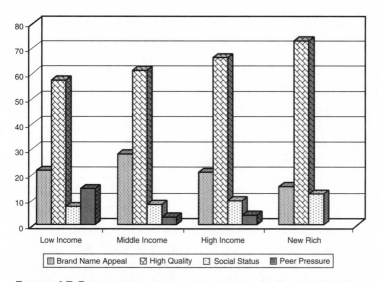

Figure 10.3
Important reasons for wearing foreign brand-name clothes for different household income categories, Shanghai, 2001.
Source: Based on analysis of data from a survey conducted by Yuan Ren and Xiangming Chen in the Pudong New Area, Shanghai in 2001.

may be more a reflection of them liking traditional Chinese fast foods better than American fast food as opposed to their differential prices.

Whereas other factors may underlie the relationship between income and food consumption, the association between income and wearing foreign brand-name clothes is also complicated by how people at different income levels perceive the meaning and value, both functional and symbolic, of foreign brand-name clothes. As Figure 10.3 indicates, people in the four income categories differ quite a bit in the reasons for wearing foreign brand-name clothes. At the low end of the income distribution, people are least concerned about the high quality and social status associated with foreign brand-name clothes but attach most importance to peer pressure in comparison to the other income groups. At the other end, the new rich value both quality and social status most highly while not caring about peer pressure at all. The middle-income group is more similar to the low-income group, whereas the high-income group resembles the new rich. This pattern reveals an interestingly mixed reaction to or perception of foreign brand-name clothes among consumers with growing income differentials. Being more responsive to the appeal of foreign brand-name clothes and the peer pressure for wearing them, people with low and middle incomes appear to place a greater emphasis on one kind of symbolic value or image embodied in foreign brand-name clothes. Whereas this may account for their weak appreciation for the high quality—a functional attribute—of foreign brand-name clothes, it is consistent with their weaker emphasis on the more symbolic social status of foreign brand clothes due to their income. In contrast, once reaching the highest income level, consumers not only care more about the real quality of foreign brand-name clothes than just their brands but also have a strong consciousness of their high social status being marked and reinforced by wearing foreign brand-name clothes.

If there is another variable that interacts with income intensively in affecting consumption, it is the simple demographic variable of age. Age is a particularly important factor in the consumption of foreign products in China as a huge generation of young consumers has come of age in an era of unprecedented openness and prosperity (Davis and Sensenbrenner 2000). As the geographic and cultural vanguard of that opening and prosperity over the last decade, Shanghai is ideal for looking at how age may interact with income in the consumption of foreign brand products.

Figure 10.4 displays the strikingly differential influence on fast-food consumption in conjunction with income. At lower incomes, younger people are much more likely to have either McDonald's or KFC, whereas people of all ages are certain to have the American fast foods beyond the middle-upper income levels. At the lowest end of the income scale, people aged 14–18 are about 2.5 times more likely to have the fast-food experience than the 51+ age group. Two factors may account for this varied age-income profile in fast-food consumption. First, younger people have higher incomes in a cosmopolitan city such as Shanghai because they tend to be better educated. A 1994 survey of young consumers in Shanghai showed that those aged 18–28 with stable jobs earned 1,085 yuan (8 yuan = one U.S. dollar) per month, compared to the average monthly income of 789 yuan for the entire work force (ages 18–59). The human capital acquired by young people makes them more useful to and better paid by employers in China today, whereas the education and experience of older workers has become less useful and translated into lower incomes (Fan 2000). Second, young people simply have a much stronger craving for McDonald's and KFC. This is particularly true of children who grow up in one-child households, numbering about 100 million (or 25 percent of the population under age 25). Strongly attracted to Western consumer goods and heavily spoiled by their parents, young people, teenagers in particular, develop an insatiable demand and even an addiction for cheeseburgers and fried chicken. Whereas age makes a huge difference in fast-food

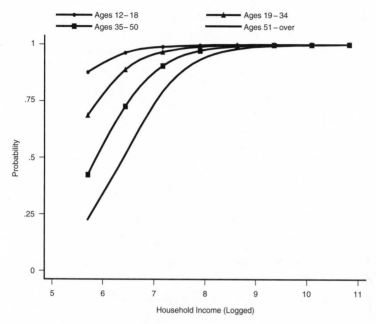

FIGURE 10.4

The probability for having had either McDonalds' or KFC, age groups by household income levels, Shanghai, 2001.

Source: Based on analysis of data from a survey conducted by Yuan Ren and Xiangming Chen in the Pudong New Area, Shanghai in 2001.

consumption, it is important to note that income is a strong interactive factor in that older people are much more likely to have American fast foods as their income rises (see the steep curves for the two oldest age groups).

Compared to fast-food consumption, age and income interact quite differently to influence the purchase of foreign brand-name clothes (see Figure 10.5). Although younger people are more likely to buy foreign brand-name clothes, higher income accelerates the probability of all age groups to do so, with the acceleration being faster for the two oldest age groups. However, the age groups differ most in their likelihood to buy foreign brand clothes across the middle range of the income distribution, whereas this difference largely disappears at the highest income level. The data show that buying foreign brand-name clothes is dependent more consistently on both age and income, whereas age-based difference in fast-food consumption disappears completely across the middle-income threshold. At the same time, it is very clear that when it comes to foreign

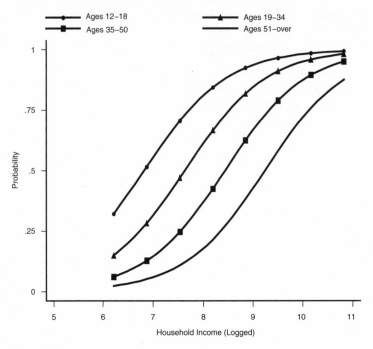

FIGURE 10.5
The probability for having bought foreign brand-name clothes, age groups by household income levels, Shanghai, 2001.
Source: Based on analysis of data from a survey conducted by Yuan Ren and Xiangming Chen in the Pudong New Area, Shanghai in 2001.

brand-name clothes, both youth and wealth are important factors, although age seems to matter even more at the same income level. This is partly reflected by young Muslim women in China of different family income levels wearing Western wedding gowns to identify themselves with images of the West, cosmopolitanness, and development (Gillette 2000).

GLOBAL CONNECTIONS AND
LOCAL CONSUMPTION

Despite their importance, age and income merely carry the basic demographic and economic influence on the consumption of global or foreign brand products. Assuming that the tendency of the young and wealthy in Shanghai to consume American fast foods and foreign brand-name clothes reflects a shift toward a global lifestyle, the next analytical step is to examine if there are global connections that may accelerate this shift. We constructed a measure of global connections based on dichotomous responses to: 1) have been abroad (yes = 1); have relatives and friends overseas (yes = 1); have worked for a foreign company locally (yes = 1); and often surf foreign Web sites (yes = 1)" (see earlier). This measure could be labeled the index of personal global connections (PGC) on a scale of 0–4, with zero indicating no global connections and four denoting a full set of global connections (also used in Lu, Ren, and Chen, this book). Since these global connections may facilitate Shanghai residents' consumption of global products by exposing them to the outside world, we first show whether the presence/absence of PGC is associated with the likelihood of having had fast foods and bought foreign brand-name clothes (see Figure 10.6) before using the index of PGC as an independent variable in the multivariate analysis later.

As Figure 10.6 indicates, the mean differences between people with or without PGC in the consumption of both fast foods and foreign brand-name clothes are striking in both graphic display and statistical terms (both chi-squares are highly statistically significant). Whereas higher percentages of the people with PGC have McDonald's or KFC and buy foreign brand-name clothes, with or without PGC makes a greater difference to having bought foreign brand-name clothes than to having had American fast foods. The large difference between the percentages of people with PGC who have McDonald's or KFC vs. buy foreign brand-name clothes, coupled with the even larger disparity between those without

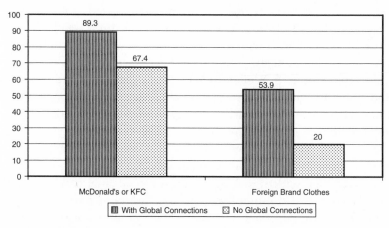

FIGURE 10.6

Percentage differences between people with or without personal global connections for having had McDonald's or KFC vs. bought foreign brand-name clothes, Shanghai, 2001.

Source: Based on analysis of data from a survey conducted by Yuan Ren and Xiangming Chen in the Pudong New Area, Shanghai in 2001.

PGC, confirm the broader spread and massive appeal of fast foods than foreign brand-name clothes in Shanghai. These differences, especially those that may be attributable to PGC, beg to be explored further in multivariate analysis.

LOGISTIC REGRESSION ANALYSIS

To ascertain the independent or potentially intervening influence of PGC on whether one consumes fast foods or foreign brand-name clothes net of demographic and socioeconomic variables beyond age and income, we estimated a paired set of logistic regression models shown in Table 10.1.

As Models 1a and 1b show, having American fast foods or buying foreign brand clothes or not is a function of the same demographic and socioeconomic variables, except gender. Men are less likely than women to have American fast foods, whereas they do not differ in their likelihood of buying foreign brand-name clothes. Younger people and people with higher education and household income are much more likely to have either McDonald's or KFC and buy foreign brand clothes. Whereas people aged 19–34 are almost nine times more likely than those aged 51 and over to have McDonald's or KFC, it is more striking that everyone in the youngest age group has had American fast foods, forcing that category to drop out of the logistic model. Only education has a slightly different effect on fast foods vs. brand clothes because only people in the highest educational category have a stronger tendency to buy foreign brand-name clothes. It is clear that besides the fully expected strong effect of age, both economic and human resources are important predictors of globally oriented consumer behaviors represented by eating American fast foods and wearing foreign brand-name clothes.

To explore other possible factors that may facilitate the pursuit of fast foods and foreign brand clothes, we included an ordinal-type measure of residential positions[2] in Models 2a and 2b while holding the other variables constant. People in three of the four urban residential positions are not more likely than rural residents to have McDonald's and KFC, whereas everyone living in luxurious apartments and villas has been to the American fast food outlets, making the highest residential rank a perfect predictor of fast food consumption (and also making it drop out of the model). Controlling for residential status, however, does not weaken the effects of gender, age, household income, and education on the likelihood of eating American fast foods. Whereas people in new residential villages and old urban settlements are slightly more likely than rural residents to buy foreign brand clothes, those at the top of the residential hierarchy are

TABLE 10.1

Odds Ratios from Logistic Regression Models Predicting the Consumption of Food at McDonald's or KFC vs. the Purchasing of Foreign Brand-name Clothes, Shanghai, 2001

	Model 1a	Model 1b	Model 2a	Model 2b	Model 3a	Model 3b
	Having Eaten at McDonald's or KFC (yes = 1)	Having Purchased Foreign Brand-name Clothes (yes = 1)	Having Eaten at McDonald's or KFC (yes = 1)	Having Purchased Foreign Brand-name Clothes (yes = 1)	Having Eaten at McDonald's or KFC (yes = 1)	Having Purchased Foreign Brand-name Clothes (yes = 1)
Gender (male = 1)	0.56*	0.97	0.55*	0.99	0.53*	0.93
	(−2.19)	(−0.17)	(−2.23)	(−0.05)	(−2.37)	(−0.32)
Ages 12–18[a]	—	20.40**	—	20.93**	—	19.32**
		(7.12)		(7.19)		(6.88)
Ages 19–34[a]	8.89**	6.56**	8.77**	6.82**	8.24**	6.38**
	(5.17)	(6.50)	(5.10)	(6.41)	(4.90)	(6.02)
Ages 35–50[a]	3.22**	3.28**	3.18**	3.11**	3.21**	3.24**
	(4.26)	(4.22)	(4.21)	(3.91)	(4.22)	(3.95)
Household Monthly Income (Logged)	5.49**	3.75**	5.33**	2.99**	4.80**	2.38**
	(6.52)	(6.84)	(6.29)	(5.34)	(5.76)	(4.08)
Vocational School and Community College[b]	3.14**	0.91	3.18**	0.94	3.12**	0.89
	(3.03)	(−0.36)	(3.05)	(−0.25)	(2.98)	(−0.43)
University and Postgraduate Study[b]	5.81**	2.01*	5.34**	1.71	3.89*	1.19
	(2.75)	(2.33)	(2.60)	(1.71)	(2.05)	(0.53)
New Residential Villages[c]			0.96	1.92*	0.90	1.73
			(−0.13)	(2.08)	(−0.31)	(1.72)
Old Urban Settlements[c]			1.10	2.56*	1.01	2.30*
			(0.19)	(2.27)	(0.01)	(1.99)

(Continues)

TABLE 10.1

(Continued)

	Model 1a	Model 1b	Model 2a	Model 2b	Model 3a	Model 3b
	Having Eaten at McDonald's or KFC (yes = 1)	Having Purchased Foreign Brand-name Clothes (yes = 1)	Having Eaten at McDonald's or KFC (yes = 1)	Having Purchased Foreign Brand-name Clothes (yes = 1)	Having Eaten at McDonald's or KFC (yes = 1)	Having Purchased Foreign Brand-name Clothes (yes = 1)
New Commercial Housing Complexes			1.35 (0.37)	1.36 (0.61)	1.28 (0.30)	1.02 (0.04)
Luxury Apartments and Villas[c]			—	28.49** (3.02)	—	20.74** (2.75)
Index of Personal Global Connections					1.02* (2.03)	1.02** (4.17)
Number of Cases	554	601	517	601	517	601
-2 Log-Likelihood	-197.03	-304.00	-196.46	-294.24	-194.21	-285.12
Degrees of Freedom	6	7	9	10	10	11

Source: Based on analysis of data from a survey conducted by Yuan Ren in the Pudong New Area, Shanghai, in 2001.

Notes: Absolute values of z statistics are in parentheses. *Significant at 5%. **Significant at 1%. [a]The 51+ age group is omitted. For models predicting "having eaten at McDonald's or KFC," all people in the youngest age group of 12–18 ($N = 47$) and those living in luxury apartments and villas ($N = 37$) chose 1 and were dropped by the statistical software (STATA) for having no variation in the dependent variable, resulting in a shortage of 83 cases from a total N of 600. [b]People educated to a senior high school level or below are omitted as the reference category. [c]People in agricultural villages and town centers are omitted as the reference category.

twenty-eight times more likely to do so relative to rural residents. Despite this strong effect, age and household income remain powerful predictors of buying foreign brand clothes, whereas the weak effect of education is crowded out of Model 2b.

Although we established the likelihood of consuming global goods being differentially dependent on such demographic and socioeconomic characteristics of gender, age, income, education, and residential status, we were more intrigued by the possibility that this also is facilitated by the strength of local consumers' ties to the outside world. We explored this with Models 3a and 3b, which include the index of PGC while holding all the other variables constant. The models indicate that people with more or stronger PGC are more likely to have McDonald's or KFC and buy foreign brand-name clothes, even though the effect is stronger on foreign brand-name clothes. This provides corroboration for the earlier descriptive statistic on the greater dependence of buying foreign brand-name clothes on PGC (see Figure 10.6). Taking PGC into account attenuates effects of education and residential areas on having fast foods and buying foreign brand-name clothes, albeit to different degrees, whereas age and household income sustain their strong effects on both dependent variables, with gender maintaining its influence on having fast foods.

DISCUSSION: FROM YOUTH AND WEALTH TO PERSONAL CONNECTIONS TO GLOBAL CONSUMPTION

The overall aim of the analysis in this chapter is to identify and estimate the relative effects of the attributes (demographic characteristics and human and economic resources) of local residents in Shanghai and their global connections on consuming American fast foods and foreign brand-name clothes. Regarding the attribute variables, whereas female and most educated consumers are slightly more likely to go to McDonald's and KFC, age and income are much stronger predictors of consuming both American fast foods and foreign brand-name clothes. Given that American fast foods in China are comparably priced as in the United States or elsewhere, with a big Mac costing as much as one quarter of the daily household income (about 100 yuan) in our sample, only the relatively wealthy can afford to enjoy it, or enjoy it more frequently. This is clearly confirmed by the finding that 100 percent of all those living in luxury apartments and villas, a clear indicator of local residents' wealth, have had American fast foods.

Just as growing wealth whets people's desire for American fast foods, youth are another powerful driver of the widespread popularity of

McDonald's and KFC in China's big cities where one in five children under eighteen suffer from obesity associated with frequently eating cheeseburgers and fried chicken. They became the majority of patients in China's fat reduction clinics and hospitals, which did not exist until 1992.[3] As they line up in McDonald's and KFC outlets in Shanghai, young people are also more enthusiastic about chasing foreign fashions. And teenagers stand out because they are a great deal more likely than any of the age groups to buy foreign brand-name clothes (see Table 10.1).

Important as they may be in predicting the consumption of American fast foods and foreign brand-name clothes, age and income still make room for personal global connections (PGC) to contribute to the explanation of globally oriented consumption. Although this relationship may be expected, it reveals a set of functional and symbolic mechanisms that transmit the broad influence of economic and cultural globalization to the local consumption of global products. Working for a foreign company not only gives one a high salary and makes American fast foods and foreign brand clothes affordable but also exposes one to a peer-pressured "global" lifestyle characterized by white-collar young professionals lunching at McDonald's and wearing brand-name clothes. In more symbolic ways, going abroad and surfing foreign Web sites stimulate and reinforce a desire and orientation toward consuming American fast foods and foreign brand clothes by providing direct or indirect contact with and information on such products. Since one's choice of goods and services indeed makes a statement about who one is and about the types of people with whom one desires to identify (Solomon 1996), stronger PGC make it easier and more "natural" for local consumers to identify with the consumption of global products as a lifestyle.

However, consumer values and behaviors are heavily shaped by traditional cultures, which have deep historical roots and a resilient hold on social institutions and practices. Traditional cultures may both filter out and cushion against the very strong force of accelerated globalization in Shanghai or other traditional societies. They maintain these functions through the sustaining power of such institutions as the family, which remains strong in China. The Shanghai Values Change Survey in the early 1990s showed that people who chose "very important" and "important" in responding to "Family is an important element in their life" accounted for 90.7 percent of the total responses (Sun 1997). This may help explain why a familial outing at a McDonald's is considered an important activity. The persistence of traditional practices and lifestyle is also reflected in older people's weaker preference for American fast foods. Nevertheless, we have uncovered strong evidence on a clear shift of high-income consumers toward global brand-name products, albeit for different reasons, such as quality vs. social status. This illustrates a mixed relationship between the materialistic and symbolic aspects of consuming foreign products in an indigenous context.

In completing a series of analyses of local transformations in Shanghai with a focus on consumer behavior, we look back and forward at a visible path of change in a rapidly globalizing city that shows the crossed marks of globalization and evolution of a modern lifestyle. Fashion is now becoming increasingly important to urban residents. As a 2006 survey[4] indicated, more than 40 percent of China's city dwellers think fashion is an important part of their life and are willing to spend more to become fashionable, whereas more than 20 percent of the people surveyed have saved for a while to buy luxury goods. People at different income levels are willing to pay for something beyond their income level. For example, those with comparatively lower incomes, such as fresh graduates and young students, allocate more than one-third of their expenditures on fashion consumption, far more than senior white-collar workers. The same survey also found that urban residents are attaching more importance to individual expression; 74.5 percent of urban residents hope their clothes, accessories, and so on are different from others and reflect their personal tastes.

If the pursuit of fashion beyond one's means reflects a crossover of modern and global lifestyles, Chinese's wealthy urban residents also become more individualistic as they chase and accumulate more material wealth. These complex processes challenge us to disentangle the broader and deeper local or internal conditions from global or external forces that jointly induce individualistic vs. materialistic values and behaviors. Shanghai, as China's most modernizing and globalizing metropolis, will continue to provide us with an excellent context for meeting this analytical challenge.

NOTES

Data used in this chapter came from a 2001 survey supported by a CCK Foundation grant to Xiangming Chen. In drafting this chapter, Xiangming Chen benefited from a Faculty Scholar Award from the Great Cities Institute of the University of Illinois at Chicago during fall 2005, and Jiaming Sun was supported by a Dean's Scholar Award from the Graduate College of the University of Illinois at Chicago during 2004–5. We thank two anonymous reviewers for suggestions and comments on earlier drafts.

1. "KFC and McDonald's—A Model of Blended Culture," *China Daily*, June 1, 2004, http://www.chinadaily.com.cn/english/doc/2004-06/01/content_335488.htm.

2. From the survey data, we were able to identify six residential areas or types: (1) agricultural villages, (2) town centers, (3) new residential villages, (4) old urban settlements, (5) new commercial housing complexes, and (6) luxury apartments and villas. In a different paper (Sun and Chen 2005), we treated these as an ordinal scale of residential stratification by assigning values of 1 (low) to 6 (high) throughout the range from rural areas to luxury apartments and villas. We later (Chen and Sun 2007) modeled a different category of these residential areas as an outcome variable via multinomial logistic regression.

3. According to one report (Chandler 2004), a couple of teenagers at a weight-reduction facility boasted about having been able to knock down up to four family-sized buckets of KFC and received a daily regimen of acupuncture, exercise, and healthy food.

4. The survey of Chinese urban residents was conducted by Horizon Research Consultancy Group, as reported in *People's Daily* online, June 27, 2007, reprinted on the Asian Development Bank Institute (ADBI) Web site at http://www.adbi.org/e-newsline/index.html.

REFERENCES

Appadurai, Arjun. 2001. "Grassroots Globalization and the Research Imagination." In *Globalization,* edited by Arjun Appadurai, 1–21. Durham, N.C.: Duke University Press.

Bocock, Robert. 1993. *Consumption.* London: Routledge.

Browning, Martin, and Annamaria Lusardi. 1996. "Household Saving: Micro Theories and Micro Facts." *Journal of Economic Literature* 34, no. 4: 1797–1855.

Chandler, Clay. 2004. "Little Emperors." *Fortune* 105, no. 7: 138–48.

Chen, Xiangming, and Jiaming Sun. 2007. "Untangling a Global–Local Nexus: Sorting Out Residential Sorting in Shanghai." *Environment and Planning A* 39, no. 10: 2324–45.

Davis, Deborah, and Julia S. Sensenbrenner. 2000. "Commercializing Childhood: Parental Purchases for Shanghai's Only Child." In *The Consumer Revolution in Urban China,* edited by Deborah S. Davis, 54–79. Berkeley: University of California Press.

Fan, Chengze Simon. 2000. "Economic Development and the Changing Pattern of Consumption in Urban China." In *Consumption in Asia: Lifestyles and Identities,* edited by Chua Beng-Huat, 82–97. London and New York: Routledge.

Gillette, Maris Boyd. 2000. *Between Mecca and Beijing: Modernization and Consumption among Urban Chinese Muslims.* Stanford, Calif.: Stanford University Press.

Held, David. 1999. *Global Transformations: Politics, Economics and Culture.* Stanford, Calif.: Stanford University Press.

McCracken, Grant. 1990. *Culture and Consumption.* Bloomington: Indiana University Press.

Pudong Social Development Bureau and Pudong-Fudan Social Development Research Center. 2002. *Social Development Report of Shanghai Pudong New Area*. Shanghai: People's Press of Shanghai.

Ritzer, George. 1996. *The McDonaldization of Society*. Thousand Oaks, Calif.: Pine Forge Press.

———. 2003. *The Globalization of Nothing*. Thousand Oaks, Calif.: Pine Forge Press.

Robertson, Roland, and Habib Haque Khondker. 1998. "Discourses of Globalization: Preliminary Considerations." *International Sociology* 13, no. 1: 25–40.

Shanghai Statistical Bureau. 2004. *Shanghai Statistical Yearbook 2004*. Beijing: State Statistics Press.

Solomon, Michael R. 1996. *Consumer Behavior*. London: Prentice-Hall International.

Sun, Jiaming. 1997. *Generational Gaps: The Background of Transition Period 1990–1994*. Shanghai: Shanghai People Press.

Sun, Jiaming, and Xiangming Chen. 2005. "Personal Global Connections and New Residential Differentiation in Shanghai." *China: An International Journal* 3, no. 2: 301–19.

Watson, James L. 1997. *Golden Arches East: McDonald's in East Asia*. Stanford, Calif.: Stanford University Press.

Wilson, David. 1997. *Globalization and the Changing U.S. City*. Thousand Oaks, Calif.: Sage.

Yan, Yunxiang. 2000. "Of Hamburgers and Social Space: Consuming McDonald's in Beijing." In *The Consumer Revolution in Urban China,* edited by Deborah Davis, 201–25. Berkeley: University of California Press.

Yu, Verna. 2002. "McDonald's Sets Its Sights on Rivals in Hong Kong." *Arlington Heights Daily Herald* (August 20): 1.

CONCLUSION

SHANGHAI AS A NEW GLOBAL(IZING) CITY

LESSONS FOR AND FROM SHANGHAI

Xiangming Chen and Anthony M. Orum

WHY SHANGHAI?

The rapid rise of Shanghai as a global(izing) city is unprecedented. If the world were not aware of Shanghai's rising global importance, it received a wake-up call from the shock waves unleashed by the Shanghai Stock Exchange's plunge on February 27, 2007. The city of Chicago, which had launched an aggressive bid to host the 2016 Summer Olympics, chose Shanghai to set up its first overseas development office in February 2007. The city of Mumbai (Bombay)—the heart of India's growing economic power—has fancied and fashioned itself to become "like Shanghai". These and other recent events not only draw continuing press coverage to Shanghai but also prompt urban scholars to inquire about the essence of the "Shanghai model" that is worthy of serving as a lesson for other cities.

This book has furnished a deeper understanding of the ways that Shanghai has become transformed by the forces both of the global economy and state power in the two most recent decades. Our central focus yields two analytical benefits that other accounts cannot provide. One is an integrated understanding of the distinctive features of Shanghai as a Chinese globalizing city and the powerful forces that have shaped its developmental trajectory. The second is a greater theoretical understanding that can be achieved by looking at Shanghai in depth and in a comparative context. In this conclusion, we highlight four broad themes from the preceding chapters and beyond that together not only yield a coherent picture of global city development, especially in Asia, but, we believe, also constitute the ground for new thinking and empirical research on globalization and global cities more generally.

BRINGING HISTORY BACK IN; PATH DEPENDENCY IS NOT OUT

First of all, the book points to the largely missing historical element in global city research and the looming shadow of history in fully understanding Shanghai as a globalizing city (see Chen, introduction; Wu, this book). Saskia Sassen (this book) suggests that although most of the global cities today were once world cities that tended to exist much earlier in Asia and European colonial centers than in the West, some global cities are not world cities of the past. This implies that world cities have been around longer than the global cities in industrialized countries today. However, more formerly world cities of developing countries could become global cities as the global economy expands. Therefore, a relatively narrow focus on global cities today would leave some historical analysis out, thus missing the temporal trajectory of a global city and the knowledge of whether and how different histories help make different global cities over time.

Detailed historical analysis of cities teaches us that cities, like states, may possess different historical trajectories from one another. Once a city takes root and begins to travel along a specific path of development, it will be difficult for it to change course. Why? In part, it is because cities develop their own specific histories and narratives about themselves, tales that help constitute the city, how it grew, and its unique and defining characteristics. The historical trajectory also lies in the creation of the mix and type of the industrial base of a city: formerly successful older industrial cities, such as Manchester, England, or Pittsburgh, Pennsylvania, find it hard to replicate that success because of an aging population and the now-empty manufacturing relics of an earlier era. These sorts of factors— the nature of the economic infrastructure as well as the local culture—are imperatives that constitute the city, as a city, and, in so doing, they set it on a course for its future development.

In light of the global city perspective (Sassen), the question arises whether the forces of globalization are so strong as to completely "flatten the world," in Thomas Friedman's (2005) catchy phrase, or, from another angle, to override the historical forces and the trajectory on which a city has been set. Dedicated advocates for the globalization thesis seem to believe that the forces of the economy are so powerful that they will obliterate the history of specific cities and thereby substantially alter the historical trajectories. But such a conclusion is premature. The truly powerful forces of globalization have only been with us for a relatively short time, and no one knows for certain what long-term effects they will have. One does not know, for example, how the particular cultural and political elements of a city are apt to modify and temper the impact of global forces. Presumably not all cities will become global cities: some will and many will not. One might therefore ask: Is it possible that those that have become, or will become, global cities, possess a different historical trajectory than those that do not?

In studying Shanghai as a globalizing city, a historical perspective is particularly valuable for showing a strong, albeit ironic, connection between Shanghai's past and present and whether new opportunities in a different era may allow the city to free itself from past political and economic constraints or to benefit from former strengths (see Wasserstrom 2008). Shanghai had reached the status of today's top-tier global city by the 1920s when it was mentioned in the same breath as New York and London and known as the "Paris of the Orient and New York of Asia" (see Chen, introduction, this book). Shanghai ranked as the world's sixth largest city behind London, New York, Tokyo, Berlin, and Chicago in this order. More importantly, it had become by far the most dominant financial, industrial, shipping, and cosmopolitan center in China.

By 1936, Shanghai had half of the number of banks, money stores, and trust companies, both foreign and domestically owned, in China. By 1933, Shanghai accounted for more than half of China's total industrial output. From 1986 to around 1930, Shanghai consistently handled about half of China's foreign trade, and it absorbed 34.3 percent of China's total foreign investment in 1931. During 1902–1904, Shanghai accounted for 69 percent of the 529 Western books translated into Chinese in China (Qi and Xiao 2005). In effect, Shanghai was dominant then because the rest of China was so underdeveloped. Today Shanghai's weight in China's economy is much smaller, accounting for only 5.4 percent of China's GDP, 9.5 percent of China's foreign direct investment, and 23.6 percent of China's total trade in 2003 (Qi and Xiao 2005).

In light of the distinction between the world and global city (Sassen, this book) and Shanghai's historical status, Shanghai was clearly a legitimate world city around 1930, and its quest to become a global city in the late twentieth century is, in a way, a reprisal of its past glory that began and evolved as a market town and cotton production center over several centuries (Johnson 1995). Despite drawing the most attention among all Chinese cities from historians of urban China, Shanghai's recent rise from its storied past confronts the double or opposite pull of path dependency on becoming a global city in the future.

On the one hand, Shanghai was remade into an overwhelmingly industrial city by rigid socialist central planning with emphasis on production rather than consumption and China's international isolation from 1949 to 1980. Although the textile industry was dominant, the broader industrial expansion in Shanghai over four decades created an entrenched manufacturing base, which accounted for two-thirds of the city's GDP by 1990 (see Table I.1 in Chen, introduction). This entrenched manufacturing economy has shifted since the early 1990s as a result of government downsizing older and inefficient industries and promoting services, which grew rapidly and contributed to half of the GDP by 2003. It thus appears that state power can loosen the severe constraint of path dependency in reshaping the economic composition of Shanghai and thus (re)turning it "back to the future" into a global city of multiple functions in finance, shipping, and trade. But path dependency carries a heavy inertia. Shanghai's service sector's share of GDP is far from the 70–85 percent range of such global cities as New York, London, Tokyo, and Hong Kong. At the current pace of growth, Shanghai's service sector gains 0.5 percent of its share in the municipal GDP annually and will reach only 58 percent of GDP by 2015 (Qi and Xiao 2005). It appears as though for the foreseeable future Shanghai will remain on its path-dependent development, one that is characterized by balanced manufacturing and services, and one that represents a new kind of global city equally shaped by its past and present.

THE STATE'S DOUBLE EDGE AS A POWERFUL BUILDER OF GLOBAL CITIES

Regardless of how far one would go with the view that globalization weakens the nation-state (see Ohmae 1995 vs. Rosenau 1997), taking this view leads to the expectation that the state has limited power to shape global cities. The opposite view sees the state as very important, if not crucial, in the development of global cities. Whereas Sassen characterizes the state as more of an enabler of global city formation (see Sassen 2006), others attribute a dominant developmental role to the state, especially in Asian global cities such as Tokyo and Seoul (e.g., Hill and Kim 2000). Irrespective of their past differences in the scope and functions of the state, both Singapore and Hong Kong governments have been involved in promoting and fostering competitiveness, with formerly laissez-faire Hong Kong adapting to and becoming more dependent on state-driven development and the internationalization of mainland China (Ho; Lui and Chiu, this book).

In building Shanghai into a global city, the Chinese state, at the municipal level in particular, has gone above and beyond its Japanese and Korean counterparts in playing a stronger and broader role (Wu; Zhou and Chen; Zhang, this book). This role distinguishes the full strength of the decentralized state in China where one might otherwise expect an erosion of state power due to the triple impact of decentralization, marketization (privatization), and globalization. Quite to the contrary, with a unique blessing by the central government, the empowered and aggressive Shanghai government has demonstrated its capacity to harness the forces of the market and foreign capital as an efficient means of upgrading the metropolitan economy at an uncommonly rapid pace.

The reconstituted and localized state power has made a tremendous difference in the speed of urban development. Exemplifying this central-to-local state-led development, the central government allowed Shanghai to be one of the first few major Chinese cities to experiment with selling the use rights of state-owned land to foreign investors in the early 1990s. By 2000, Shanghai had raised over US$13 billion from leasing land for infrastructure construction and urban redevelopment. As a former mayor of Shanghai commented then, if Shanghai depended on the central government for traditional budget allocation instead of raising funds through land lease, the urban renewal projects completed from 1990 to 2000 would have taken 100 years to complete. That was not necessary considering that Shanghai has attracted over US$120 billion in foreign investment since 1992 (see Chen, introduction).

There is no doubt that the concentration of power and decision-making in China's Party-state is chiefly responsible for the unparalleled rapidity at which the building of Shanghai as a global city has occurred. It simply would not have happened elsewhere. But is the same Chinese state capable of managing the adverse consequences of globalization that can happen just as rapidly? What must and should the state do to offset them? In a democratic society there is a system of rights and a history of local popular participation that limits the extent to which any government can suddenly reverse course. Democratic institutions such as a constitution put limits on these matters. In contrast, the state's handling of the "backlashes" of marketization and globalization in Shanghai continues to rely on top-down macro-control and administrative interference.

At the same time, there are significant differences and tensions emerging between the operations of government at the local and national levels in China. Consider this episode, for example. In Shanghai, the very high rate of private ownership (close to 80 percent by 2005) became a dominant factor in dictating housing supply and demand and keeping the property market very "hot" and prices sky high, which makes housing increasingly unaffordable for more people. The central government first introduced cooling measures in 2005 targeting a few coastal cities such as Shanghai, but the market showed few signs of cooling. Further measures were introduced in May 2006. These included raising down payments on loans for luxury homes from 20 to 30 percent, taxing proceeds from reselling homes within five years, instead of the existing two, and ending bank loans to developers unless they funded at least 35 percent of project costs from their own capital. The government also introduced rules to increase low-cost housing, requiring developers to designate 70 percent of the units in a property project to apartments of no more than ninety square meters. Eventually, the Shanghai real estate market slowed with a 10 percent drop in property prices in mid 2006, but it partly resulted from the municipal government's big push to promote more sales of lower-priced apartment units in the city's outskirts to lower the average city-wide property price (Chen 2006). However, the still-hot real estate market cooled in 2008, largely as a result of the global financial crisis and credit crunch rather than any state intervention.

This particular episode exemplifies the increasingly divergent interests and priorities of the central and municipal governments. Whereas the central government is concerned about macro-issues such as inflation and other symptoms of overheating, local governments target growth because it means more jobs and less risk of social unrest, and, in turn, it helps local officials advance their political careers through rewarding promotions. The inability of the Chinese state to reassert itself fully is closely tied with China's economic development becoming more and more led by the local government. Local governments have essentially become like businesses that compete among themselves to maximize GDP, which forces them to maximize their revenues through multiple channels to maintain high property prices, highway tolls, and sales taxes.

In the foreseeable future, there is likely to be a continuing tension between the interests of the central government and those of the municipal government in Shanghai. And, in the end, it will be the power and authority of the central government that is likely to be decisive. No better example of this tension, and the assertion of authority by the central government, exists than in the case of the pension scandal in Shanghai, which led to the oust of its Party secretary in late 2006. Groomed as China's global city for the future, Shanghai faces a bigger dilemma than all other cities in China in balancing the continued power of the local state in city building and its increasing tension and contention with the central state in sustaining market- and global capital-driven economic growth and dealing with its undesirable socioeconomic consequences. The tension between the central state and the powerful Shanghai government will only grow as more downsides of rapid marketization and globalization catch up and spill widely. This not only will test the tolerance level of both political actors but also further complicate and compromise their capacities of managing their relationship and solving local problems. Shanghai offers a sobering lesson about how the powerful Party-state builds a global city and is increasingly unable to cope with its repercussions. The initial strength of the state as a global-city builder has turned into a delayed weakness in managing Shanghai as a galloping global city. Further complicating this process is how Shanghai under the new Party secretary will balance sustaining its nationally prominent position against its role in "serving" the national interests as expected by the central government.

REDISCOVERING THE REGIONS OF GLOBAL CITIES

By emphasizing the themes of Shanghai's past and the double-edged role of the powerful Chinese state, we have addressed two weak elements in global city research. We now tackle another deficient aspect—the largely overlooked connection of global cities to their broader regional contexts and conditions. The literature on global cities teaches us a lot about their functional influence as control and command centers, relative positions in worldwide hierarchies and networks, and local social and spatial inequalities. But it shows us relatively little about the global cities' relations with their immediate and broader regional hinterlands, even though there was clear evidence that globalization via foreign investment and transnational migration had long spread beyond the central city and penetrated the suburban areas of American metropolises such as New York and Chicago (Greene 1997; Muller 1997). This insufficient attention to the city-region nexus could be attributed to two strong emphases of the global city literature on (1) the external positions and functions of global cities in the world economy and (2) the structure and consequences of their globalized local economy and society.

The paucity of empirical research on the concept of the global city-region introduced by Scott et al. (2001) also means that we know very little about the different types of cases that would fit under the global city-region rubric. What is known is based much more on global city-regions in industrialized economies where we find more established global cities (e.g., New York, London) integrated with their metropolitan regions. There is limited empirical knowledge about the regions around cities in developing countries that are globalizing at different paces instead of having already reached global city status. Compared to mature global city-regions with dominant international service functions such as finance, globalizing cities have very different mixes of economic sectors and functions that foster the growth of their own distinctive regional spaces and activities. Shanghai again provides an important illustrative example of how both history and the state have come together to produce key spatial and socioeconomic relations characterizing a new globalizing city-region.

From the late 1800s to the 1930s, Shanghai attracted a steadily growing amount of capital, labor, and goods from southern China (Guangdong in particular), interior China, and the surrounding Yangtze River Delta (YRD) region, especially from Ningbo, due to the famine and unrest in many of these places and the relative stability associated with the presence of the International Concessions in Shanghai (Qi and Xiao 2005). This process eventually consolidated Shanghai as the dominant economic and shipping node for the YRD and much of China. Now more than a century later, Shanghai's rise as a globalizing city features a similar and yet different relationship with this region.

The investment-driven economic boom of Shanghai since the early 1990s has driven up land and labor costs in its densely populated central city, where land has become more scarce and thus more difficult and expensive for investors to lease. The average wages of both factory workers and technicians in Shanghai are now more than double those of their counterparts in interior cities, whereas the average pay for managers and senior managers in Shanghai is three times higher. In 2005, the annual pay of manual labor in Shanghai averaged US$2,979 compared to the large interior cities of Chongqing and Chengdu at US$1,787 and US$1,489, respectively. Land cost in Shanghai approximately doubled that in some secondary cities in the YRD. So development began to spill into the surrounding YRD region, especially to booming secondary cities such as Suzhou and Kunsan, and even smaller cities such as Wujiang (see Map I.1 in Chen, introduction). Today the total GDP of the Shanghai region amounts to US$450 billion, equivalent to half of the GDP of the entire Indian economy.

Since 1999, Suzhou has attracted over 1,000 industrial enterprises set up by Shanghai-based companies with a total capitalization of over

US$5 billion. Shanghai became the largest investor in Suzhou, accounting for over 35 percent of the total capital investment by 2004. In 2005, Suzhou's GDP ranked fifth in the country at US$50.8 billion, and its industrial output totaled US$150 billion, good enough for second place behind Shanghai (Chen 2007). More generally, the Suzhou government officially adopted the strategy of more actively linking with Shanghai through both competition and cooperation across different industries and services. But the loss of capital and companies was seen by Shanghai as a threat to its broad manufacturing base, prompting the Shanghai government to launch an initiative of keeping old manufacturing jobs and growing new ones in Jiading and Qingpu Districts bordering Jiangsu province (see Map I.1 in Chen, introduction).

Although the policy of protecting noncompetitive manufacturing may be unwise and ineffective, the Shanghai government has maintained the traditional practice of top-down, large-scale spatial planning and population redistribution. With the most densely populated central city in China, Shanghai's central Huangpu district has an astonishing 126,500 people per square kilometer, giving each person less than eight square meters. In addition, the average housing price in central Shanghai is quadruple that of the far outlying areas. To reduce this density and take advantage of the large housing price differential, the Shanghai municipal government in 2001 drew up a massive plan to build one new city and nine new towns (each of which is themed after a European country, including Germany and Britain) with a combined population of 5.4 million and sixty new small towns with populations of around 50,000 each outside the outer ring road. The expansion of the transport network including the metro and roads will allow people to live away from downtown Shanghai but easily commute into the center for work in about one hour.

Although these towns may become home to many more families displaced from the city center, many of the over 1 million families already displaced face the tough choices of moving out to the new and more spacious suburban housing or staying put in the old and crowded central-city dwelling. Those families who have moved like the lower mortgage payment, larger living space, better air quality, green parks, modern facilities, and diminished noise in the suburban towns of Pudong, but they also miss the familiar social networks, shopping and transport convenience, and even the lively activity in downtown Shanghai. Despite the compensation they receive from the government and real estate developers for vacating their housing units, some residents refuse to move because they simply do not like the idea of a long commute to and from downtown Shanghai. Others do not like the inconvenience in lagging commercial facilities and social services (Chen 2006). The small number of wealthy people with cars from central Shanghai who have bought high-end apartments and luxury villas in the German (Anting New Town in Jiading) and British (Thames Town in Songjiang) towns generally use these properties as second, weekend homes (Chen, Wang, and Kundu 2009).

Shanghai's changing regional links provide clear evidence of the reactive role of the municipal government in maintaining the city's slipping manufacturing advantage relative to lower-cost nearby cities as well as its proactive role in creating a form of integrated metropolitan development. Hong Kong also has become more integrated with the Pearl River Delta region in its move back into (the return of sovereignty in 1997) and forward from China's enlarged global orbit more recently (see Lui and Chiu, this book). Singapore's symbiotic relations with the neighboring regional growth triangle involving parts of Malaysia and Indonesia remains strong; it has extended its global reach through the key agency of the Economic Development Board (Ho, this book). By considering Shanghai within its broader regional context, and having shown parallel developments both in Hong Kong and Singapore, we have shown yet another direction in which research on global cities may be extended (see Ren, Chen, and Läpple 2009).

A GROUNDED RELATIONAL VIEW ON GLOBAL CITIES

In addition to those three theoretical themes already identified here, we advocate yet another, final, one—the effort to incorporate a grounded relational view into global city research as a substantive and methodological lesson from Shanghai. Though it is easy to characterize and criticize global city research as being strong on the macro level but weak "on the ground," this is true especially when we look for evidence to establish links between community- and individual-level phenomena and the large-scale structural and spatial dynamics of globalizing cities. We also know relatively little about the ways in which the differential effects of global, national, and local forces become manifest in communal life and individual behavior. The absence of such information reveals an important lacuna in the global city research agenda. And it can be partly, if not wholly, attributed to the methodological difficulties of measuring and modeling the small-scale effects of globalization, particularly in comparison to the increasingly sophisticated macro-level quantitative measures and analysis of global city networks.

By including two chapters—chapters 9 and 10—that focus specifically on community (re)building and consumer behavior in globalizing

Shanghai, this book makes some progress in redressing these deficiencies in global city research. As chapter 9 indicates, globalization leaves many foot-prints on communities in Shanghai, including the involvement of foreign capital in building gated luxury communities, foreigners marrying locals and becoming long-term residents, and the presence of foreign fast food restaurants and convenience stores in a large number of traditional neigh-borhoods. These global influences, however, are entangled with and filtered through state-initiated housing and community governance reforms that exert both independent and interactive effects on community development.

Moving from a grounded view to an explicit microscopic relational approach, Chapter 10 shows that although globalization facilitates the rapid growth and broad availability of a variety of consumer goods in Shanghai, there are personal attributes and qualities that affect the reach of global forces into the everyday lives of local residents. In particular, con-sumers with stronger global connections are more likely to consume global products. The global connections of people also make a difference to how they feel about the environment and services of their communities. More recent evidence suggests that people with global connections are also more likely to live in high-end and more exclusive residential areas in Shanghai (Chen and Sun 2007). At both the community and the individual levels, in other words, Shanghai is rapidly becoming tied to global events and transactions, so much so, in fact, that we can no longer conclude that the local is simply local.

Besides adding to the distinctiveness of Shanghai as a globalizing city, the findings from chapters 9 and 10 also contribute to the literature on global cities by demonstrating the value of a grounded relational approach as a means of bridging the divide between the large- and small-scale levels in all global or globalizing cities. Some of the seemingly dis-tinctive attributes of Shanghai look far less so when seen in the light of the broader comparative perspective displayed in the non-Shanghai chapters of the book. These materials thus help in identifying a set of general opportunities and constraints on global city development under any national and local circumstances. These include the path-dependent tra-jectory of a city's history, the double-edged role of the state, and the regional context of a global or globalizing city.

CONCLUDING OBSERVATIONS

As we bring the book to a close, we want to leave the reader with two final observations. One concerns the distinctive way in which the two halves of the book are linked. The entire book could have been about

Shanghai with more chapters dealing with other facets of its local trans-formations. This exclusive focus on Shanghai would have been easily justified given the tremendous attention on and interest in the city. But to have done so would have been at the expense of advancing the global city literature and highlighting the distinctive features of Shanghai. By embedding Shanghai in the theoretical and comparative frames of Part I, we not only have eschewed "Shanghai exceptionalism" but we also have established more useful reference points for the more focused analyses of Shanghai in Part II.

And the other is that the four themes, in combination, can provide new elements and insights into research on global cities. History is deeply etched into a global or globalizing city, as Shanghai has demonstrated. Constrained by being the center for the Yangtze River Delta region, on the one hand, and a broadly industrialized city under state planning, on the other, Shanghai has traveled a difficult path to become a global city. Its experience thus illuminates the continuing tension between its own his-torical roots and the efforts by the state to overcome this history. The struggle, itself, marks the Shanghai experience as fundamentally different from the experience of global cities in advanced industrialized countries and should provide a sobering lesson for globalizing cities in developing countries. Through and beyond the broad structures of history, state power, and regional context, global forces penetrate to the very bottom of cities by altering the consumption patterns and lifestyles of local residents. Shanghai provides another lesson that illustrates using a grounded rela-tional approach to understanding the mechanisms by which the global-local social and cultural nexus emerges.

Where do we go from here? In exploring and extending new avenues of global city research, Shanghai will remain a source of new evidence and ideas that beg to be evaluated through further research. How will Shanghai respond to and emerge from the current global economic crisis, which has taken a particularly heavy toll on global financial centers, which Shanghai aspires to become? As we learn more about Shanghai itself, it will help us better appreciate and understand how global forces shape metropolitan growth and development. This book, we hope, provides an important step on this long journey.

NOTE

We thank Dennis Judd for his helpful comments and suggestions for develop-ing and improving the structure and substance of this chapter through its earlier versions.

REFERENCES

Chen, Xiangming. 2006. "Rising Cities and the Restructured State: Local Autonomy in the Name of Economic Development is Changing China." *Internationale Politik* (November): 62–65.

———. 2007. "A Tale of Two Regions in China: Rapid Economic Development and Slow Industrial Upgrading in the Pearl River and the Yangtze River Deltas." *International Journal of Comparative Sociology* 48, no. 2: 79–113.

Chen, Xiangming, and Jiaming Sun. 2007. "Untangling a Global–Local Nexus: Sorting out Residential Sorting in Shanghai." *Environment and Planning A* 39, no. 10: 2324–45.

Chen, Xiangming, Lan Wang, and Ratoola Kundu. 2009. "Localizing the Production of Global Cities: A Comparison of New Town Development Around Shanghai and Kolkata." *City & Community* 8, no. 4: (Forthcoming).

Friedman, Thomas. 2005. *The World Is Flat: A Brief History of the Twenty-first Century.* New York: Farrar, Straus, and Giroux.

Greene, Richard P. 1997. "Chicago's New Immigrants, Indigenous Poor, and Edge Cities." *The ANNALS of the American Academy of Political and Social Science* 551: 178–90.

Hill, Richard Child, and June Woo Kim. 2000. "Global Cities and Developmental States: New York, Tokyo, and Seoul." *Urban Studies* 37, no. 12: 2167–95.

Johnson, Linda Cooke. 1995. *Shanghai: From Market Town to Treat Port, 1074–1858.* Stanford, Calif.: Stanford University Press.

Muller, Peter O. 1997. "The Suburban Transformation of the Globalizing American City." *The ANNALS of the American Academy of Political and Social Science* 551: 44–58.

Ohame, Kenichi. 1995. *The End of the Nation State: The Rise of Regional Economies.* London: HarperCollins.

Qi, Weiping, and Zhaoqing Xiao. 2005. "The Historical Background and Contemporary Implications of the Establishment of Shanghai's Central City Position in Modern China." In *A Collection of Modern Shanghai Studies* (in Chinese), edited by Xiaomin Feng, 1–31. Shanghai: The Century Publishing Group.

Ren, Yuan, Xiangming Chen, and Dieter Läpple, eds. 2009. *The Era of Global City–Regions: Diversity and Dynamics in Asia and Europe.* Shanghai: Fudan University Press.

Rosenau, James N. 1997. *Along the Domestic-Foreign Frontier: Exploring Governance in a Turbulent World.* New York: Cambridge University Press.

Sassen, Saskia. 2006. *Territory, Authority, Rights: From Medieval to Global Assemblages.* Princeton: Princeton University Press.

Scott, Allen J., John Agnew, Edward W. Soja, and Michael Storper. 2001. "Global City–Regions: An Overview." In *Global City–Regions: Trends, Theory, Policy,* edited by Allen J. Scott, 11–32. Oxford: Oxford University Press.

Wasserstrom, Jeffrey N. 2008. *Global Shanghai, 1850–2010: A History in Fragments.* Oxford and New York: Routledge.

CONTRIBUTORS

Xiangming Chen is founding dean and director of the Center for Urban and Global Studies and Paul E. Raether Distinguished Professor of Sociology and International Studies at Trinity College, Hartford, Connecticut. He is also a distinguished professor in the School of Social Development and Public Policy at Fudan University, Shanghai. He is author of *As Borders Bend: Transitional Spaces on the Pacific Rim* (2005) and coauthor of *The World of Cities: Places in Comparative and Historical Perspective* (2003, with Anthony Orum).

Stephen W. K. Chiu is a professor in the department of sociology and director of the Public Policy Research Centre at the Chinese University of Hong Kong. He has published widely in international journals and is coauthor of *East Asia and the World Economy* and *City-States in the Global Economy: Industrial Restructuring in Hong Kong and Singapore* and coeditor of *The Dynamics of Social Movement in Hong Kong.*

K. C. Ho is an associate professor of sociology at the National University of Singapore. He is coauthor of *City-States in the Global Economy: Industrial Restructuring in Hong Kong and Singapore* and coeditor of *Globalization, the City, and Civil Society in Pacific Asia Cities, Capital Cities in Asia-Pacific, Service Industries, Cities, and Development Trajectories in the Asia-Pacific,* and *Critical Reflections on Cities in Southeast Asia.*

John D. Kasarda is Kenan Distinguished Professor of Management and director of the Kenan Institute of Private Enterprise at the University of North Carolina at Chapel Hill. He has published more than seventy scholarly articles and nine books on aviation infrastructure, logistics, urban development, and commercial real estate.

Hanlong Lu is a professor and director of the Institute of Sociology at the Shanghai Academy of Social Sciences. He is an elected representative of Shanghai's Municipal People's Congress and a consultant to the Shanghai Municipal Government. He is the editor of *2001–2002 Shanghai Social Development Report: Urban Governance and Quality of Citizen, 2000–2001 Shanghai Social Development Report: System Reform and Social Transformation,* and *Shanghai Community Development Report, 1996–2000.*

Tai-lok Lui is a professor of sociology at the Chinese University of Hong Kong. His publications include *City-States in the Global Economy: Industrial Restructuring in Hong Kong and Singapore, Consuming Hong Kong,* and *Hong Kong, China: Learning to Belong to a Nation.*

Ann R. Markusen is a professor and director of the Project on Regional and Industrial Economics at the Humphrey Institute of Public Affairs at the University of Minnesota. Her recent publications include *Reining in the Competition for Capital, From Defense to Development,* and *Second Tier Cities: Rapid Growth beyond the Metropolis* (University of Minnesota Press, 1999).

Anthony M. Orum is a professor of sociology and political science at the University of Illinois at Chicago. He is the author of *Black Students in Protest: A Study of the Origins of the Black Student Movement* (1972), *City-Building in America* (1995), and *The World of Cities: Places in Comparative and Historical Perspective* (2003, with Xiangming Chen) and the coeditor of *A Case for the Case Study* (1991, with Joe Feagin and Gideon Sjoberg). His most recent books are *Political Sociology: Power and Participation in the Modern World* (2008, 5th edition, with John S. Dale) and *Common Ground? Readings and Reflections on Public Space* (forthcoming, coeditor with Zachary Neal). He also is the founding editor of the journal *City and Community.*

Yuan Ren is professor of demography and urban studies in the School of Social Development and Public Policy at Fudan University, Shanghai. He is author of *Employment in Transition Society: Community-based Employment and Social Policies in Urban China* (2007), coauthor of *Long-term Care Insurance and Ageing Society* (2005, in Chinese), and editor of *Re-observe the Labor Market: Chinese Informal Employment Report* (2007, in Chinese).

Saskia Sassen is the Robert S. Lynd Professor of Sociology and a member of the Committee on Global Thought at Columbia University. Her recent books include *Territory, Authority, Rights: From Medieval to Global Assemblages, Cities in a World Economy* (3rd ed.), and *A Sociology of Globalization.* She is editor of *Deciphering the Global: Its Spaces, Scales, and Subjects* and coeditor of *Digital Formations: New Architectures for Global Order.* Her books have been translated into nineteen languages.

Jiaming Sun is associate professor of sociology and criminal justice at Texas A&M University–Commerce. He is author of *A Generational Gap: The Background of a Transitional Period, 1991–1994* (in Chinese) and *Global Connectivity and Local Transformation: A Micro Approach to Studying the Effect of Globalization on Shanghai.*

Fulong Wu is professor of East Asian Planning and Development in the School of City and Regional Planning at Cardiff University, United Kingdom. He is coeditor of *Restructuring the Chinese City,* editor of *Globalization and the Chinese City* and *China's Emerging Cities,* and coauthor of *Urban Development in Post-reform China.*

Pingkang Yu is a Ph.D. candidate in economics at the George Washington University. He has published widely accredited refereed journal articles on high-tech economic policy, defense spending, and rankings of economics journals. His expertise within economics lies in open-macroeconomics and urban and regional economics. He has served as an economic policy analyst at the Federal Reserve Bank of Boston and has provided economic consultancies to the World Bank and the International Monetary Fund. As an urban planner, he participated or managed around thirty urban development projects in China.

Tingwei Zhang is director of the Asia and China Research Program in the Great Cities Institute of the University of Illinois at Chicago. He has published more than one hundred papers and book chapters and has authored or coauthored seven books on urban China. His recent publications include *Comparison of Chinese and American Cities, Shopping Mall Today,* and *Design and Development of Waterfront Areas.*

Zhenhua Zhou is director of the Development Research Center of Shanghai Municipal People's Government. He is editor of the journal *Shanghai Economic Research* and the author of several books in Chinese, including *The Economic Analysis of Industrial Policy, The Structural Effect in Modern Economic Growth, The Structure of Industries, System Change and Economic Growth: Chinese Experience and Analysis,* and *Informatics and Industrial Convergence.*